INTERNATIONAL BUSINESS AND GLOBAL INTEGRATION

UNIVERSITY OF READING EUROPEAN AND INTERNATIONAL STUDIES

Published by Macmillan in association with the Graduate School of European and International Studies, University of Reading.

General Editor: George N. Yannopoulos
Associate Editor: Malcolm B. Hamilton

Zygmunt G. Barański and Robert Lumley (*editors*)
CULTURE AND CONFLICT IN POSTWAR ITALY

Zygmunt G. Barański and Shirley W. Vinall (*editors*)
WOMEN AND ITALY: ESSAYS ON GENDER, CULTURE AND HISTORY

Mark Casson (*editor*)
INTERNATIONAL BUSINESS AND GLOBAL INTEGRATION: EMPIRICAL STUDIES

Jeremy Clegg
MULTINATIONAL ENTERPRISE AND WORLD COMPETITION

Anne Deighton (*editor*)
BRITAIN AND THE FIRST COLD WAR

Malcolm B. Hamilton
DEMOCRATIC SOCIALISM IN BRITAIN AND SWEDEN

D.L. Hanley and A.P. Kerr
MAY '68: COMING OF AGE

Robert D. Pearce
THE INTERNATIONALISATION OF RESEARCH AND DEVELOPMENT BY MULTINATIONAL ENTERPRISES

Robert D. Pearce and Satwinder Singh
GLOBALIZING RESEARCH AND DEVELOPMENT

George N. Yannopoulos (*editor*)
EUROPEAN INTEGRATION AND THE IBERIAN ECONOMIES
GREECE AND THE EEC

INTERNATIONAL BUSINESS AND GLOBAL INTEGRATION

Empirical Studies

Edited by

MARK CASSON
Professor of Economics
University of Reading

M

in association with
THE GRADUATE SCHOOL
OF EUROPEAN AND
INTERNATIONAL STUDIES
UNIVERSITY OF READING

First published in 1992 by
THE MACMILLAN PRESS LTD
Houndmills, Basingstoke, Hampshire RG21 2XS
and London
Companies and representatives
throughout the world

ISBN 0–333–56035–3

A catalogue record for this book is available
from the British Library

Printed in Great Britain by
Billing and Sons Ltd, Worcester

Contents

Preface

The 1970s and 1980s have witnessed significant advances in our theoretical understanding of international business operations. One of the great strengths of economic theories of international business has been their relevance to policy and practice. This derives from the way that theoretical development has been driven by the desire to explain 'stylised facts', such as the concentration of international business activity in innovative oligopolistic industries. If economic theories of international business have lacked some of the elegance of more abstract theories, they have more than compensated for this in the way they have successfully handled the complexities of real world phenomena.

There is a danger, however, that as a result of recent advances theory may outstrip empirical evidence. Some of the most significant early evidence that guided theoretical development was collected by John Dunning. His study of US investment in British manufacturing industry was a seminal work. This tradition of combining theoretical development with empirical study has been maintained in the Department of Economics at the University of Reading since then. This book reports some of the most recent work, much of it carried out by PhD candidates at Reading. Although united by their association with Reading, they are a fairly cosmopolitan group, drawn from India, China, Portugal and Greece as well as from the UK.

One of the aims of this collection is to show how the study of international business is moving on from the themes that dominated the 1970s and 1980s, such as the role of foreign direct investment as an import-substituting strategy in manufacturing industry. The focus now is on contractual relations as a whole – including joint ventures and management contracts – and on the service sector rather than the manufacturing sector. There is also greater interest in going right inside the multinational enterprise to analyse how instruments such as corporate culture can help to make internal markets work better. The world economy of the 1990s is more highly integrated than the world economy of the 1960s, and the policy agenda is rather different as a result. Rivalry between geopolitical economic powers in a polycentric trading system is emerging as the key policy issue. It is important to keep up to date in our factual grasp of underlying trends in business practice if recent theoretical insights are to be brought to bear successfully on these new policy issues.

University of Reading MARK CASSON

Acknowledgements

Chapter 1. Thanks are due to Peter Buckley for comments on an earlier draft. John Dunning and Matthew McQueen kindly provided some useful references.

Chapter 2. The authors are grateful to Colin Thirtle for the invitation to present the paper to the Economic and Social Research Council Development Economics Study Group Conference at the University of Leicester, June 1990. Helpful comments were received from John Thoburn and other participants.

Chapter 5. The author is grateful for comments received from J.A. Cantwell, A. Chester, E.P. Davis and R. Heath. The views expressed are solely those of the author and not necessarily those of the Bank of England.

Chapter 6. The authors are grateful to the ESRC for funding the project from which the main results were derived. They are also grateful to John Cantwell, and to the Science Policy Research Unit of the University of Sussex for providing the patent data used in some of the regressions.

Chapter 8. The author is grateful to Robert Pearce for supplying the data for Table 8.3 in an already processed form.

Notes on the Contributors

Paul Campayne is Research Analyst in the International Finance, Economy and Debt Division of the Bank of England. He holds MA and PhD degrees from the University of Reading, where his supervisor was John Cantwell.

Mark Casson is Professor of Economics at the University of Reading. He has recently published *Enterprise and Competitiveness: A Systems View of International Business* (1990) and *Economics of Business Culture: Game Theory, Transactions Costs and Economic Performance* (1991). He is also the editor of *Global Research Strategy and International Competitiveness* (1991).

Jose-Paulo Esperanca is a PhD candidate at the European University Institute, Florence. He is jointly supervised by Peter Hertner and Mark Casson.

Christos Nicolaidis is a PhD candidate in the Department of Economics, University of Reading. His supervisors are Mark Casson and Chistopher Nobes. He holds a BA in Economics from the Graduate Industrial School of Thessaloniki, Greece, and an MBA from the Birmingham Business School, University of Birmingham. His professional experience includes consultancy work for several major UK and Greek firms.

Robert D. Pearce is Senior Research Fellow in the Department of Economics, University of Reading. He has published numerous papers on multinational enterprises, technology and economic development, and co-authored several books. His most recent book is *The Internationalisation of Research and Development by Multinational Enterprises* (1990).

Satwinder Singh is Senior Research Fellow on the ESRC-funded project on Strategic Behaviour by Dominant Firms directed by

Michael Utton and Michael Waterson at the University of Reading. He is the author of *Multinational Corporations and the Indian Drug Industry* (1985) which is based on his PhD work at the Gokhale Institute of Politics and Economics, Pune. Between 1988 and 1989 he researched the global R & D strategies of multinational firms on another ESRC-funded project at Reading.

Allan Webster is Lecturer in Economics at the University of Reading. He has published various articles on international trade and industrial economics and is co-editor (with John Dunning) of *Structural Change in the World Economy*. He has carried out consulting assignments in Africa under the auspices of both the UN and the World Bank.

Jurong Zheng is a PhD candidate in the Department of Economics, University of Reading. She holds an MBA in Export Management and International Business from the City University Business School and a BSc in Textile Industrial Management from the China Textile University, Shanghai.

1 Introduction

MARK CASSON

1.1 A HISTORICAL PERSPECTIVE

Economic integration can be defined in various ways (Machlup, 1977). Economists have traditionally emphasised that integration is effected through the growth of commodity trade. Their initial focus was on tariff reductions, though more recently it has switched to the elimination of non-tariff barriers such as discriminatory government procurement. The modern world economy manifests many other forms of integration, however: capital mobility effected through international capital markets, and labour mobility effected through migration, not to mention technology transfer and the transfer of management skills.

In Victorian times many writers saw the growing integration of the world economy as one of the clearest indicators of economic progress. Popular British works on political economy are full of references to the variety of products imported and exported through the great ports of that time. The Lancashire cotton industry was extolled for the way that imported cotton was transformed into clothing exports through the ingenuity of the steam-powered mechanised factory.

Historically, of course, progress through integration has been intermittent rather than steady. Indeed, world history could be naively interpreted in terms of cycles of integration, disintegration and reintegration. In each cycle the market area encompassed seems to increase. The trading activities of the Roman empire stretched further than did those of the Greeks, for example. More recently, US trade and investment activities encompassed not only most of the pre-war British empire but much of Europe and Latin America too.

As the territory encompassed by trading empires has increased, so the methods of organisation have tended to change. Progressive integration has to some extent gone hand in hand with progressive decentralisation. The Roman empire was more centrally governed than the British empire, for example. The British often economised on governance costs by making treaties with local leaders. Commercial activities in the British empire were organised mainly by expatriate merchants who had emigrated voluntarily rather than by state officials posted overseas.

Trading empires have also become more open over time. The Roman empire was a reasonably self-contained territorial unit, whilst the British empire was integrated with the US and European economies too, although the British still made strenuous efforts to reserve certain trades for British merchants and British ships. After the Second World War, however, US hegemony sustained a trading system that was open to everyone. The Japanese, in particular, took a 'free ride' on the US role of 'international policeman' in the Pacific rim to develop off-shore processing in support of their export trade.

The simultaneous growth of decentralisation and openness is no coincidence. Centralisation tends to isolate each local territorial unit from its neighbours, strengthening its ties with the centre at the expense of its links with other territorial units close by. Centralisation also enhances the centre's power to enforce prohibitions on local cross-border trade. If such prohibitions do not exist, or cannot be enforced, then there is a natural tendency for trade to develop between the territorial units of adjacent empires. Such units share the problems of being peripheral to their respective empires, so that with effective decentralisation they will naturally exploit the mutual gains from local trade. Historically the most centralised empires have been the most concerned to discourage external trade – China being a conspicuous case – whereas decentralised empires have been most tolerant of it (for example, the US-dominated GATT – General Agreement on Tariffs and Trade – regime of the 1960s).

Some of the most dynamic trading empires have been those that have concentrated on pushing back their frontiers. The excitement of discovering new territories and new resources has led to a highly speculative approach to the expansion of investment and trade. The gains from discovery have been most remarkable where the exploitation of the frontier was largely decentralised and deregulated (Britain in Africa and the US mid-West) and least successful when central control was tight (Spain in Latin America).

Where frontiers could not be pushed back without difficulty – because, for example, of a land frontier with a powerful neighbour –

a more defensive attitude has tended to prevail. Military considerations have argued for strengthening communications between the centre and the frontier, and for maintaining strategic industrial and agricultural self-sufficiency. By and large, the maritime countries have had much greater choice over where to focus their frontier activity, whilst island countries generally have less need to be preoccupied with defensive considerations. This suggests that land-locked countries with powerful neighbours will tend to be defensive, closed and centralised, whilst maritime countries (and especially islands) will tend to be more expansion-oriented, open and decentralised. While there are plenty of historical counter-examples, this principle is nevertheless quite relevant in explaining the rise of some of the great trading empires of the past.

1.2 THE TRIAD

Open trading systems organised by neighbouring countries tend to overlap. They may, indeed, interpenetrate quite significantly, so that systems based upon different hubs (see below) compete with each other in several different locations. So long as political relations are basically cordial, this can stimulate a progressive form of competition, in which each country seeks out improvements in technology and management in order to improve the quality and reduce the cost of services. This outcome was achieved for a time by Renaissance city-states in the Mediterranean. The Papacy exercised a kind of moral hegemony which kept the worst excesses of rivalry under control.

Deteriorating political relations can create military instability, however. The more deeply different networks interpenetrate, the greater are the number of locations at which conflicts can flare up. Problems in one area can quickly spill over to others. Thus the European imperialists' 'scramble for Africa' at the end of the nineteenth century was a source of escalating rivalry which contributed to the political breakdown that culminated in the First World War.

The present world trading system is largely an open system although the prospects for the 1990s as a whole are not good (see below). There are three major interpenetrating blocs, based in the European Community (EC), USA and Japan. These blocs constitute the 'Triad'. Table 1.1 illustrates the structure of world trade in 1987. It shows that the trade of most countries is dominated by exports

TABLE 1.1 *Value of annual exports between major groups of countries, 1987 (US$billion)*

Origin	*EC*	*USA*	*Japan*	*EFTA*	*Other developed*	*E. Europe*	*Socialist Asia*	*OPEC*	*Other LDCs*	*Total*
EC	550.7	82.7	15.7	104.4	42.9	22.2	6.6	34.2	87.0	951.2
USA	57.2	–	26.9	6.1	67.2	2.2	3.5	10.4	65.5	245.3
Japan	36.4	84.2	–	7.2	15.8	3.3	8.6	11.4	62.3	229.2
EFTA	88.4	12.3	3.4	23.7	4.6	8.5	1.1	4.1	13.9	160.3
Other developed market economies	23.3	80.4	18.1	2.9	5.3	1.9	2.9	3.5	20.2	160.6
E. Europe	29.3	1.8	1.9	10.5	5.0	119.0	8.1	3.8	20.6	204.7
Socialist Asia	5.1	3.6	7.3	0.7	0.8	4.8	0.4	0.7	17.0	40.4
OPEC	34.0	20.8	21.6	1.7	1.5	3.1	0.4	4.1	31.9	119.8
Other LDCs	79.7	105.1	35.5	7.8	13.8	18.7	15.4	17.5	72.1	368.9
Total	904.0	390.9	130.5	165.1	152.2	183.7	47.0	89.7	390.5	2480.4

NOTE: Row totals contain a residual element.
LDC = Less developed country.
Numbers do not add up correctly due to rounding.
SOURCE: United Nations Conference on Trade and Development (UNCTAD, 1989), Table 3.1.

and/or imports with one or more of the three main blocs. In some cases just one of the blocs has a paramount role. For example, over half of European Free Trade Association (EFTA) exports are destined for the EC, and an even larger proportion of EFTA imports come from the EC. EFTA trade with the EC is about four times as large as intra-EFTA trade.

Japan is by far the smallest of the Triad members but its long-term rate of growth of exports has been the highest, so that if recent trends continue the discrepancy is likely to diminish. Japan is running a substantial balance of trade surplus, which finances Japanese overseas investments. The USA, on the other hand, is running a substantial deficit, which is mainly accounted for by the deficit on bilateral trade with Japan. Even so, it is worth noting that the whole of the US deficit cannot be accounted for in this way.

Trading relations have a parallel in the cross-holdings of foreign direct investments. Figure 1.1 illustrates the role of Triad members in sourcing investment in 1987–8. There are major cross-investments between the USA and the EC, although the proportion of EC investment directed to the USA is much higher than the proportion of US investment that is directed to the EC. Japan directs a higher proportion of its investment to the USA than to the EC, while the USA and EC direct a relatively small (but rapidly increasing) proportion of their investments to Japan.

The figure shows that the USA sourced more than 50 per cent of all foreign direct investment in several Latin American countries and the Philippines, while the EC similarly dominated Nigeria, Kenya, South Africa, Bangladesh and Vietnam. Some countries were heavily dependent on just two Triad members for inward investment: Thailand and Taiwan were dominated by the USA and Japan, and Argentina and Pakistan by the USA and the EC. Only a few countries are dominated by neighbours which are not Triad members: China by Hong Kong, and Papua New Guinea by Australia, for example.

The statistical evidence shows that while there are substantial cross-flows of both trade and investment, the world economy is still not fully integrated in the sense that some groups of countries have far stronger links with some partners than they do with others. Triad members act as hubs, often with long 'spokes' linking the hub to the 'remote outposts' of a colonial empire of the past. In other cases a Triad member dominates neighbouring economies, which are far more closely integrated with the Triad member than they are with each other.

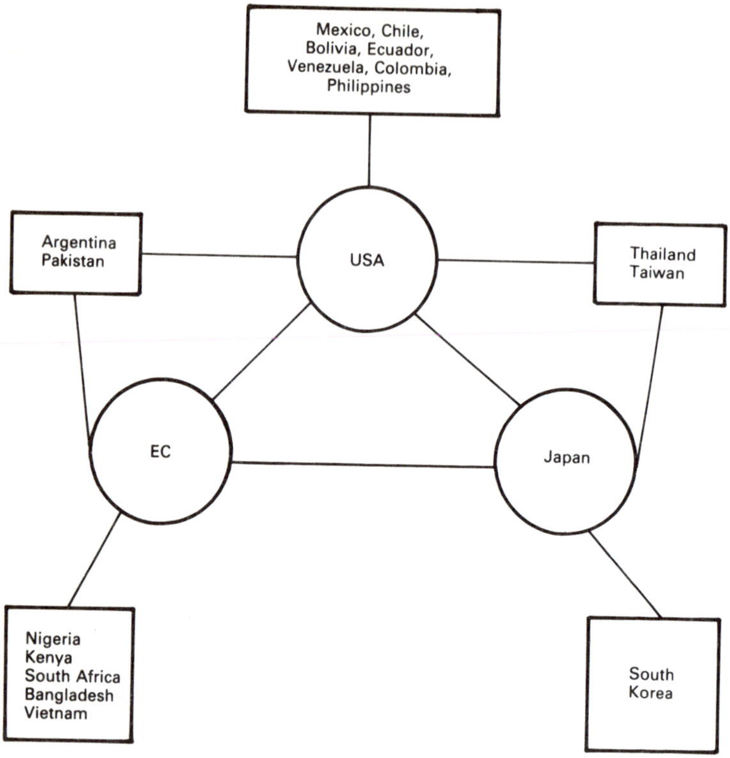

SOURCE: United Nations Centre on Transnational Corporations (UNCTC, 1991), Table 4.

FIGURE 1.1 Countries in which Triad members contributed more than 50 per cent of the foreign direct investment stock in 1987–8

A progressive view of economic integration would therefore emphasise the continuing opportunities for strengthening trade and investment links. Such optimism would be unjustified, however, in the light of the political rivalries developing between the Triad members during the late 1980s and early 1990s. Increasing political hostility could yet have a devastating effect on integration, as the historical record makes only too clear.

The USA and EC have repeatedly expressed concern about the apparent slowness with which barriers to imports and foreign investment are being dismantled in Japan. It is not just a question of eliminating formal legal obstacles, but of changing the culture of

Japanese officialdom to exercise administrative discretion in a more impartial way. The reluctance of the EC to phase out the Common Agricultural Policy (CAP), and even to make significant concessions over agricultural protection in the Uruguay Round, has antagonised the USA, which has a comparative advantage in arable agriculture. The USA also objects to the emerging technological protectionism in Europe, and in particular to the strategic subsidisation of aircraft and information technology R & D. At the same time Europe and Japan object to the continued attempts of the USA to implement its anti-trust policies, and other aspects of its industrial and trade policies, on an extraterritorial basis. They suspect that this is a covert way of coping with declining US competitiveness. They deny that successful foreign exporters or investors are merely benefiting from hidden subsidies provided by their home governments. Even if such subsidies exist, it is claimed, they are often smaller than the subsidies the USA gives to own 'national champions' through lucrative defence contracts. Unless the political will exists to resolve these conflicts through negotiation, the natural tendency of an open and deregulated system to become more integrated may well be undermined, and the process of integration put into reverse.

1.3 INTERNAL AND EXTERNAL INTEGRATION

Each of the Triad members derives much of its economic strength from its own internal integration. This is particularly obvious in the case of the EC. The benefits of tariff reduction within the EC are believed to come mainly from the exploitation of economies of scale. The traditional focus of economic theory on the gains from international specialisation according to comparative advantage seem to apply mainly to trade between countries at different stages of development (for example, between Britain and the colonies in the nineteenth century, and Japan and some of her poorer South-East Asian neighbours today). The founding member states of the EC were at fairly similar levels of development, and the enlargement of each producer's potential market produced intra-industry specialisation on different varieties of product, rather than interindustry specialisation based upon differences in cost. As a result, the variety of products of each type available to consumers in each country increased, and each country sourced the other's market through cross-flows of intra-industry trade.

As the EC has expanded to absorb some of the Southern Mediterranean countries, however, it seems likely that comparative advantage will play a greater role in internal integration. The traditional division of labour between town and country – based on the exchange of agricultural and manufactured products – will extend to trade between the industrial north and the predominantly agricultural south. So far such specialisation has been inhibited by the CAP, which has protected agricultural producers in the industrialised countries. However, the balance of benefits and costs for traditional supporters of the CAP, such as France, is shifting adversely, partly as a result of the redistribution of income to farmers in the new member countries. A reduction in the effective protection of European agriculture would allow comparative advantage to play a larger role in the internal integration of the EC than it has done so far.

Integration occurred much earlier in the USA, of course, when the expansion of railroads not only developed interstate trade but also encouraged the growth of multistate enterprises (Chandler, 1977). They were the forerunners of the US multinational enterprises (MNEs) of today. Many were formed as a result of mergers and acquisitions designed to achieve nationwide monopoly power, but as anti-trust legislation began to bite they were forced to divest many of their core operations. In many cases the funds were reinvested in diversification, leading to a situation where many leading firms interpenetrated one another's markets and so came into conflict with each other on many different fronts. The divisional organisation increasingly adapted to streamline the management of these enterprises became a useful model when US businesses subsequently expanded into multinational operations on a large scale.

Japan is less dependent on internal integration, and correspondingly more dependent on external integration, than either the USA or the EC. Lacking its own raw materials, it is obliged to import them from resource-rich neighbours; and in order to pay for them it is obliged to export the resulting finished products. The need for internal integration arose indirectly from a Western initiative which, under the 'unequal treaties', obliged Japan to open its ports to Western trade. Faced with the prospect of becoming just another Western colony the Japanese elite closed ranks, and began to promote industrialisation in order to catch up both economically and militarily with the West. Following the Meiji restoration, internal integration in Japan was promoted by centrally planned investment in transport infrastructure and utilities. Enterprising Japanese travelled abroad to identify best-practice Western technology and management that could be adapted and improved to meet Japanese needs.

The Japanese experience is not dissimilar to that of Germany, and to other countries which, feeling threatened by external economic and military power, have sought to 'catch up' through planned industrialisation. The German genius for original scientific research meant that the import of foreign technology was less significant, but the role of internal integration through a customs union, and external integration through the military conquest of sources of raw material supply, has parallels with Japan.

Other countries have tended to have much less success in catching up by these means, however. African countries, for example, have by and large failed to absorb advanced technologies successfully, and attempts at territorial expansion within Africa have become bogged down in military stalemate. Attempts to organise a common market foundered because of traditional local rivalries and differences of political ideology. Decolonisation has, in some cases, adversely affected the maintenance of infrastructure and utilities.

Failure to achieve economies from internal integration has inhibited external integration in Africa. A shortage of domestic savings encouraged attempts to finance industrialisation from the taxation of agriculture (a policy legitimated on the grounds that there is a long-term secular trend for the terms of trade to move against agricultural exporters). But failures in product quality and marketing meant that industrial exports did not expand to make good the decline in agricultural exports, and the desperate attempt to finance trade deficits by borrowing from Western banks precipitated the debt crisis of the mid-1980s. Not only, therefore, is there no integrated African market on a scale commensurate with that of the leading powers, but most of the individual national markets are now reduced because of the burden of debt repayment.

Current World Bank policies are concerned mainly with reintegrating African economies into the world economy by eliminating the distortion of incentives created during periods of planned industrialisation. Historical precedents suggest, however, that external integration must go hand-in-hand with internal integration if it is to be properly successful. External integration without internal integration simply leads to the development of enclaves – such as plantations and off-shore processing zones – which have negligible linkages with the rest of the economy. Moreover, as Western governments become increasingly strict over environmental standards, there is a growing danger that such zones merely attract pollution-intensive activities which take advantage of a lax regulatory regime. Even where such enclaves may, from an economic point of view, be better than nothing, there remain substantial losses from the failure of African political leaders to achieve stronger internal integration.

1.4 THE GEOGRAPHY OF INTERNAL INTEGRATION

However large or small the territory, integration is not an even process. Some places are more heavily integrated into the rest of the system than are others. The movement of passengers and freight, for example, typically involves a trunk system connecting major hubs from which local feeder services emanate. These feeders typically serve local hubs at which smaller-scale feeder operations are based, and so on.

It seems to be a characteristic of relatively undeveloped networks that there is a single centre which has a crucial role. Communication between the minor centres is almost invariably through the major one. As the volume of traffic on the network develops, however, congestion increases around the major hub, whilst at the same time the amount of traffic flowing between certain pairs of minor centres reaches the level that will justify a direct link between them.

Under the original configuration traffic tends to build up as the major centre is approached, so the volume of both passengers and freight is greatest at the hubs nearest to the major one. These hubs are therefore the ones that are likely to have the greatest amount of direct traffic between them. They are also the hubs that are the shortest distance apart. The deepening of the network is therefore likely to begin with direct links between adjacent pairs of hubs in the vicinity of the major centre. When this process is complete the links will connect up to form an orbital structure around the centre, affording a bypass facility.

This dramatically alters the role of the centre because through traffic is largely eliminated, and so the demand for warehousing and transhipment is reduced. The importance of markets where physical products are displayed and inspected also declines, but such markets can often be replaced by trade in claims instead. Samples rather than actual supplies are exhibited, and the negotiation of each contract is separated from the physical collection or delivery of the product. The key issues handled at the centre therefore concern price comparisons, means of payment and the enforcement of contracts. These are handled by specialists in the service sector – wholesalers and retailers, bankers and lawyers – who in turn rely on other specialists, such as computer personnel, for support. The centre therefore evolves from an entrepôt into a service centre. Personal travellers now visit the centre specifically to do business there (or for tourism) rather than on a through journey, so that the demand for accommodation and catering, while still buoyant, is of a slightly different nature. On balance, though, the demand for leisure and tourism services increases.

As the centre and its hinterland develop further, so a finer subdivision of activities can be made, with the entrepreneurial and innovative components being retained in the centre while more routine clerical activities are spun off to the suburbs. This tendency may be accelerated by recent developments in telecommunications, which allow 'screen working' to be decentralised not merely from the centre to the suburbs, but even from the office to the suburban home.

This heavily stylised picture is somewhat complicated by geographical idiosyncrasies, of course. Major entrepôt centres are typically connected to other centres of similar status by maritime trade (the sea being the cheapest long distance mode of freight transport). For this reason they often occupy a coastal position, where there is a natural harbour at the estuary of an inland river system. The coastline is convenient for the disposal of pollutants created by the processing of materials passing through the port. As the infrastructure around the centre improves, the port and the processing tend to move further out along the coast, so that the minor centres around the entrepôt become more heavily industrialised.

In this way economic development through integration spreads outwards from the centre until, in a developed country, the whole of the territory is affected (Casson, 1990). In an undeveloped country, on the other hand, the centre may have very little impact on the hinterland. Instead of developing into a service centre with many satellite centres it remains an entrepôt: connected to the rest of the world by shipping, but starkly urban in contrast to its predominantly rural and inaccessible hinterland.

While a small country such as Britain, Belgium or the Netherlands may be dominated by a single centre, a large country such as the USA may have several such centres, although one of them (such as New York) may be rather more important than the others. This distinction is important when considering links between the world's major centres because it is not always the case that such links are international, although it is often assumed that they are. The drawing of national boundaries is sometimes a fairly arbitrary process – reflecting, for example, the disposition of troops at the termination of a war – and does not therefore respect the logic that each nation should be an economic unit with a 'geocentric' service centre.

1.5 INTERNATIONAL BUSINESS AS AN INTEGRATING FORCE

One of the main themes of this book is that international business operations facilitate economic integration. It was emphasised at the outset that economic integration benefits greatly from political stability. Political stability also favours the growth of multinational operations, as it reduces the risks of expropriation and discrimination against foreign-owned firms. These operations in turn expedite the integration process. Commodity trade, factor mobility and technology transfer all benefit from intrafirm linkages created by MNEs.

The pre-eminent motive for multinational corporate expansion is the exploitation of a competitive advantage in technology or marketing. By avoiding the transaction costs of licensing and franchising, multinational strategies increase the profitability of researching and developing global technologies and products. To accommodate local tastes, a modular product design is frequently adopted which allows different product varieties to be created through various permutations of components. This approach maximises the economies of scale available from the mass production of components, and encourages an international division of labour in which the production of different components is concentrated on different sites according to local comparative advantage.

Technology transfer assists newly industrialising countries to catch up with the leaders, although the leaders themselves will at the same time be forging ahead through further innovation. The development of global products increases rivalry between MNEs since no firm's domestic market is now safe from competition. Even where there is protection, foreign firms can 'jump the tariff wall' using foreign direct investment.

In the absence of such protection, large segments of the world market can be sourced by third-country production. This allows countries with small domestic markets but outward-looking trade policies to attract significant export-oriented foreign investment.

Multinational operations also promote intermediate product trade. Economies of vertical integration reduce the transaction costs of international trade in raw materials, components and semi-processed goods, and hence promote the international division of labour described above. Labour-intensive assembly operations can be relocated to low-wage countries while capital- and skill-intensive operations are retained in the more advanced economies.

The reputation gained by MNEs through their global operations allows them to raise capital in different countries. This provides MNEs with considerable flexibility to avoid capital controls. For example, US government attempts to limit the export of capital from the USA led many US-owned MNEs to raise funds in London (on the Eurodollar market) instead.

Raising funds from different sources allows different aspects of corporate risk to be borne by different nationalities of shareholder. Thus investors in countries where risk-aversion is high can concentrate on holding debentures, whilst investors in countries where risk-aversion is low can concentrate on holding equities instead. In this way not only the operation of the enterprise, but also its ownership, becomes multinational (Casson, 1982). Furthermore, because of intermediation by mutual funds (pension funds, insurance companies, and so on) in this process, it is actually quite difficult to establish the true nationality of ownership (if any) of some firms.

Nationality of firms is often inferred from the location of the headquarters instead, but even this can sometimes be a poor guide. Some European MNEs, for example, have extremely powerful US subsidiaries. Because of its privileged access to a large consumer market the US subsidiary is in a stronger position to make key decisions about product development than is the European headquarters, so that while the headquarters may have the nominal authority, it normally acts upon recommendations from the USA.

1.6 MANAGERIAL MOBILITY AND CORPORATE CULTURE

Another key to nationality is the citizenship of the chief executive. As a consequence of the geographical mobility of personnel within large firms it cannot be assumed that chief executives are nationals of the country in which the firm is headquartered (and even if they are, they may have dual nationality, or have been born and/or educated outside the country). The internal mobility of management is particularly conspicuous in the case of MNEs based in the smaller European economies – the Netherlands, Switzerland, Sweden, and so on – where many of the key executive posts are outside the home country (for example, in the USA; see above). This means that home-country nationals cannot get to the top in the company without extensive first-hand overseas experience, and equally that they face potential competition for top jobs from the many foreign citizens recruited by the foreign subsidiaries. These recruits expect promotion (including promotion to the headquarters) as a reward for good performance.

The management of personnel within MNEs is a large subject which has, until recently, received only limited attention from academics. An early concern expressed by host-country governments was that subsidiary managers were too ethnocentric, transferring the cultural values of the source country without suitable modification. This may, of course, reflect little more than the inexperience of the managers concerned. Certainly, well-established MNEs have made special efforts to become good 'corporate citizens' in the host country. There is, however, a trade-off between appointing a host-country citizen as manager, who may have a limited familiarity with the organisation as a whole, and a foreigner from headquarters who has greater familiarity with the organisation but less with the host country.

As MNE operations become more complex, the amount of direct contact between subsidiary and subsidiary tends to increase relative to the contact between the subsidiary and the parent. This is an organisational analogy with the process of 'bypassing the centre' described earlier. If the firm places too much emphasis on being a good corporate citizen in each country then subsidiary operations will become so non-standard that intersubsidiary linkages will become difficult to manage. One possible response to this is to establish a corporate culture which allows managers to invoke common beliefs and assumptions when communicating with each other.

The difficulty with engineering a corporate culture along these lines is that it is liable to be a relatively superficial one. Most of the world's leading cultures have evolved through frequent face-to-face contact within reasonably stable, geographically compact social groups. The values embodied in the cultures have evolved from one generation to the next through parental guidance and incremental adaptation. The middle managers of an MNE are a scattered group of individuals, many of whom are mobile between firms as well as within them, and who communicate with each other chiefly by impersonal telecommunication. Only the elite managers based at headquarters are likely to function as a traditional social group. There is a danger, therefore, that the elite managers become cliquish, and disseminate to middle management a rather crude form of propaganda based upon a charismatic image of the chief executive.

The most satisfactory way of engineering a corporate culture is probably to reduce interfirm managerial mobility by relying heavily on internal promotion, and then to encourage managers to pursue a varied career path within the firm. Regular face-to-face contact with managers from different divisions can be organised under the auspices of senior management. This, of course, requires mobility of personnel not only through overseas postings but also through short visits, corporate convention trips, and so on. It is worth adding that, at more senior levels, functional mobility as well as geographical mobility is useful as it serves to reduce the individual's allegiance to technical and professional groups external to the firm. Clearly, though, while such measures are a useful corrective to individual managerial motivations which would otherwise conflict with corporate performance, overzealous application of them may actually undermine performance by turning managers into conformist 'organisation men'.

1.7 SERVICES TO TRAVELLERS

Managerial mobility is a special case of a more general phenomenon, namely labour mobility. MNEs have promoted mobility not only at the managerial level, but amongst unskilled workers too. Although small firms rather than large firms are notorious for the operation of 'immigrant sweatshops', MNEs are major employers of immigrants, particularly in service industries like hotels. The hotel industry is interesting because it employs 'mobile' unskilled workers to support the mobility of professional people and tourists through the provision of travellers' accommodation. Other travel-related industries in which MNEs are well represented are banks and car rental.

The concentration of travellers around major hubs means that, for multinational service firms, the key requirement is not necessarily representation in every country but representation at every major hub. This implies, for reasons noted above, that they may require several facilities in certain countries and none in others. Service firms require full coverage of major hubs for the same reason that manufacturing firms benefit from full range in terms of product variety. Customers at one facility are potentially subsequent customers at other facilities, and *economies of mutual recommendation* mean that they are more likely to patronise any one facility if they have enjoyed their experience at a previous one. In providing banking facilities for tourists, *economies of mutual recognition* are important too; the customer needs to be confident that a credit instrument (bank deposit, say, or traveller's cheque) purchased at one facility will be recognised and accepted at another, and this confidence is increased if the other facility is a branch of the same bank rather than just an independently-owned 'correspondent' bank. A firm that provides a comprehensive coverage of locations visited by the regular traveller relieves the traveller of any need to seek out alternative suppliers at any location. The traveller's lack of experience of alternative suppliers deters experimental switching and so creates brand loyalty that acts as a barrier to the entry of rival firms.

1.8 KEY ISSUES IDENTIFIED BY THE EMPIRICAL WORK

It is, of course, impossible to illuminate all of these issues within the context of a single book. Nevertheless the range of source and host countries discussed, and the number of different sectors covered in this book, is quite large. Several chapters draw comparisons between foreign investments sourced from different parts of the Triad. The coverage of host countries is quite extensive, with a particular focus on two of the larger and more populous LDCs: China and India. There is also a strong coverage of the service sector, with a particular focus on banking, while high-technology manufacturing industries, such as pharmaceuticals, are also examined in detail.

Six main themes can be identified from the empirical work.

The view of the world economy as a hierarchy of centres in which the most important centres are concentrated in the Triad countries is borne out well by evidence on service activities. It is clearest in the case of multinational banking, where trading is split into three time zones, and each Triad member hosts the leading centre in each zone: New York, London, and Tokyo (see Chapter 5). These three financial centres offer the widest variety of financial services, and specialise in offering the more specialised services which minor centres cannot afford to provide at all.

The hierarchy is also apparent in the field of R & D, where

innovative activity tends to cluster around the major centres. The USA, as the world's largest single national market, hosts the largest amount of 'near market' product development work. Quite a lot of this is nowadays undertaken by European firms – particularly German and Swiss firms – who carry out their more basic research elsewhere. Within countries, laboratories geared to development work tend to cluster round the periphery of the major service centres, suggesting that the concentration of market information in these centres attracts innovative activity. Laboratories geared to basic research can survive in a more solitary environment. Countries which have a strong university system are regularly used for more basic research even though they do not have large indigenous markets: Canadian affiliates, for example, are regularly allocated specific research tasks by their US parents.

The Triad groups have promoted very different degrees of external integration amongst their neighbouring countries. Because the EC has been preoccupied with exploiting opportunities for internal integration, the traditional links of its major industrial powers with their former colonies have been neglected. Whilst the USA and Japan have expanded off-shore processing in their 'back yard', to utilise low-wage labour in the countries of the Pacific rim, EC countries have done much less of this except in a few countries such as Tunisia and Morocco (see Chapter 8). The continued expansion of the EC through the accession of the Southern Mediterranean countries, and the prospect of further expansion as a result of German unification and the proposed accession of Turkey, will tend to perpetuate this inward-looking attitude.

In so far as EC outward investment expands, it may well be channelled into Eastern Europe rather than to its traditional destination in Africa. European investment in Africa has been geared more to the exploitation of mineral deposits than to the utilisation of cheap labour, and new minerals projects are discouraged by memories of the earlier nationalisations and expropriations which occurred after decolonisation. Similarly, import-substituting manufacturing investments are discouraged by the small size of the domestic markets in debt-ridden countries, and by the dismantling of protection as part of, or in imitation of, World Bank structural adjustment programmes. These same programmes, however, may serve to stimulate agricultural production and labour-intensive manufacturing for export by aligning domestic prices in these countries more closely with international prices. The main barriers to foreign investment in these sectors are social and political: the limitations of indigenous entrepreneurship on the one hand, and the need to negotiate tariff preferences for wider access to the European market on the other.

The growth of Japanese exports and investment has led to major changes in management practices amongst Western MNEs. In industries such as motor vehicles and consumer electronics, the dramatic loss of market share to Japanese imports has encouraged Western producers to learn from the Japanese. Particular attention has been paid to the concept of total quality management as applied to mass production processes based on a component manufacture-assembly sequence. Long-term 'relational contracting' between assemblers and component-subcontractors has been employed to improve communication, leading to better control of component flow and quality, and thence to lower buffer inventory stocks. Within the enterprise, quality circles and flexible working practices reduce machine down-time and minimise disruption to material flow.

Learning from the Japanese has also affected technology itself. Western R & D is now far more oriented to development, and less to basic research, than it was in the 1970s (see Chapter 6). Development is perceived as a continuous process of incremental improvement, with shorter lead-times associated with each project.

These learning effects show that the greater integration of final product markets achieved through Japanese exports of 'global products' has induced greater integration in the intermediate product market for management skills. Expertise no longer flows one way (outward from the West) but is a two-way flow in which the West has learned much from the Japanese. The Japanese, for their part, continue to learn selectively from the West. Their major firms are undertaking more basic research than they did before, so that there is an international convergence of practice in R & D. They are also re-evaluating their education system in order to strengthen their indigenous capability for imaginative pure research, without excessively diluting their traditional emphasis on practical engineering skills.

The market for management skills is now much more sophisticated than it was in the early days of US multinational expansion. At that time equity ownership was closely identified with management control. Majority ownership of a subsidiary was deemed necessary in order to coordinate the subsidiary's operations with those of the parent company.

Nowadays it is recognised that equity has a dual role: it not only secures control but also allocates responsibility for risk. Control and risk-bearing are two distinct functions and can, in principle, be separated. Such separation affords gains to specialisation through comparative advantage. A risk-averse enterprise with effective management skills can exercise control of an overseas project without significant exposure to risk, while a less risk-averse local partner can take on the risks without having to exercise control.

The mechanism that permits this separation of functions is the management contract. It is particularly useful when the management skills are embodied in routine office procedures which can be reliably implemented by suitably trained managers. This allows the risk-taker to forecast managerial performance fairly easily on the basis of management's track record on other projects. It is also particularly useful when each project requires local expertise to evaluate the risks and obtain statutary permission to proceed.

Both of these conditions are satisfied by several service industries (see Chapter 4). It is not the command of advanced technology but the detailed supervision of employees carrying out tightly specified programmes of work that is crucial in car rental, hotels and fast food, for example. In the first two cases the operation of a global computerised reservation system is important too. Command of such a system gives the management contractor a strong advantage over independent indigenous management when international travellers constitute a significant proportion of the clientele.

Joint ventures can function reasonably well both as a transitional arrangement with a private partner and as a long-term arrangement with a public partner. The high rate of dissolution of private joint venture partnerships (Kogut, 1988) does not mean that they are normally unsuccessful. It may simply mean that they are more appropriate as a transitional rather than a permanent arrangement. Joint ventures can be an effective way for the partners to learn from each other, and even if one partner eventually buys out the other it does not mean that the other partner has lost, provided that the sale price reflects the value added to the partner's stake as a result of the operation. It is really only when the venture ceases trading altogether that there is prima facie evidence of failure.

The role of local partners in the expansion of the MNE is again well illustrated by the service sector (see Chapter 4). A service MNE has a choice, when entering a new country, of confining its activities to just the major centre(s), or expanding them to gain greater depth of penetration. A single facility located at a major hub is not too difficult to manage at a distance because the hub itself is so accessible from headquarters. Managing at a distance is much more problematic so far as the hinterland is concerned, however. It is less well known and less accessible, and on both these criteria a local partner may be required. Because service MNEs facilitate travel, however, the collective effect of such partnerships within the service sector is to open up the hinterland to the traveller, making managing at a distance easier than it was before. Coupled with the greater experience gained by the firm through opening up new territories in conjunction with local partners, this encourages the reintegration of the partnership into the firm. Such reintegration is particularly likely in those areas such as insurance and advertising where the management contract is not particularly suitable as a means of maintaining control.

In some countries, however, outright ownership is not really an option (except, sometimes, in government-designated high priority sectors) and joint ventures are expected to be in partnership with the state. Joint venturing *per se* does not seem significantly to reduce the risk of expropriation or political interference, as some Western investors in LDCs initially hoped, but the ability to invoke management contracts helps to insulate the Western partner from day-to-day interference. It also appears that large Western MNEs with long experience of overseas operations are well versed in harnessing political forces for their protection. Whether they bring pressure to bear on the host government directly – by threatening to stop importing components and technology – or indirectly – by lobbying their own government to make wider threats of a political or military nature – is not clear. In any case, a belief amongst Western investors that they have such power may well explain why such investors often seem to take less than the maximum permitted stake in joint ventures with public-sector partners (see Chapter 2). The choice of equity stake seems to be governed more by the desire to limit exposure to risk (particularly where the project is large in relation to the firm's global operations) than by the desire to strengthen control at the boardroom level. While the exercise of political power in defence of foreign economic interests may, in one sense, be deplored, its influence on economic efficiency seems on balance to be benign. It represents a rational 'second best' response to intervention which might otherwise inhibit integration by deterring technology transfer.

Western MNEs share certain common elements of corporate culture which integrate much better with local cultures in some countries than in others. Today's largest MNEs are to some extent the firms that have grown most rapidly in the past. As a result they are likely to have a corporate culture that is conducive to growth. To avoid diseconomies of bureaucracy, such a culture must support decentralised organisational structures by stressing individual autonomy. It must also encourage loyalty amongst managers who are working far away from the parent company and sometimes (particularly in the service sector) far away from the subsidiary headquarters as well. Reconciliation of autonomy and loyalty can be achieved through a team ethic which stresses the importance of internal competition. The object of each competitor is to become not the best individualist, but the best 'team player'. In a firm that expands through internal growth this culture may permeate even the lowest levels of management. In a firm that expands by acquisition it is more likely to be confined to the higher levels of management, with the acquired groups retaining more of their traditional (and probably less growth-oriented) ethos.

This kind of corporate culture resonates well with national cultures in certain countries. By and large these are the developed countries where the influence of major market centres is paramount. However, because the corporate culture is oriented to the internal markets of the firm as well as to the external markets in which it competes, the culture is normally more team-oriented than the extremely competitive individualism that permeates some of the arm's-length markets at network hubs.

Many countries, however, have cultures which emphasise the importance of harmonious social relations in which everyone treats everyone else with great respect. Internal competition is regarded as divisive, and the idea that the group must have a team mission external to itself is alien. Groups are modelled closely on the family, so that the intergenerational reproduction of the group and its traditional authority relations is the paramount consideration (see Chapter 7). Such a culture is not necessarily inimical to business success; small family firms may be able to 'free ride' on this family structure quite well, provided there is sufficient flexibility to allow the most able of the inheritors to succeed to the senior management position. But it generates very high costs to growth, preventing the firm from capitalising fully on any success.

MNEs operating in such countries may have to rely heavily on expatriates, and even fill relatively junior management positions with people seconded from the parent firm. Backward linkages with indigenous firms may be difficult to develop because, even with a secure corporate customer, the indigenous firms may be reluctant to grow at the customer's pace.

Cultures can, of course, change in the long run, and a large MNE presence can be a powerful agent of change. In the UK, for example, US management practices diffused quite quickly from foreign investors to indigenous firms, and the same thing seems to be happening with respect to recent Japanese investors (as indicated above). In India, by contrast, the presence of many Western MNEs in the pharmaceutical industry has elicited little response from the private sector, even though India is regarded by Western firms as a satisfactory place not only to undertake production for export, but also to undertake research (see Chapter 3).

Cultural change within a country is most likely to emanate from the major centres, which is in any case where most MNEs (particularly those in the service sector) are likely to locate. Economic integration and cultural change are therefore closely linked, as development economists have often observed. Private foreign direct investment is unlikely to be profitable until cultural change has occurred, but cultural change may well not occur until private investment has developed local market access and promoted travel. It may require a powerful indigenous elite to break this potential stalemate. The historical evidence reviewed earlier suggests that some kind of external pressure, such as a military threat, or the rise of a new technological competitor, may be necessary to galvanise such an elite into action.

1.9 CULTURAL CONVERGENCE THROUGH ECONOMIC INTEGRATION

The link between economic integration and cultural change raises the broader issue of whether economic integration is really desirable in the first place. The material benefits conferred by integration may be outweighed by social costs. In this case, governments who have sought to restrict international business operations simply because they are agents of cultural change may well have been in the right.

The very existence of cultural differences makes it difficult to arrive at any consensus on the relative merits of different cultures, since it is in the nature of a culture to command unquestioning commitment to certain beliefs and values. On the other hand, the fact that global integration is now more advanced than at any time in history means that there are better opportunities for communication and for sharing different views. Whether this opportunity is exploited properly is, of course, another matter.

It seems unlikely that economic integration will ever completely eliminate cultural diversity. People like to identify themselves with particular groups and will therefore create cultural diversity, just as young people continually evolve subcultures to differentiate themselves from older people. However, while diversity may be sustained through innovation, the sense of continuity and tradition that older people in particular value in a culture may well be undermined. There is no easy solution to this, because it is unrealistic to believe that a traditional culture can be preserved, say, as a tourist attraction without turning it into a commercialised 'museum piece'. The preservation of a living culture really depends on the young people who inherit it placing sufficient value upon it that they wish to sustain it through their lifestyle, even though material sacrifices may be involved.

There is one particular aspect of economic integration which, above all, threatens traditional culture, and that is the greater opportunity it provides for mobility. Most traditional cultures are sustained through individual participation in community activities on a recurrent basis. In an isolated society the opportunity cost of commitment to the local community is very low but, as mobility increases, the cost rises and so the emotional benefits of participation must increase to match. There is, however, an externality problem, because the value of participation depends on the number of other participants, but participants do not necessarily consider the impact on other participants when they decide whether to participate. For this reason traditional cultures may be excessively vulnerable to disintegration.

On balance it seems likely that some cultural convergence is an unavoidable consequence of integration. Indeed, such convergence is probably desirable on highly practical grounds. In a highly-integrated world the political, economic and military consequences of intercultural rivalry are much more severe than in a less integrated world where each culture enjoys exclusive dominion over a defensible territory. Thus while diversity may well be desirable at a superficial level, it is increasingly important to have consensus over a core set of fundamental values. Toleration of other people's views, for example, is a fairly obvious requirement for peaceful coexistence in a highly integrated economic system.

If the maintenance of the present material benefits of economic integration is deemed necessary, then the set of core values is quite tightly constrained. It may be supposed, for example, that a broadly-based commitment to economic liberalism is necessary to sustain integration of the present kind. The difficulty here seems to be that economic liberalism has become identified in the twentieth century with a rather aggressive kind of competitive individualism. It would be very useful to be able to convince hardened Western individualists that it is often more productive to compete as a team rather than as an individual, and that a really rewarding team game requires cooperation in respecting the rules. Competition is not merely a means of engineering economic efficiency, but a cooperative exercise that helps each player to give of his best. The principles of competition and cooperation are both helpful in maintaining discipline and social order: the former exerts an external discipline on the individual and the second an internal discipline based on self-restraint. While cultures differ considerably in the relative emphasis placed on these two principles, an economic liberalism which emphasises their complementary roles might provide a satisfactory cultural compromise compatible with continued integration.

2 Western Joint Ventures in China

MARK CASSON AND
JURONG ZHENG

2.1 INTRODUCTION

The liberalisation of foreign investment regulations in many developing countries has led to a proliferation of joint ventures involving Western firms (Contractor and Lorange, 1988). The People's Republic of China is no exception to this. The 'open door' policy is designed to promote technology transfer in industries of strategic importance for national development, and to stimulate hard currency exports and local employment (Hsu, 1989). Liberalisation reflects host-government recognition that Western firms are reluctant to transfer proprietary technology without an equity stake (Thoburn *et al.*, 1990).

This chapter presents new evidence on Western investment in China, derived from 79 questionnaire responses by Western firms. It is supplemented by a comprehensive analysis of official statistics for the period 1979–86. The evidence is used to test a theory of joint ventures derived from the internalisation approach to international business (Buckley and Casson, 1976, 1985). The data were collected from two main sources: official publications – in particular, the China Investment Guide (CITIC, 1984, 1985, 1986) and Almanac of China's Foreign Economic Relations and Trade (MOFERT, 1987) – and a questionnaire survey of Western investors. The first source generates a data base of 2136 equity joint ventures (EJVs) over the period 1979–86. A separate data base for 120 wholly-owned ventures (WOVs), 1979–85, was also established. Together, they provide a reasonable coverage of Western ventures in China, as seen in Table 2.1.

TABLE 2.1 *Data collection*

	1979–83	*1984*	*1985*	*1986*	*Total*
EJVs*	190	741	1300	892	3123
EJVs database	190†	651†	835†	460‡	2136
WOVs*	48	26	46	18	138
WOVs data base	48†	26†	46†	–	120

* Chen (1986).
† CITIC (1984, 1985, 1986).
‡ MOFERT (1987).

TABLE 2.2 *Composition of survey sample*

	USA	*UK*	*Other European*	*Other OECD*	*Total*
Usable replies	30	19	18	12	79
Sample population	115	41	52	28	236
Response rate(%)	26.1	46.3	34.6	42.8	33.5

(OECD = Organisation for Economic Co-operation and Development.)

The second source provides more detailed information both on the projects themselves and on the attitudes of the Western partners. A sample of 236 Western firms in 15 countries received a questionnaire. The response rate after one reminder was 32.6 per cent (see Table 2.2). The response of UK and Australian firms was relatively good and that of the USA was relatively poor.

The theory is summarised in section 2.2. Chinese policy towards foreign investment is briefly reviewed in section 2.3. Official statistics are used to profile EJVs in China in section 2.4. A preliminary attempt to test the theory using official data is made in section 2.5. A comparison between EJVs and WOVs is made in section 2.6. Evidence from the questionnaire is introduced in section 2.7 and the tests are re-run using this additional evidence in section 2.8. These tests generally validate the theory. Comparisons between Hong Kong and Macao (HKM) and Western firms are made in section 2.9. Future prospects for foreign direct investment (FDI) in China are considered in section 2.10. The conclusions are summarised in section 2.11.

2.2 THEORY

A foreign investor engaged in technology transfer demands an equity stake not merely as a means of appropriating rents but, most importantly, as a means of acquiring influence and control. Licensing is not usually an acceptable alternative because of the well-known difficulty of monitoring compliance. In a non-Western environment the firm will be particularly concerned that the technology may be passed on to unauthorised users. The more valuable the technology transferred, the stronger will be the firm's desire for a significant equity stake.

Where exportable goods are concerned, it will wish to regulate competition between different users of the technology attempting to source the same market (Casson, 1987, Chapter 2). The greater the export potential, therefore, the higher is the desired equity stake. Where a brand name is involved as well, it will also be concerned that an inferior quality product from one source will damage its overall reputation. Quality control is particularly important for goods produced with sophisticated technology and exported to high-income markets. Quality control is easiest to enforce when the equity stake is high.

Technology transfer is not the only motive for foreign involvement in a developing country. Backward linkages into natural resources may be stimulated by economies of vertical integration. In this context, high sunk costs and opportunities for transfer pricing may be the dominant considerations. They are also relevant to technology transfer, but tend to show up more in the context of resource-based investments. The higher are sunk costs as a proportion of total costs, and the greater the discrepancies between the fiscal regimes in home and host countries, the higher will be the desired equity stake.

Foreign investors not only transfer their knowledge into a country, but also acquire through experience important knowledge of the local market. Investors with only a transitory involvement in a single project may have little motive for learning about the domestic market as a whole. A firm with a long-term commitment to serving the local market, however, most certainly does. Firms attracted on a long-term basis will normally learn more if they have a high equity stake, because this will give them better access to confidential marketing information.

A foreign investor who traditionally relies on centralised management and strict hierarchical control will normally desire a higher equity stake than a decentralised conglomerate firm. This is because some styles of management require stronger authority structures than others. Another factor is that investors based in countries with only weak cultural and political links with the host country may perceive excessive expropriation risks. The exaggeration of risk through 'psychic distance' will tend to reduce the desired equity stake.

The actual equity stake may differ from the foreign firm's desired equity stake because of the attitude of the host government. The actual equity stake can be regarded as the outcome of a bargaining process. The conventional bargaining literature (Fagre and Wells, 1982) emphasises an exchange of threats between the foreign firm, with its monopoly of technology, and the host government, with its monopoly of the allocation of production sites. The party that can make the biggest threat gets the biggest stake according to this view.

A different approach is adopted here. It reflects the view that there is an international market in which governments can choose between various foreign investors, and foreign investors can choose between various production locations. Given such a market environment, the normal procedures of negotiation subject to competitive constraints apply. Each party is restricted by the need to better the deal its competitors offer. The government, for example, can insist on a higher equity stake than its competitors only if it offers some compensating advantage (such as lower taxes) in return. The competitive process means that the foreign investor gets the equity stake that other investors in the same line of business would also require. He or she only settles for less if the host government offers some other benefits in return. The net effect is that the actual stake is equal to the stake normally required by investors with similar technologies to offer, less a discrepancy which reflects the host government's willingness to offer worthwhile inducements to settle for less.

It is often difficult to obtain direct measurements of the value of proprietary technology, the importance of quality control and the other variables identified by theory as key determinants of the equity stake. These variables may, however, be systematically related to the industry in which the venture is involved, and to the source country in which the foreign firm is headquartered. Industries such as pharmaceuticals and office equipment, for example, are dominated by high-technology firms, whereas in agriculture and construction much less proprietary technology is involved. Although technological sophistication is often modest in the service sector, proprietary brand names in car rental, hotels and financial services may create a similar desire for equity control. The sophistication of the technology may also be related to the source country. US firms, for example, typically have more advanced technology than those in the Asia/Pacific region (with the possible exception of Japan). Thus, within a high-technology industry, the incentive to demand a high equity stake may be strongest for US firms. Cultural attitudes to management can also vary between source countries. US firms, for example, tend to rely more heavily than European firms on hierarchical control, possibly because of the higher level of distrust within their source country culture (Casson, 1990, Chapter 5). Thus US firms may desire higher equity stakes than European firms even when the technology transferred is the same. European firms may demand a lower equity stake both because of their management culture and because their greater distance from China makes close supervision more difficult anyway.

The location chosen for the project within the developing country will also reflect hidden factors concerned with the nature of the technology and management style. Firms with a high propensity to export, and with considerable concern over international collusion and quality control, will tend to locate near the coast and particularly in zones where fiscal incentives for off-shore production are strong. Firms with a long-term commitment to the domestic market are likely to select a fairly central location, such as Beijing. Firms that are heavily dependent on state contracts may also locate close to Beijing for customer liaison and political lobbying.

Other observable characteristics related to hidden variables include the duration and size of the venture. High-technology projects, for example, may be longer term than others. Duration is also important in its own right, because a long-term venture is more likely to involve a sequence of managerial decisions and so increase the foreign investor's desire for control. The role of size is more ambiguous. When a project is large in relation to the foreign investor's global operations, the foreign investor may be happy to lay off a significant proportion of the financial risks on to the Chinese partner. Not only does this reduce the risk that the failure of the venture may bankrupt the firm as a whole, but it also reduces the amount of additional capital that the firm has to raise in the first place. On the other hand, the greater strategic importance of the venture to the firm may actually increase its desire for control. On balance, though, it seems likely that risk reduction will outweigh other factors, and that an increase in the size of project will normally reduce the foreign equity stake. The main exception will be where a very large investor is concerned.

2.3 POLICY ENVIRONMENT

Foreign investment has played an important role in the modernisation of the Chinese economy. In fact, despite various adjustments in government policy since the open door policy of 1979, the Chinese government has shown increasing commitment to foreign investment as an integral part of national development strategy (Campbell, 1988, 1989).

Forms of Investment

The main forms of foreign investment in China are EJVs, contractual joint ventures, compensation trade, WOVs and joint off-shore exploration. Contractual joint ventures involve a wide range of projects, often vaguely specified, which involve no equity stake; they are excluded from this study. The Chinese government prefers EJVs to WOVs as it desires some control over investment for ideological, political and historical reasons. It was not until 1986 that the Chinese government began to promote WOVs, following a significant reduction in foreign investment in China during that year.

In theory, WOVs have been permitted in a restricted form since 1980 but, although the promulgation of the law on joint ventures using Chinese and foreign investment (JVL) stipulated only a minimum 25 per cent of foreign investment, the government seldom approved more than a 50 per cent foreign equity stake. Until 1984 WOVs were in practice allowed only in the Special Economic Zones (SEZs). Later, the 14 coastal cities also became proposed sites of WOVs.

Geographical Priority

Four SEZs were established in the late 1970s and early 1980s – Shenzhen, Zhuhai, Shantou and Xiamen – on an experimental basis. The Hainan Island SEZ was set up in late 1987. They offered preferential treatment in terms of reduction of, or exemption from, enterprise income tax and consolidated industrial and commercial tax, tax incentives on repatriated profits, and reduced land use fees as well as simplified administrative procedures. For example, income is subject to a 15 per cent tax for EJVs in the SEZs while 30 per cent tax plus a 10 per cent local surcharge is payable outside the SEZs.

In 1984 preferential treatment was extended to the 14 coastal cities: Dalian, Qinhuangdao, Tianjin, Yantai, Qingdao, Lianyungang, Nantong, Shanghai, Ningbo, Wenzhou, Fuzhou, Guangzhou, Zhangjiang and Beihai. However, it was only available for production enterprises whereas the SEZs give preferences to services as well. The 14 coastal cities were designed to attract scientific and technological research. Dalian, Guangzhou, Tianjin and Shanghai were given special autonomy in allocating foreign exchange and approving projects. The Tianjin and Shanghai governments can approve a project up to US$30 million (compared to US$5–10 million elsewhere) without the need for further authorisation. This reflects a significant decentralisation of foreign investment policy implementation.

The JVL also permits preferential treatment to be extended on a case-by-case basis to projects of a developmental nature in economically underdeveloped areas, but this provision has proved less successful.

In 1985, further liberalisation accorded preferences to other economic regions along the coast, each consisting of several dozen small cities and counties.

Technologically-Advanced and Export-Oriented Ventures

According to the Provisions on Encouragement of Foreign Investment of October 1986, special preferences can be accorded to export-oriented and technologically-advanced enterprises. For example, export-oriented ventures in the SEZs or the 14 coastal cities already paying income tax at a rate of 15 per cent enjoy a reduced rate of 10 per cent. As for technologically-advanced ventures, they can enjoy an extended period of 3 years' tax holiday.

Import-Substitution

EJVs are encouraged to sell their products on the international market. However, the domestic market may be open to EJVs only when their product is urgently needed or presently imported. China's import-substitution policy, promulgated in October 1987, enables EJVs to earn hard currency directly by supplying their products as import substitutes to Chinese enterprises (such as foreign trade corporations) which would otherwise use their currency allocation for imports.

Venture Duration and Size of Investment

There is no statutory limit on the duration of an EJV. However, informally there is a difference between so-called 'productive' projects, for which up to 25 years is acceptable, and 'non-productive' projects, such as hotels, where 10 years is the norm. In 1986 the emphasis was switched away from promoting small- and medium-scale EJVs towards large-scale, complex ventures.

There is no doubt that, for Western firms, the policy environment in China has improved over the period 1979–86. However, foreign investors remain restricted in terms of some decisions. Most fundamentally, the ever-changing Chinese policy environment continues to create business uncertainty and political risks.

2.4 STATISTICAL SUMMARY OF EJVs: 1979–86

Sectoral Distribution

Table 2.3 shows that during the period 1979–86 EJVs were mainly concentrated on electricals, food and drink, other manufacturing, textiles, chemicals and hotel industries. These six industries accounted for 60.3 per cent of foreign investment in terms of number of projects, while their share of capital value was 43.7 per cent of total investment. Over the period there was a decline of investment in hotels and other service industries while investment in building materials, chemicals, electricals, textiles, clothing and other manufacturing increased. This is due to a change in government policy designed to promote export-oriented projects.

Country of Origin

HKM is the dominant source of foreign investment in China over the period 1979–86, as shown in Table 2.4. Although its share fell from

TABLE 2.3 *Equity joint venture by industrial sector: summary*

	Number of projects	*Total investment (US$m)*	*Average investment (US$m)*	*Average foreign equity(%)*	*Average duration (years)*
Extractive					
Agriculture	58	138.9	2.4	45.5	14.6
Mining	1	1.3	1.3	40.0	25.0
Oil	55	84.5	1.5	43.5	10.3
Subtotal	114	224.7	2.0	44.5	12.7
Manufacturing					
Building materials	67	307.3	4.7	45.2	15.1
Chemicals	180	348.7	1.9	41.6	12.6
Computers	38	50.4	1.4	41.1	11.6
Construction	54	49.9	0.9	43.6	11.4
Electricals	312	543.9	1.7	39.2	12.1
Food and drink	142	422.1	3.0	44.2	14.0
Mechanicals	43	4 096.3	95.3	42.5	14.2
Metals	86	215.9	2.6	38.7	13.3
Motor vehicles	23	367.7	16.0	45.1	17.1
Paper	53	54.8	1.0	40.4	10.9
Pharmaceuticals	38	84.0	2.2	42.3	12.9
Telecommunications	20	141.5	7.1	37.8	12.5
Textiles	232	426.4	1.9	40.5	12.3
Wood and furniture	61	118.1	1.9	40.7	12.1
Other manufacturing	223	286.2	1.3	40.4	11.8
Subtotal	1 572	7 512.9	4.8	41.0	12.6
Services					
Hotels and tourism	170	2 893.7	17.1	43.3	13.9
Transportation	68	187.4	2.8	42.2	9.6
Retail trade	112	157.5	1.5	40.9	11.1
Business services	20	103.2	5.2	44.0	14.7
Financial and insurance	9	38.7	4.3	43.1	14.2
Science and technology	7	11.9	1.7	46.8	13.6
Other services	28	129.6	5.0	46.5	12.9
Subtotal	414	3 522.0	8.7	42.8	12.5
Total*	2 100	11 260.0	5.4	41.6	12.6

* Among 2136 observations, there are 36 observations with missing industry, 19 observations with missing values of amount of total investment, 38 observations with missing values of foreign equity percentage and 36 observations with missing values of duration.
Numbers do not add correctly due to rounding.
SOURCE: EJV data base.

71.7 per cent in 1979–83 to 67 per cent in 1986, its share of capital commitment increased from 36.3 per cent in 1979–83 to 51.9 per cent in 1986. On the other hand, both the Japanese and Other Asian shares have increased. There appears to be little change for US investment. The USA and Japan were the second and third largest

TABLE 2.4 *Equity venture by country of origin: summary*

	Number of projects	*Total investment (US$m)*	*Average investment (US$m)*	*Average foreign equity(%)*	*Average duration (years)*
HKM	1 623	8 733.8	5.4	40.9	11.9
Japan	146	569.0	3.9	45.9	13.4
Other Asia*	102	301.4	3.0	43.7	16.2
USA	166	844.0	5.1	43.0	14.3
UK	12	157.5	13.1	45.3	15.8
Other European†	57	499.3	8.8	42.1	14.3
Other OECD‡	18	74.4	4.1	44.3	18.1
Rest of world	6	103.5	17.2	42.5	19.2
Total§	2 130	11 280.0	5.3	41.7	12.5

* Asia includes Singapore, Thailand, Indonesia, Malaysia and Philippines.
† European includes Austria, Belgium, France, Denmark, West Germany, Italy, Netherlands, Norway, Sweden and Switzerland.
‡ Other OECD includes Australia, Canada and New Zealand.
§ Among 2136 observations, there are 6 observations with missing country, 19 observations with missing values of amount of total investment, 38 observations with missing values of foreign equity percentage and 36 observations with missing values of duration.
Numbers do not add correctly due to rounding.
SOURCE: EJV data base.

investors, while European and Other OECD investment, including Australia, Canada and New Zealand, was relatively small.

Geographical Distribution

The location classification used in Table 2.5 is designed to reflect both geographical factors and fiscal preferences. The 'Other Coasts' category refers to all the provinces on the coast with the exception of the 14 coastal cities. There was a dramatic change in geographical distribution of foreign investment over the period. SEZs accounted for 52.2 per cent of investment in 1979–83, but only 28 per cent in 1986. This was partly due to the extension of preferential treatment to other coastal areas. Investment in the 14 coastal cities increased from 16.1 per cent in 1979–83 to 26.1 per cent in 1986 (a level similar to that of the SEZs). Investment in inland areas increased dramatically from 3.9 per cent in 1979–83 to 14.7 per cent in 1986.

TABLE 2.5 *Equity joint venture by location: summary*

	Number of projects	*Total investment (US$m)*	*Average investment (US$m)*	*Average foreign equity(%)*	*Average duration (years)*
SEZ*	573	5 193.1	9.4	42.8	13.1
14 Coastal Cities	519	2 396.8	4.6	41.0	13.5
Other Coasts†	651	1 221.7	1.9	41.8	11.8
Beijing	114	1 762.5	15.5	46.1	12.5
Inland‡	276	720.4	2.6	38.3	11.5
Total§	2 133	11 290.0	5.3	41.7	12.5

* SEZ includes: Shenzhen, Zhuhai, Shantou and Xiamen.
† Other coast comprises these provinces: Liaoning, Jilin, Heilongjiang, Hebei, Shandong, Jiangsu, Zhenjiang, Fujian, Guangdong, Guangxi and Hainan.
‡ Inland comprises these provinces: Jiangxi, Henan, Hubei, Hunan and Sichuan, etc.
§ Among 2136 observations, there are 3 observations with missing location, 19 observations with missing values of amount of total investment, 38 observations with missing values of foreign equity percentage and 36 observations with missing values of duration.
Numbers do not add correctly due to rounding.
SOURCE: EJV data base.

Foreign Equity Participation

Only about 10 per cent of foreign firms in the EJV data base enjoy majority ownership, while about one-third share ownership equally (see Table 2.6). However, the proportion of foreign majority stakes has increased from 7.2 per cent in 1979–83 to 11.5 per cent in 1986, while equal sharing has declined from 42 per cent in 1979–83 to 26.5 per cent in 1986.

There is not much difference between industries in the level of

TABLE 2.6 *Foreign equity participation: 1979–86 (percentages)*

	1979–83	*1984*	*1985*	*1986*	*Total*
0–25	6.1	15.9	16.7	16.3	15.4
25–49	44.4	47.5	44.1	45.7	45.5
50	42.2	27.1	30.2	26.5	29.5
51–99	7.2	9.5	9.1	11.5	9.6
Total	100	100	100	100	100
(Number of projects)*	(180)	(623)	(835)	(460)	(2098)

* There are 38 observations with missing values of foreign equity percentage.
SOURCE: EJV data base.

foreign equity participation. However, it is somewhat higher than average in motor vehicles, building materials, food, and pharmaceuticals. It is worth noting that the average level of foreign equity stakes was relatively smaller for HKM investors and at inland locations (see Tables 2.4 and 2.5).

Size of Investment

Fifty-one per cent of foreign investments were small projects worth less than US$1 million, while only about 7 per cent were valued above US$10 million. Over the period, the proportion of large projects was reduced while that of medium-size projects valued between US$1 million and $5 million increased.

Small projects were dominant in textiles, electricals, wood, furniture and other manufacturing. By comparison, investments in motor vehicles and hotels were relatively large. Asian and Japanese projects appear to be relatively small compared to those of other countries (see Table 2.4).

In terms of location, projects in Beijing and the SEZs tend to be large while those in inland and other central areas are relatively small (see Table 2.5).

Venture Duration

About 8 per cent of EJVs were planned to last for less than 10 years. Ventures exceeding 15 years' duration account for 14 per cent. Between 1979 and 1986 there was a decline in the proportion of ventures with shorter duration (below 10 years) as policy began to favour longer-term ventures.

Longer than average duration was found in building materials and the motor industry. HKM projects appear to be relatively short term compared to those of other countries (Table 2.4). Investments in the SEZs and the 14 coastal cities seem to be of relatively longer duration (Table 2.5).

Industry and Country of Origin

HKM investment is mainly focused on hotels, chemicals, electricals, textiles and other manufacturing. In comparison, US investment focuses not only on chemicals, electricals, textiles and other manufacturing but also on food and pharmaceuticals.

Summary

In conclusion, the pattern of foreign investment over the period of 1979–86 seems to be changing. This may be due partly to changes in Chinese government policy, and partly to changes in foreign firms' behaviour. Foreign investment in the early period 1979–83 appears to be rather more diversified than it was later.

Overall, foreign investment tends to concentrate in export-oriented industries, such as textiles, electricals, food, other manufacturing, and so on. There is a relatively small proportion of investment in high-technology industries, though it is increasing. Most projects were small with only a foreign minority stake. Initial locational concentration on the SEZs has given way to a more even spread across the country. HKM investment remains dominant in terms of the number of projects, but it involves on average a smaller foreign equity stake as well as shorter duration.

2.5 EMPIRICAL FINDINGS FROM REGRESSION ANALYSIS

In this section, a multiple regression model is used to test the effects of some of the determinants of foreign equity participation identified in section 2.2. The independent variables include size of investment, venture duration, industry, location and country of origin. Size of investment was logarithmically transformed to improve the linearity of the relationship with the dependent variable; other variables, such as industry, location and country, were treated as zero/one dummy variables. Other relevant variables had to be excluded because of data limitations. They appear in section 2.8 below.

The tests presented here were based on the data reviewed above. The model was tested for each time period as well as for the whole period.

Size of Investment

Table 2.7 shows that the size of investment has a significant negative effect on foreign equity participation for each time period. As

TABLE 2.7 *Multiple regression on foreign equity participation for each time period*

	1979–83	*1984*	*1985*	*1986*	*1979–86*
Constant	38.225	54.663	53.096	42.216	45.596
	(7.299)	(14.083)	(11.324)	(6.540)	(3.949)
Log.(size)	-3.014***	-2.829***	-1.955***	-2.629***	-2.284***
	(0.843)	(0.621)	(0.414)	(0.633)	(0.278)
Duration	0.465**	0.297**	0.369**	0.692***	0.455***
	(0.199)	(0.133)	(0.121)	(0.166)	(0.071)
Agriculture	7.733	3.346	4.885**	5.479	3.972**
	(8.077)	(3.526)	(2.496)	(4.690)	(1.758)
Oil	15.009***	1.458	2.157	–	3.001
	(4.521)	(3.256)	(2.981)	(–)	(1.836)
Building materials	19.686***	3.573	3.661	4.542	4.721***
	(5.558)	(4.324)	(2.393)	(3.348)	(1.695)
Chemicals	7.025*	2.075	-1.163	0.229	0.839
	(3.996)	(3.000)	(1.822)	(2.086)	(1.189)
Computers	1.634	2.601	-1.756	-11.090	0.540
	(9.616)	(3.599)	(3.117)	(12.483)	(2.111)
Construction	0.830	-3.483	3.538*	–	2.381
	(7.198)	(5.189)	(2.068)	(–)	(1.784)
Electricals	9.247***	-0.002	-1.639	-3.934**	-0.983
	(3.361)	(2.448)	(1.601)	(1.953)	(1.042)
Food and drink	4.831	1.793	2.826	1.871	2.722**
	(4.018)	(3.117)	(2.033)	(2.313)	(1.285)
Mechanicals	–	4.644	-2.736	4.929	1.773
	(–)	(5.337)	(2.926)	(3.362)	(1.987)
Metals	5.872	0.657	-2.765	-3.516	-1.994
	(6.147)	(3.582)	(2.309)	(2.786)	(1.526)
Motor vehicles	2.562	8.692***	14.588***	1.979	3.747
	(4.406)	(4.981)	(8.111)	(5.279)	(2.592)
Paper	1.858	-2.775	-0.837	-1.000	-0.545
	(4.837)	(5.645)	(2.374)	(3.857)	(1.793)
Pharmaceuticals	12.734**	-3.600	-0.796	3.246	1.035
	(5.961)	(4.943)	(3.049)	(4.415)	(2.088)
Telecommunications	12.799	-0.429	-2.010	-1.550	-0.799
	(7.968)	(4.336)	(6.540)	(8.928)	(2.827)
Textiles	1.002	1.316	-0.360	-0.673	0.042
Wood and furniture	4.411	1.552	0.583	-8.107**	-0.581
	(4.461)	(4.584)	(2.419)	(3.518)	(1.701)
Other services	13.273**	5.287	-2.263	16.772	5.481**
	(5.473)	(3.684)	(11.313)	(12.453)	(2.461)
Beijing	0.276	7.272*	6.508***	3.036	4.839***
	(4.299)	(4.302)	(2.272)	(3.735)	(1.619)
Inland	1.589	-4.313*	-1.064	-0.679	-1.784*
	(6.545)	(2.397)	(1.429)	(1.956)	(1.004)
SEZ	5.889**	1.929	3.619***	0.607	2.342***
	(2.855)	(1.822)	(1.432)	(1.652)	(0.853)
Other coast	5.238*	2.386	2.801***	0.753	2.091***
	(2.915)	(1.869)	(1.140)	(1.655)	(0.794)
HK/Macao	4.134	-7.288	-10.993	1.829	-2.304
	(5.678)	(13.132)	(11.175)	(5.674)	(3.602)
Japan	10.921	-5.559	-6.269	7.028	2.114
	(7.035)	(13.383)	(11.262)	(6.003)	(3.749)
Other Asia	-0.864	-5.793	-7.823	3.075	-0.761
	(8.412)	(13.361)	(11.317)	(6.042)	(3.791)
USA	8.855	-2.107	-4.866	-0.019	0.526
	(5.841)	(13.225)	(11.293)	(5.847)	(3.704)

	1979–83	*1984*	*1985*	*1986*	*1979–86*
Other European	4.708	−2.394	−8.964	0.046	−0.019
	(6.031)	(13.799)	(11.517)	(6.628)	(3.944)
Other OECD	2.667	1.629	−7.988	5.857	1.528
	(13.097)	(18.163)	(11.937)	(7.138)	(4.577)
Rest of world	–	– 21.827	9.427	−1.048	−1.807
	(–)	(15.859)	(13.679)	(13.826)	(6.379)
$F_{industry}$	1.73*	0.76	1.38	1.61*	3.35***
$F_{location}$	1.08	2.92**	5.22***	0.31	7.57***
$F_{country}$	1.02	1.08	3.30***	1.15	2.86***
N	112	389	712	454	1667
R^2	0.366	0.126	0.133	0.141	0.101
F_{value}	1.71*	1.72*	3.50***	2.50**	6.12***

*** significant at 1 per cent level.
** significant at 5 per cent level.
* significant at 10 per cent level.
NOTE: Other Manufacturing is industry control group; 14 coastal cities is location control group; UK is country control group.
SOURCE: EJV data base.

mentioned in section 2.2, this effect may reflect the relative importance of risk reduction on large projects. This interpretation is supported by the fact that the size of the coefficient tends to diminish over time, suggesting that risk reduction may have become less important as foreign investors become better informed about local conditions and as the progress of liberalisation raised investor confidence.

Duration

Duration has a significant positive effect for each time period. This result supports the theoretical argument in favour of securing greater control over relatively long-term ventures.

Industry

Using other manufacturing as the control industry, there was a significant positive effect on foreign equity stake in building materials and other services in 1979–83 and in 1979–86. Other Services comprises a wide range of professional services (for example, conference organisation, photography) where technology and management skills are quite sophisticated, and so its positive significance is broadly in line with the theory. Disaggregation of the building materials category reveals two distinct types of project: high-technology projects involving glass, ceramic decoration and so on, and low-technology products involving bricks, cement and so on. The result remains problematic because the highest levels of foreign participation are found in the low-technology projects (in glass, for example, some foreign firms have only a minority stake). A possible explanation in terms of the size of the foreign investor is given in section 2.8.

Location

According to Table 2.7, inland EJVs have significantly lower foreign equity participation than the control group (14 coastal cities) in 1984 and 1985, while the SEZs and Other Coastal areas have higher participation, especially in 1979–83 and 1985. It is probable that location is here acting as a proxy for the propensity to export (and import, too, perhaps). Thus inland EJVs are likely to have fewer problems of quality control for export, and fewer opportunities for transfer pricing. This interpretation is supported by results reported later, which show that when the model is tested using not only EJV data but also WOV data, there is an increasingly significant positive relationship between foreign equity participation and location in the trade-oriented SEZs. It is rather a surprise that Beijing EJVs also have relatively higher foreign equity participation during the period. It might be because there is relatively high investment in hotel and other services in Beijing, which is associated with higher foreign equity participation as mentioned earlier.

Country

There was no clear effect of country on the dependent variable. This is rather surprising. The relatively high level of sophistication in US technology, for example, would be expected to provide a significantly positive coefficient for US ownership. Although the coefficient of USA is negative relative to the UK control group, it is still relatively higher than that of HKM and other Asia. It is worth noting that there was only a small number of UK investments, especially in 1984 and 1985.

2.6 COMPARISON OF THE PATTERN OF WOVs AND EJVs OVER 1979–85

Industrial Sector

Tables 2.3 and 2.8 show that 40 per cent of WOVs are invested in the service sector as compared to 19.7 per cent of EJVs. However, WOV investment in hotels and other services declined from 47.5 per cent in 1979–83 to 29.5 per cent in 1985. On the other hand, WOV investment in manufacturing increased from 45 per cent in 1979–83 to 70.5 per cent in 1985. WOV investment began to appear in chemicals, mechanical, pharmaceuticals and telecommunications by 1985.

The average size of total investment in WOVs is relatively small in both manufacturing and services, compared with that of EJVs. However, average planned duration of WOVs is relatively longer, particularly in electricals, building materials, telecommunications and other manufacturing.

Country of Origin

HKM projects are dominant in both EJVs and WOVs, where they account for 76.2 per cent and 85 per cent of projects respectively. But the HKM share of WOV investment fell from 93.0 per cent to 82 per cent in 1985. Other Asian projects constitute a relatively high proportion (8.3 per cent) of WOVs compared with 4.8 per cent of EJVs, as shown in Tables 2.4 and 2.9.

In terms of average size of investment, US and Other European projects seem to be relatively small in WOVs compared to EJVs, while for Japanese projects the reverse is true. As for venture duration, HKM, Japanese and US projects seemed to be relatively longer in WOVs than in EJVs.

Location

Tables 2.5 and 2.10 reveal that 87.4 per cent of WOVs were located in the SEZs as compared to 26.9 per cent of EJVs. There was a declining investment in the SEZs from 100 per cent in 1979–83 to 77.3 per cent in 1985. Also, the proportion of WOVs in the 14 coastal

TABLE 2.8 *Wholly-owned ventures by industry: summary*

	Number of projects	*Total investment (US$m)*	*Average investment (US$m)*	*Average duration (years)*
Extractive				
Agriculture	2	28.9	14.5	25.0
Mining	1	0.2	0.2	0.0
Subtotal	3	29.1	9.7	25.0
Manufacturing				
Building materials	4	8.2	2.7	22.5
Chemicals	5	1.9	0.5	13.7
Electricals	9	11.5	1.3	16.6
Food and drink	8	10.3	1.3	9.3
Mechanicals	3	1.5	0.5	11.7
Metals	4	6.6	1.7	12.5
Motor vehicles	2	2.9	1.4	0.0
Pharmaceuticals	6	20.5	4.1	11.7
Telecommunications	1	0.9	0.9	30.0
Textile and clothing	12	17.1	1.4	13.2
Wood and furniture	2	3.7	1.9	20.0
Other manufacturing	5	95.7	19.1	24.4
Subtotal	61	180.8	3.1	14.9
Services				
Hotels and tourism	24	194.8	8.9	18.5
Transportation	2	1.3	0.7	6.5
Retail trade	4	23.4	5.9	14.5
Business services	3	1.9	0.9	25.0
Financial and insurance	4	0.8	0.2	2.7
Other services	5	2.5	0.5	35.0
Subtotal	42	224.7	5.8	18.1
Total*	106	434.5	4.3	16.5

* Among 120 observations, there are 14 observations with missing industry, 6 observations with missing values of amount of total investment, and 19 observations with missing values of duration.
Numbers do not add correctly due to rounding.
SOURCE: WOV data base.

cities was relatively small – 7.1 per cent and 24.5 per cent for WOVs and EJVs respectively – but increasing. WOVs based in the SEZs and the 14 coastal cities were relatively small compared with EJVs in the same area, although their duration was longer.

TABLE 2.9 *Wholly-owned ventures by country of origin: summary*

	Number of projects	*Total investment (US$m)*	*Average investment (US$m)*	*Average duration (years)*
HKM	102	467.4	4.9	16.5
Japan	3	15.1	5.0	21.7
Other Asia*	10	22.4	2.2	16.6
USA	4	5.4	1.4	23.8
European†	1	0.1	0.1	3.0
Total	120	510.3	4.5	16.8

* Other Asia includes Singapore, Thailand, Indonesia, Malaysia and Philippines.
† European includes Austria, Belgium, France, Denmark, West Germany, Italy, Netherlands, Norway, Sweden and Switzerland.
Numbers do not add correctly due to rounding.
SOURCE: WOV data base.

TABLE 2.10 *Wholly-owned ventures by location: summary*

	Number of projects	*Total investment (US$m)*	*Average investment (US$m)*	*Average duration (years)*
SEZ*	104	479.8	4.9	17.0
14 coastal cities	8	5.4	0.7	13.7
Other coasts†	5	7.9	1.6	16.6
Beijing	1	0.4	0.4	10.0
Inland‡	1	0.4	0.4	15.0
Total§	119	493.8	4.4	16.7

* SEZ includes Shenzhen, Zhuhai, Shantou and Xiamen.
† Other coasts comprises these provinces: Liaoning, Jilin, Heilongjiang, Hebei, Shandong, Jiangsu, Zhenjiang, Fujian, Guangdong, Guangxi and Hainan.
‡ Inland comprises these provinces: Jiangxi, Henan, Hubei, Hunan and Sichuan, etc.
§ There is 1 observation with missing location.
Numbers do not add correctly due to rounding.
SOURCE: WOV data base.

Size of Investment and Venture Duration

There was a relatively high proportion of large projects (valued above US$5 million) among WOVs: 20.1 per cent and 13.4 per cent for WOVs and EJVs respectively. However, the proportion of large projects in both EJVs and WOVs declined over the period 1979–85. A relatively high proportion of WOVs were planned to last for either a short time (below 10 years) or a long time (above 15 years), as compared with EJVs, which are typically medium term.

Regression Analysis for Both EJVs and WOVs, 1979–85

The rather different pattern exhibited by WOVs might arise because the factors influencing the choice of a WOV are different from those governing the level of foreign participation in an EJV. It is quite possible, though, that the differences observed might be explained by the very kind of differences in the nature of the projects which would, according to theory, cause firms to insist on a high equity stake. Could it be that, from a behavioural point of view, the WOV is no more than an EJV in which the foreign equity stake takes the limiting value of 100 per cent?

To test this view, the regression reported in Table 2.7 was re-estimated using a consolidated sample of EJVs and WOVs, with the dependent variable set equal to 100 for each WOV. Because of data limitations the regression for 1986 could not be replicated. The results are shown in Table 2.11. They clearly support the view that the WOV is essentially a limiting case of the EJV. Although there are differences of detail – particularly in the regression for the earlier period 1979–83 – the regressions for the entire period are remarkably similar. Both the R^2 and the overall F-value are considerably improved by the inclusion of WOVs. Size again has a significant negative effect on foreign equity participation, and duration a significant positive effect. Building materials and food and drink again have positive effects. Interestingly, the high-technology pharmaceutical industry now carries a positive sign, as theory predicts it should. It was insignificant before because relatively few pharmaceutical firms were represented in the EJV sample as they normally refuse to settle for less than 100 per cent ownership. Mechanical engineering also carries a significant positive sign, and the significance level associated with Other Services is increased too.

Some minor alterations occur in connection with location factors. The inland region is no longer significantly disposed to low levels of equity participation. The SEZs, however, now appear more significantly disposed to foreign participation in each time period, as would

TABLE 2.11 *Multiple regression on foreign equity percentage of EJVs and WOVs: 1979–85*

	1979–83	*1984*	*1985*	*1979–85*
Constant	28.486 ***	41.767 *	48.341 ***	45.171 ***
	(13.062)	(16.294)	(15.679)	(4.938)
Log (size)	–1.541	–0.067	–0.488	–3.139 ***
	(1.299)	(0.672)	(0.555)	(0.333)
Duration	0.969 ***	–0.025	0.107	0.676 ***
	(0.232)	(0.153)	(0.156)	(0.080)
Agriculture	9.784	3.152	5.210	4.611 **
	(10.130)	(4.162)	(3.462)	(2.180)
Oil	9.412	0.642	2.886	1.559
	(7.991)	(3.843)	(4.139)	(2.309)
Building materials	6.279	1.507	6.043 *	4.710 **
	(9.211)	(5.098)	(3.275)	(2.103)
Chemicals	–7.605	2.656	–0.021	0.189
	(6.886)	(3.518)	(2.512)	(1.484)
Computers	–5.522	2.469	–0.849	–0.517
	(17.728)	(4.249)	(4.324)	(2.658)
Construction	–9.737	–2.776	3.798	0.668
	(13.115)	(6.126)	(2.872)	(2.244)
Electricals	–3.874	–0.249	0.682	–1.124
	(5.539)	(2.885)	(2.204)	(1.297)
Food and drink	5.384	2.402	7.126 ***	3.887 ***
	(6.397)	(3.679)	(2.737)	(1.583)
Mechanicals	–	5.654	5.365	4.723 **
	(–)	(6.299)	(3.814)	(2.425)
Metals	–19.974 *	3.429	0.367	–1.666
	(10.811)	(4.157)	(3.169)	(1.901)
Motor vehicles	–8.389	6.993	15.069	1.844
	(7.815)	(5.878)	(11.251)	(3.259)
Paper	–10.712	–0.267	–0.950	–1.929
	(8.665)	(6.653)	(3.297)	(2.257)
Pharmaceuticals	2.576	7.094	6.989 *	6.216 ***
	(10.674)	(5.381)	(3.952)	(2.492)
Telecommunications	1.661	–2.215	11.217	0.974
	(14.301)	(5.113)	(7.926)	(3.474)
Textiles	–5.651	2.005	4.363 **	1.352
	(8.219)	(3.314)	(2.192)	(1.386)
Wood and furniture	–12.461	6.979	3.581	–0.124
	(7.797)	(5.194)	(3.324)	(2.115)
Other services	9.281	4.130	–7.738	7.932 ***
	(7.736)	(4.342)	(15.707)	(2.915)
Beijing	–0.517	5.881	7.009 **	5.198 ***
	(7.625)	(5.074)	(3.112)	(2.028)
Inland	–4.375	–3.401	–0.977	–1.903
	(11.768)	(2.823)	(1.969)	(1.259)
SEZ	14.711 ***	5.194 ***	13.149 ***	6.992 ***
	(5.152)	(2.115)	(1.877)	(1.049)

(continued on page 46)

TABLE 2.11 *continued*

	1979–83	*1984*	*1985*	*1979–85*
Other coast	1.978	2.837	2.333	1.823 *
	(5.363)	(2.190)	(1.570)	(0.994)
HKM	12.464	−3.813	−12.632	−0.632
	(10.336)	(15.496)	(15.514)	(0.889)
Japan	21.172	−2.529	−9.225	2.999
	(12.489)	(15.794)	(15.635)	(0.525)
Other Asia	13.779	5.361	−3.890	3.626
	(13.630)	(15.692)	(15.686)	(0.446)
USA	10.042	0.989	−4.965	2.395
	(10.536)	(15.604)	(15.674)	(0.607)
Other European	3.636	−4.704	−12.245	1.036
	(11.091)	(16.286)	(15.987)	(0.835)
Other OECD	4.015	4.116	−11.192	2.324
	(23.625)	(21.439)	(16.571)	(0.687)
Rest of world	–	−20.572	6.764	−1.239
	(–)	(18.723)	(18.989)	(0.878)
$F_{industry}$	1.96 **	0.80	1.44	4.07 ***
$F_{location}$	4.26 ***	3.05 **	17.36 ***	17.27 ***
$F_{country}$	0.84	1.52	3.13 ***	2.15 **
N	130	396	742	1722
R^2	0.481	0.093	0.146	0.149
F_{value}	3.34 ***	1.25	4.04 ***	9.83 ***

*** significant at 1 per cent level.
** significant at 5 per cent level.
* significant at 10 per cent level.

NOTE: Other manufacturing is industry control group; 14 coastal cities is location control group; UK is country control group.

SOURCE: EJV data base and WOV data base.

be expected not only from their export orientation but also from the special incentives they provide.

2.7 DETERMINANTS OF WESTERN INVESTMENT IN CHINA

This section reviews evidence from a sample of 79 Western firms. It examines their reasons for investing in China, for selecting EJVs, and for selecting a particular Chinese partner. It also considers their choice of location within China. Differences between large MNEs and other Western investors are examined too. It is worth noting that 54 of the Western firms in the sample were not included in the EJV data base described earlier.

Profile of EJVs in the Sample

The sectoral distributions of the sample and total population of EJVs are broadly similar. For example, chemicals, electricals, food and drink, textiles and other manufacturing, which together accounted for 52.2 per cent of EJV projects in the population, accounted for 44.3 per cent of all projects in the sample. However, three particular industries – motor vehicles, pharmaceuticals and oil – were significantly overrepresented in the sample.

In terms of country of origin, the sample was entirely focused on Western firms, which included 30 US, 19 UK, 18 Other European and 12 Other OECD. As for location, EJVs located in the 14 coastal cities and other coastal provinces were well represented, accounting for 67.1 per cent of the total. However, EJVs in the SEZs appear to be underrepresented as compared with that of total population in the EJV data base.

Regarding size of investment, foreign equity stake and venture duration, their average seems to be relatively high. For example, 17.5 per cent of EJVs in the sample were planned to last over 20 years whereas only 3.9 per cent in the EJV data base were of this length. There were 18.5 per cent of EJVs with a foreign majority stake compared to 9.6 per cent in the total population, while 60 per cent of projects in the sample invested above US$5 million as compared to 13.4 per cent in the population.

Reasons for Investing in China

The reasons for investing in China can be divided into five major categories: better access to a large Chinese market, establishment of an export base, use of low cost labour, access to natural resources and the availability of tax incentives. The reasons are not, of course, mutually exclusive. Table 2.12 shows that the large Chinese market was perceived as the most important factor; low-cost labour was also relatively important. These two factors were particularly significant in building materials, electricals, textiles and pharmaceuticals.

On the other hand, a good export base was perceived as important by EJVs in chemicals, textiles and motor vehicles. Natural resources were a factor in oil, foods and other manufacturing.

TABLE 2.12 *Reasons for investing in China by industry*

	Large Chinese market	*Good export base*	*Low cost labour*	*Natural resource*	*Tax incentive*
Agriculture	3	1	1	2	1
Mining	1	2	2	2	2
Oil	14	1	5	6	5
Building materials	6	3	5	3	0
Chemicals	15	6	5	3	2
Electricals	14	4	7	1	4
Food and drink	17	3	5	6	6
Mechanicals	4	3	5	1	1
Metals	7	2	4	1	3
Motor vehicles	16	10	9	3	4
Paper	2	2	2	0	0
Pharmaceuticals	13	1	6	3	3
Telecommunications	4	2	3	0	2
Textiles	9	6	7	2	1
Other manufactures	6	2	4	5	4
Business services	3	0	1	0	1
Total	134	48	71	38	39

NOTE: Respondents were asked to classify the factors as either 'of major importance', 'of some importance' or 'of no importance'. A response indicating major importance carries a weight of two in the table.
SOURCE: Questionnaire Survey.

Reasons for Selecting EJVs

The seven possible reasons for selecting EJVs identified in the questionnaire were: host-government pressure, establishing a long-term presence; acquiring a local facility; developing a local identity; protecting proprietary technology; serving the Chinese market; and taking advantage of tax incentives. Establishing a long-term presence was perceived as the most important factor. Local identity was also ranked high. Rather surprisingly, host-government pressure appears relatively unimportant. In fact, about 60 per cent of the Western partners in the sample claimed to have a free choice in selecting their investment mode.

Protecting technology was perceived as important by firms in building materials, motor vehicles, food and drink and pharmaceutical industries. Establishing a local facility was important for pharmaceutical EJVs, probably because of the importance of clinical trials in gaining product acceptance and the importance of industrial discipline in maintaining factory hygiene. Servicing the Chinese market, together with long-term presence and local identity, was important in electricals, motor vehicles, pharmaceuticals, telecommunications, textiles, chemicals and other manufacturing.

Reasons for Selecting a Particular Chinese Partner

The reasons for selecting a particular partner can be grouped into: past relationship; availability of a suitable facility as a going concern; access to partner's technology; access to partner's marketing network; and the partner's strategic location. Overall, access to a marketing network, suitability of location and convenience of the facility were found to be relatively important. Access to a marketing network was relatively important in electricals and pharmaceuticals, while suitability of location was ranked relatively higher by EJVs in food and drink, textiles and business services. On the other hand, the past relationship was important in metals and textiles. Partner's technology was regarded as particularly important in pharmaceutical and metal EJVs.

Reasons for Selecting a Location

Six main reasons for choosing a particular location were identified: investment incentive; proximity to the target market; availability of trained labour; availability of a qualified partner; access to local raw materials; and the quality of local infrastructure. Overall, the availability of a qualified partner was found to be the most important factor. Proximity to the target market and the quality of infrastructure were more important than investment incentive. At the industrial level, availability of a qualified partner and proximity to the target market were relatively important in motor vehicles, pharmaceutical and textiles. Sources of raw materials were particularly important in chemicals, food and drink and metal; availability of trained labour was found to be relatively important in electricals, motor vehicles and other manufacturing EJVs.

EJVs along the coast, including those in the 14 coastal cities and other coastal provinces, reckon the availability of a qualified partner

TABLE 2.13 *Reasons for Selecting Location by Location*

	Investment incentive	*Proximity to target market*	*Availability of trained labour*	*Location of qualified partner*	*Sources of raw materials*	*Infrastructure*
SEZ*	3	7	2	3	2	6
14 Coast†	21	39	27	45	26	37
Other Coast‡	8	13	10	20	12	10
Beijing	2	12	14	14	3	9
Inland$	4	11	13	7	8	7
Unspecified Location	0	3	2	4	2	3
Total	38	82	66	89	51	69

* 'SEZ' includes: Shenzhen, Zhuhai, Shantou and Xiamen.
† '14 Coast' include these cities: Dalian, Qinhuangdao, Tianjin, Yantai, Qingdao, Lianyungang, Nantong, Shanghai, Ningbo, Wenzhou, Fuzhou, Guangzhou, Zhangjiang and Beihai.
‡ 'Other Coast' comprises these provinces: Liaoning, Jilin, Heilongjiang, Hebei, Shandong, Jiangsu, Zhenjiang, Fujian, Guangdong, Guangxi and Hainan.
$ 'Inland' comprises these provinces: Jiangxi, Henan, Hubei, Hunan and Sichuan, etc.
Respondents were asked to classify the factors as either 'of major importance', 'of some importance' or 'of no importance'. A response indicating major importance carries a weight of two in the table.
SOURCE: Questionnaire Survey.

to be the most important. Infrastructure and proximity to the target market were also perceived to be relatively important by EJVs in the 14 coastal cities. By contrast, EJVs inland and in Beijing perceive the availability of trained labour and proximity to the target market to be important (see Table 2.13). The availability of a qualified partner was also one of main motives for selecting Beijing. Sources of raw materials was perceived to be relatively important by EJVs in other coastal provinces and inland. This suggests that the major factor encouraging the agglomeration of Western enterprises along the coast is not so much the ease of exporting but the quality of the workforce and the physical infrastructure.

Large MNEs and Others

Forty-three per cent of Western partners in the sample were large MNEs listed in Stafford and Purkis (1989). They are mainly involved in chemicals, pharmaceuticals, textiles and other manufacturing.

Geographically, large MNE involvement is quite diversified (a relatively high proportion of projects are inland).

Large MNEs appear to have a higher equity stake: 25 per cent of large MNEs have a majority stake but only 13.5 per cent of others. Also, 61.6 per cent of large MNE projects were valued above US$10 million, compared to 23.5 per cent for others. In terms of duration, 73.3 per cent of large MNE projects were planned to last over 15 years compared to only 40 per cent for others. Finally, 47 per cent of large MNEs had their first business engagement with China before 1949, compared to 27.3 per cent of other foreign investors.

The behaviour of large MNEs in selecting the investment mode, the Chinese partner and the location was found to be different from that of other companies (see Table 2.14). Thus, the protection of technology was perceived to be particularly important by large MNEs, as was access to the partner's marketing network. Proximity to the target market was the most important location factor for large MNEs whereas the availability of a qualified partner was most important for others.

The survey also found that large MNEs are more willing to increase their equity stake, or move all the way to a WOV. They are also more willing to extend the venture duration.

Nature of Chinese Partner, Size of Investment and Selection Method

Table 2.15 shows the relationship between the Chinese partners selected and the selection method. The data refer to all the ventures in which a partner has participated, and so any one respondent may indicate that several types of partner have been used. Central government has a relatively high commitment to large-scale projects compared to other Chinese partners. This probably reflects the central government's perception of the strategic importance of these large projects, and its consequent desire for direct control.

The most frequent selection method was through an approach from the Chinese; previous contact follows in popularity, with third-party mediation least favoured. An approach from the Chinese was particularly important where industrial and trade corporations are concerned. It probably reflects their heightened motivation to explore the new business opportunities afforded by foreign trade liberalisation.

TABLE 2.14 *Reasons for investing in China: large MNEs versus others*

	Large MNE	*Others*	*Total*
Reasons for investing in China			
Large China market	63	71	134
Good export base	20	28	48
Low cost labour	32	39	71
Natural resource	17	21	38
Tax incentive	19	20	39
Reasons for selecting EJVs			
Host government pressure	22	31	53
Establish long-term presence	60	68	128
Local facility	28	37	65
Local identity	44	56	100
Tax incentive	18	22	40
Protect technology transfer	37	30	67
Service China market	33	43	76
Reasons for Selecting a Partner			
Past relationship	20	21	41
Facility and resource	23	26	49
Partner's technology	19	17	36
Partner marketing network	29	24	53
Locations	29	23	52
Reasons for selecting a location			
Investment incentive	21	18	39
Proximity to target market	41	42	83
Availability of trained labour	31	36	67
Location of qualified partner	39	54	93
Sources of raw materials	25	28	53
Infrastructure	32	40	72

NOTE: Respondents were asked to classsify the factors as either 'of major importance', 'of some importance' or 'of no importance'. A response indicating major importance carries a weight of two in the table.
SOURCE: Questionnaire Survey.

On the other hand, previous contact was relatively important where central government rather than local government was involved. This could be explained by the fact that Chinese foreign trade was tightly controlled under the auspices of the Ministry of Foreign Trade and Economic Relations until 1978.

Due to the complexity of Chinese bureaucracy, the Western firm's choice between partners at the national and provincial levels is crucial. A foreign firm can be adversely affected by the internal

TABLE 2.15 *Type of Chinese partner versus selection methods*

	Central government	*Local government*	*Bank and other financial institution*	*Industrial and trade corporation*	*State enterprise*	*Collective enterprise*	*Total*
Previous contact	9	11	2	5	12	0	39
Approach from Chinese	10	19	5	16	12	1	63
Through third party	5	6	4	5	4	1	25
Others	1	2	1	3	2	0	9
Total	25	38	12	29	30	2	136

NOTES: Projects may have multiple Chinese partners.
SOURCE: Questionnaire Survey.

bargaining between central and provincial authorities. The firm faces a trade-off between access to nationwide markets and the greater foreign business experience of central authorities on the one hand, and access to local resources and the greater motivation and reduced bureaucracy of the provincial authorities on the other.

2.8 REGRESSION ANALYSIS OF QUESTIONNAIRE DATA

The regression results for the questionnaire data in Table 2.16 present a more convincing account of the determinants of foreign equity participation than do those in Tables 2.7 and 2.11. Five new explanatory variables are introduced. Concentrating on the full regression reported in column 1, note that the propensity to export carries a significant positive sign. The Beijing and inland locations carry negative signs (relative to the 14 coastal cities control group), with the Beijing location being significantly negative at the 10 per cent level for the period 1979–86 as a whole. Since non-coastal locations are less conducive to exports than coastal ones these results, overall, support the theory's prediction that the foreign equity stake will be positively associated with export orientation. It is also worth noting that, as in the population regression, SEZ location carries a positive (though now insignificant) sign.

The second variable introduced is a direct measure of the importance to the Western partner of protecting technology. This carries a significantly positive sign, as theory predicts. It is worth noting that the introduction of the technology variable has a major impact on the signs of the industry dummies, as compared with Table 2.7. The inclusion of technology means that the industry-specific effects now reflect other non-technological factors, such as the importance of high-quality standards in the domestic market. Thus indigenous tolerance of low standards may explain why, after controlling for the importance of protecting technology, the level of foreign equity stake is significantly lower in building materials while before it was the reverse. Some of the changes in sign may also be explained as the consequence of aggregation: the balance of constituent activities appearing in the questionnaire may be different, in some crucial respect, from the population. In particular the composition of the Other Manufacturing control group is different from that of the population because the sample contains some rather sophisticated ventures in this group.

TABLE 2.16 *Multiple regression on foreign equity participation: questionnaire sample*

	Equation (1)	*Equation (2)*	*Equation (3)*	*Equation (4)*
Constant	38.075***	40.511***	40.441***	25.966**
	(11.069)	(9.856)	(9.595)	(9.413)
Log.(size)	−1.610*	−1.699**	−1.743**	−
	(0.896)	(0.756)	(0.701)	(−)
Duration	0.695**	0.611**	0.613**	0.617**
	(0.269)	(0.251)	(0.244)	(0.285)
Export	0.111*	0.067*	0.067*	0.108*
	(0.056)	(0.039)	(0.038)	(0.060)
Technology	6.056**	5.995***	5.904***	6.443**
	(2.560)	(2.103)	(1.993)	(2.734)
Long-term presence	1.489	2.526	2.515	6.308
	(5.350)	(4.546)	(4.429)	(4.962)
Government policy	6.128**	5.651***	5.613***	5.835**
	(2.064)	(1.952)	(1.891)	(2.206)
Large MNE	−0.777	−0.368	−	−2.743
	(2.389)	(1.973)	(−)	(2.276)
Agriculture	−29.616***	−25.785***	−25.574***	−28.007***
	(8.950)	(7.423)	(7.147)	(9.544)
Mining	−0.432	−0.079	0.039	−6.269
	(7.972)	(6.970)	(6.762)	(7.802)
Oil	0.005	−1.818	−1.591	1.880
	(5.629)	(4.627)	(4.349)	(5.929)
Building materials	−17.112***	−16.392**	−16.142***	−18.610***
	(5.186)	(4.443)	(4.126)	(5.486)
Chemicals	−5.449	−4.738	−4.646	−5.317
	(4.776)	(4.452)	(4.310)	(5.118)
Electricals	−5.106	−6.530	−6.362	−5.004
	(5.402)	(4.449)	(4.244)	(5.789)
Food and drink	−12.889**	−12.029**	−11.844**	−11.931**
	(5.072)	(4.652)	(4.434)	(5.406)
Mechanicals	−16.387***	−14.174**	−14.054***	−15.955**
	(5.463)	(5.044)	(4.873)	(5.849)
Metals	−19.157***	−18.343***	−17.944***	−20.939***
	(6.231)	(5.398)	(4.828)	(6.593)
Motor vehicles	−13.759**	−15.884***	−15.764***	−14.108**
	(6.166)	(4.753)	(4.589)	(6.605)
Paper	4.909	1.231	1.593	6.233
	(8.230)	(6.401)	(5.943)	(8.785)
Pharmaceuticals	−0.271	0.475	0.668	0.012
	(4.905)	(4.532)	(4.299)	(5.254)
Telecommunications	−0.153	−1.022	−0.777	−1.206
	(5.221)	(4.762)	(4.459)	(5.559)
Textiles	1.699	3.249	3.248	0.550
	(7.082)	(6.213)	(6.054)	(7.559)
Business services	−31.416***	−24.807***	−24.582***	−27.369***
	(10.515)	(7.516)	(7.228)	(11.008)

continued on page 56

TABLE 2.16 *continued*

	Equation (1)	*Equation (2)*	*Equation (3)*	*Equation (4)*
European	−8.818**	−8.884***	−8.779***	−9.468**
	(3.327)	(2.987)	(2.859)	(3.545)
USA	5.915**	4.423*	4.523**	5.929**
	(2.507)	(2.167)	(2.045)	(2.687)
Other OECD	19.753***	18.346***	18.448***	18.743***
	(4.396)	(4.099)	(3.958)	(4.673)
Beijing	−3.613	–	–	−6.307*
	(3.735)	(–)	(–)	(3.666)
Inland	−4.344	–	–	−4.808
	(5.033)	(–)	(–)	(5.387)
SEZ	5.103	–	–	1.994
	(5.923)	(–)	(–)	(6.071)
Other coastal	−0.617	–	–	−0.987
	(2.838)	(–)	(–)	(3.034)
$F_{industry}$	5.08***	5.96***	6.28***	4.99***
$F_{location}$	2.54*	–	–	1.17
$F_{country}$	10.60***	11.83***	12.47***	9.59***
N	44	44	44	44
F-value	5.10***	6.24***	6.85***	4.50***
R^2	0.914	0.897	0.896	0.894

*** significant at 1 per cent level.
** significant at 5 per cent level.
* significant at 10 per cent level.

NOTE: Other Manufacturing is industry control group; 14 coastal cities is location control group; UK is country control group.

SOURCE: Questionnaire Survey.

The third variable is the desire for a long-term presence. This is positive, in line with the predictions of the theory. However, it fails to be significant at the 10 per cent level.

The two final variables are more problematic. Host-government policy has a significant effect on foreign equity participation, but it takes the wrong sign. If interpreted literally, the positive coefficient suggests that host-government pressure leads, on average, to about a 6 per cent *increase* in the foreign equity stake. The most probable explanation is that two-way causation has led to a simultaneous equation bias. More specifically the level of host-government pressure is probably directly related to the *desired* foreign equity stake. Western investors who want very high equity stakes encounter pressure which results in slightly lower stakes, but with the actual stake being higher than for those who did not want a high stake to begin with. Thus the true interpretation may be that those who experienced host-government pressure wanted an equity stake that was on average 12 per cent higher than others, say, but that they settled for one that was only 6 per cent higher. Consequently the effect of pressure may actually have been to reduce the equity stake by 6 per cent, although statistically the opposite appears to be the case. To some extent, the positive effect of host-government policy may support the enhanced bargaining power of those foreign firms that contribute to high technology or great export potential in terms of their equity stake percentage.

It is also puzzling that large MNEs appear to settle for a lower equity stake than other firms, though the effect fails to be significant at the 10 per cent level. It was noted earlier that firms involved in the largest projects may wish to reduce their equity stake to improve the overall corporate diversification of risk. MNEs have a greater propensity than other firms to become involved in mega-projects, and hence, perhaps, have a greater propensity to reduce exposure by taking a smaller equity stake.

The counter-argument, of course, stresses that MNEs are already well diversified because of their size, and because of the international scope of their operations. Nevertheless, other evidence suggests that some MNEs are moving towards greater involvement generally in joint ventures, for a variety of reasons, so that even if risk-reduction is not a dominant factor, their greater experience with this contractual arrangement may encourage them to take a lower equity stake.

A related point, which is particularly significant in the case of China because of the complex pattern of representation on joint venture management boards, is that the mere size of the Western investor may give it much more influence in the management process than a small investor would have, even though it holds a lower equity stake. Thus size of firm may directly substitute for size of equity stake where Western partners are concerned. This may explain the paradoxical results about building materials noted earlier. The large size of the Western investors in high-technology glass means that they are willing to concede the national government's demand for a large equity stake of its own because they believe their size itself gives substantial leverage. This leverage can be further enhanced by supplementing their own equity stake with a management contract. This emphasises the general point that while foreign equity is correlated with control, it is not the sole determinant of it. Moreover, as shown in the third column, the effect of MNE-specific seems to be marginal compared with the second column.

It is also worth noting that the duration variable, as well as the size variable, is still significant even when the new variables are introduced.

Finally, it should be noted that the effect of country dummies now become more significant than in the previous population. For example, European firms hold significantly lower equity stakes than firms from elsewhere, using UK firms as a control group. This confirms the theoretical view that the greater problems of control at a distance encourage them to take a less active role in management than, say, US investors who are based much closer.

2.9 COMPARISON BETWEEN HKM AND WESTERN FIRMS

Since HKM accounts for 71.7 per cent of foreign EJV investment, it will be interesting to see whether HKM behaviour differs from that of Western firms. In fact, the results of a Chow test show that they do (F-value = 2.057, $p < 0.01$, $n1 = 26$, $n2 = 1411$). Table 2.17 compares the major similarities and differences between the HKM and Western firms.

There is clear difference in the role of industry and location factors in foreign equity participation. HKM firms take a relatively high equity stake in agriculture, building materials and the motor industry. On the other hand, Western firms appear to take a relatively high stake in computers, pharmaceuticals and other services. So, to some extent, the results from both Table 2.7 and Table 2.11 appear to be mainly reflecting the HKM segment of the population.

As for location-specific factors, their effect on foreign equity stake seems to be more significant for HKM firms than for Western firms. HKM firms account for more than 85 per cent of foreign investment in the SEZs as well as the Other coast, while Western firms are more diversified (except into Inland areas). For HKM investment, the SEZs and Other coast carry a significant positive sign, whereas for Western investment they do not.

The final columns in the table compare the results for the Western-only population with the results of the Western-only questionnaire sample. It can be seen that the five additional variables introduced in the questionnaire sample lead to considerable improvement in the overall goodness of fit and, of course, the smaller number

TABLE 2.17 *Multiple regression on foreign equity participation*

	Population HKM 1979–86	*Population Western (1) 1979–86*	*Population Western (2) 1979–86*	*Western questionnaire (1)*	*Western questionnaire (2)*
Constant	44.624***	35.126***	32.424***	48.753***	38.075***
	(1.850)	(3.373)	(4.556)	(10.797)	(11.069)
Log.(size)	−2.501***	−0.638	−0.579	−1.545	−1.610*
	(0.336)	(0.576)	(0.588)	(0.962)	(0.896)
Duration	0.337***	0.686***	0.671***	0.744*	0.695**
	(0.094)	(0.144)	(0.148)	(0.368)	(0.269)
Export	–	–	–	–	0.111*
	(–)	(–)	(–)	(–)	(0.056)
Technology	–	–	–	–	6.056**
	(–)	(–)	(–)	(–)	(2.560)
Long-term presence	–	–	–	–	1.489
	(–)	(–)	(–)	(–)	(5.350)
Government policy	–	–	–	–	6.128**
	(–)	(–)	(–)	(–)	(2.064)
Large MNE	–	–	–	–	−0.777
	(–)	(–)	(–)	(–)	(2.389)
Agriculture	7.947***	−1.897	−2.274	−26.621**	−29.616***
	(2.156)	(4.605)	(4.634)	(11.582)	(8.950)
Mining	–	–	–	−3.179	−0.432
	(–)	(–)	(–)	(10.967)	(7.972)
Oil	1.764	9.498**	9.886***	−2.364	0.005
	(2.119)	(3.832)	(3.908)	(7.086)	(5.629)
Building materials	5.699***	3.676	3.755	−18.802**	−17.112***
	(2.047)	(3.346)	(3.509)	(6.957)	(5.186)
Chemicals	0.919	2.291	2.313	−4.578	−5.449
	(1.421)	(2.388)	(2.408)	(6.984)	(4.776)
Computers	−1.224	10.762***	10.635***	–	–
	(2.563)	(3.731)	(3.786)	(–)	(–)
Construction	2.326	7.302	7.063	–	–
	(1.993)	(5.040)	(5.090)	(–)	(–)
Electricals	−0.479	−4.112	−3.573	−8.790	−5.106
	(1.189)	(2.573)	(2.665)	(7.219)	(5.402)
Food and drink	2.304	3.819	3.462	−13.955*	−12.889**
	(1.593)	(2.677)	(2.708)	(6.876)	(5.072)
Mechanicals	3.418	0.791	0.716	−8.083	−16.387**
	(2.513)	(3.590)	(3.612)	(7.579)	(5.463)
Metals	−2.323	−1.781	−1.649	−18.002**	−19.157***
	(1.835)	(3.516)	(3.704)	(8.426)	(6.231)
Motor vehicles	8.949***	−7.372	−7.725*	−16.342**	−13.759**
	(3.457)	(4.458)	(4.476)	(7.604)	(6.166)
Paper	−2.075	5.720	5.604	1.539	4.909
	(2.105)	(3.938)	(3.952)	(10.474)	(8.230)
Pharmaceuticals	−2.840	4.508*	4.684*	0.474	−0.271
	(2.669)	(3.624)	(3.647)	(6.937)	(4.905)
Telecommunications	−2.887	−1.440	−1.558	−4.077	−0.153
	(3.901)	(4.596)	(4.619)	(7.247)	(5.221)
Textiles	0.155	0.635	1.409	−1.958	1.699
	(1.272)	(3.005)	(3.095)	(9.308)	(7.082)
Business service	–	–	–	−34.905**	−31.416***
	(–)	(–)	(–)	(14.301)	(10.515)
Wood and furniture	1.540	−3.546	−4.192	–	–
	(2.033)	(4.249)	(4.329)	(–)	(–)

continued on page 60

TABLE 2.17 *continued*

	Population HKM 1979–86	*Population Western (1) 1979–86*	*Population Western (2) 1979–86*	*Western questionnaire (1)*	*Western questionnaire (2)*
Other services	4.336	9.744***	10.056***	–	–
	(3.356)	(3.636)	(3.714)	(–)	(–)
Beijing	5.612	1.609	1.887	−1.664	−3.613
	(2.603)	(2.249)	(2.308)	(4.060)	(3.735)
Inland	−1.491	−3.584*	−3.889*	3.905	−4.344
	(1.219)	(2.133)	(2.162)	(4.594)	(5.033)
SEZ	3.494***	−1.125	−1.048	3.396	5.103
	(1.027)	(2.035)	(2.106)	(8.232)	(5.923)
Other coast	3.321***	−1.779	−2.133	−4.344	−0.617
	(0.977)	(1.730)	(1.758)	(3.533)	(2.838)
European	–	–	2.649	−0.192	−8.818**
	(–)	(–)	(3.310)	(4.309)	(3.327)
USA	–	–	2.887	3.217	5.915**
	(–)	(–)	(3.125)	(3.624)	(2.507)
Other OECD	–	–	4.371	20.042***	19.753***
	(–)	(–)	(3.914)	(6.601)	(4.396)
$F_{industry}$	3.10***	2.34***	2.21**	1.72	5.08***
$F_{location}$	8.39***	1.14	1.35	0.97	2.54*
$F_{country}$	–	–	0.42	3.65*	10.60***
N	1240	223	218	46	44
F-value	6.13***	3.08***	2.69***	1.95*	5.10***
R^2	0.104***	0.263***	0.268	0.690	0.914

* significant at 1 per cent level.
** significant at 5 per cent level.
*** significant at 10 per cent level.

NOTE: Other Manufacturing is industry control group; 14 coastal cities is location control group; UK is country control group.

SOURCE: EJV data base and Questionnaire Survey.

of degrees of freedom also helps to improve the fit as well. Note also that country-specific factors are much more powerful in the case of the questionnaire.

2.10 FUTURE PROSPECTS

By the end of 1987, the number of enterprises with foreign investment had soared to over 10 000 with a committed capital value of US$21.4 billion. Despite political uncertainty, there are several factors which suggest that foreign investment will continue to play an increasingly important role in China's industrial development. One obvious factor is that import demand is constrained by the shortage of hard currency. The substantial trade deficit is unlikely to be offset by the income from services, such as tourism. Growing foreign indebtedness makes conservative politicians reluctant to finance imports by foreign borrowing. Thus utilisation of foreign investment, particularly in the form of direct investment, appears to be fundamental.

The political unrest in June 1989 seems to have had no direct change on the open door policy. Rather, the liberalisation of foreign investment policy in respect of joint venture management and venture duration has continued, with important revisions being announced at the National People's Congress in March 1990. For example, the chairmanship of the management board of a joint venture can now be taken by a foreigner. Control over venture duration has also been loosened so that longer duration is now acceptable.

Economic growth in China has slowed down significantly under the economic austerity programme of 1988–1991. The impact on foreign investment has ranged from a shortage of local capital and raw materials to a slump in the domestic market. Recentralisation of decision-making could also reduce the overall efficiency of the system.

Nevertheless, even in this adverse climate, most Western partners are expected to maintain their operations, but to be much more cautious in their long-term investment plans. Overall, the inflow of foreign investment is not expected to increase as rapidly as in the previous decade, but not to decrease dramatically either.

2.11 CONCLUSION

A simple comparison of theoretical predictions and empirical outcomes is presented in Table 2.18. It shows that certain crucial aspects of the theory – notably the role of technology and export-orientation – are confirmed, but that on others 'the jury is still out'. The results are, however, sufficiently promising to suggest that the present research agenda should be pursued further.

It is, of course, true that contractual arrangements in general, and the size of the foreign equity stake in particular, constitute only a limited aspect of the wider issue of technology transfer as a tool of economic development. The selection of a suitable method of training foreign workers is arguably more significant than the choice of contractual method, and the informational and political asymmetries between partners of greater importance than the relative size of their equity stakes. But equity stake has the great advantage, from an

TABLE 2.18 *Summary of predictions and results*

Explanatory variable	*Theory prediction*	*Population* EJVs	EJVs plus WOVs	HKM	Western	*Questionnaire sample*
Log.(size)	+/−	−	−	−	0	−
Duration	+	+	+	+	+	+
Technology	+					+
Export percentage	+					+
Long-term commitment	+					+
Government policy	−					+
Large MNE	+					−
Industry dummies						
High-technology industry	+	0	+	0	+	0
Ownership dummies						
USA	+	0	0			+
European	−	0	0			−
Location						
Coastal	+	+	+	+	0	0
Non-coastal	−	−	−	0	−	0

academic point of view, that it is readily measured, and there is no particular reason to believe that it is seriously misleading as an indicator of the importance the foreign partner attaches to control.

So far as policy is concerned, the results suggest that the liberalisation of foreign investment in China has been an enlightened strategy, in the sense that it has addressed the legitimate concerns of Western investors regarding the protection of technology and the implementation of quality control (particularly on export products). By decentralising the authorisation of small projects, and promoting labour training and infrastructure development in the key coastal regions, it has not only 'opened the door' to the domestic market, but has successfully attracted Western investment for export that might otherwise have gone to other off-shore processing zones in Asia.

3 Western Multinationals in the Indian Pharmaceutical Industry

MARK CASSON AND
SATWINDER SINGH

3.1 INTRODUCTION

One of the manifestations of the increasing integration of the world economy is the emergence of certain regional centres of expertise in which foreign firms locate production, to serve not only the domestic market but also the markets of neighbouring countries. The UK, for example, became an important centre in the 1950s for US firms wishing to serve the European market. About the same time, India emerged as a potential location from which US and European MNEs could serve markets in South-East Asia, the Middle East and East Africa.

India has considerable entrepôt potential because of its geographical position, and because good domestic infrastructure makes much of the hinterland accessible. It has an effective educational sector and a reasonably professional civil service. The ability of the Indian economy to take full advantage of its potential seems to have been inhibited by two main factors. The first was the inward-looking attitude of the Indian government, which was more concerned with controlling domestic prices and restricting transfer pricing than it was with developing the export potential of Indian industry as a whole. The second was the inability of Indian firms to imitate their high-technology Western competitors and develop new varieties of product better suited to local conditions. This criticism applies not only to the small-firm sector which, like that in many countries, found it difficult to change traditional practices and expand quickly to meet new opportunities, but also to large indigenous enterprises (both public and private). These larger enterprises had good access to highly skilled professional scientists, but were unable to transform these technical resources into commercially successful products. Although India has exported some high-technology products, often through international joint ventures (Lall, 1982), such exports have been more of an exception than a rule. This failure may be related to the stifling effect of overcentralised decision-making, reflected not just in the power of government to restrict market forces but also in the internal structure of the large firms themselves. Whatever the cause, it has quite possibly led many Indian industries to be more dominated by foreign firms than they would otherwise have been. While foreign participation may have been larger in absolute terms in a deregulated domestic environment, it may have been smaller in relative terms because of the differential impact on domestic production of fewer market restrictions and greater scope for 'intrapreneurship' within large indigenous firms.

3.2 THE PHARMACEUTICAL INDUSTRY

The Indian pharmaceutical industry makes an interesting case study because the importance of scientific quality control means that production for export is effectively restricted to countries, like India, which have a good indigenous supply of scientific personnel. Because the sunk costs of R & D are such an important component of overall cost there is ample opportunity for transfer pricing of imported materials and specialist services. The life-saving nature of many drugs, and their consequent price-inelastic demand, encourages governments to exercise domestic price control. Thus the potential conflict between inward-looking concerns relating to income distribution and equity and outward-looking concerns relating to efficiency is particularly great in the pharmaceutical industry (Burstall, Dunning and Lake, 1981).

According to the UNCTC (1979, p.2):

> the modern pharmaceutical industry was generated by a revolution in drug therapy, first heralded by the advent of the sulfa drugs in the late 1930s and later confirmed by the introduction of penicillin in the mid-1940s. These medicines ushered in the 'age of wonder drugs' by establishing with certainty the fact that man-made drugs

could seek out and destroy target germs without harming the living host. New technologies were developed to produce these new medicines in large quantities, and patents were granted to pharmaceutical manufacturers which gave them 17-year monopoly privileges over their innovations.

As a result, by the late 1950s the major companies were transformed from full-line commodity houses, which manufactured and sold a complete range of the medicaments required by the pharmacist to compound the doctor's multi-ingredient prescriptions, into vertically-integrated R & D-intensive speciality manufactures heavily reliant on patents and brand names (Temin, 1979).

During the 1960s the rate of innovation declined as the most profitable research opportunities were exhausted, and as increasing regulation – particularly in the US – caused the costs of pre-launch trials to escalate. The problems were compounded by the expiry of many of the patents granted to drugs developed in the 1940s and 1950s, on which the profitability of the leading firms was critically based. Some firms attempted to diversify into related lines of business such as private health care, while others sought to internationalise their operations, gaining privileged access to national markets overseas by producing locally and undertaking clinical trials there (B.G. James, 1977; Schnee and Caglarcan, 1978; Hansen, 1981). While the USA became a leading centre for product innovation in many industries during this period, pharmaceuticals were a notable exception. Many products were innovated overseas to avoid the stringent requirements and costly delays imposed by the US Food and Drug Administration (Parker, 1984, 1989).

The socialisation of health care inspired by the concept of the welfare state meant that in many countries an increasing proportion of demand was financed by government. During the 1970s governments became increasingly cost-conscious and sought to use their monopsony power against the drug companies to reduce prices. Doctors were urged to substitute generic products, whose patents had expired, for patented products and, within the generic market, to substitute unbranded 'commodity' generics for their branded equivalents. The financial squeeze created by increasing regulation on the one hand and escalating R & D costs on the other hand encouraged even the most powerful firms to cut back their expenditures on basic R & D and to investigate mergers with rivals conducting related lines of research.

3.3 THE PHARMACEUTICAL INDUSTRY IN LDCs

Demand

The patterns of demand for drugs in developed and less-developed countries differ because of demography, culture and the physical environment. Life in an affluent society may be marred by sicknesses arising from work-related stress and geriatric conditions. The common ailments in such a society involve cardiovascular complications, arthritis, respiratory problems and cancer. Excessive use of drugs also causes health hazards in such a society. In contrast to this, the majority of diseases in all age groups in a poor country result from a lack of clean water supply, poor sanitation, low levels of education, inaccessibility to and also poor maintenance of public health centres but, above all, from poverty and malnutrition. As a result the pattern of demand for drugs in such a country is more in the nature of anti-infective drugs like broad- and medium-spectrum antibiotics, general anti-bacterial antiseptics, corticosteroids with anti-infective, vitamins and hematinics. Natural calamities, a frequent phenomena of developing countries, also add their share to the demand for drugs. In totality, however, LDCs account for only a marginal share (14 per cent in 1985)[1] of the global consumption of drugs primarily because of their low purchasing power.

Whereas for most consumer goods both the choice of the product and the payment of the price are performed by the consumer, the demand for drugs stems from the decision of the prescribing physician, whose decision is not necessarily guided by the patient's income and product prices. Payment, moreover, is often made by the state, local authority, insurance company or charity. This is certainly the case for the ethical drugs (as opposed to the proprietary drugs sold over the counter in shops) which are the focus of this study.

This separation between the decision-maker, the consumer and the spender tends to reduce the price-elasticity of demand for any given drug. This inelasticity is reinforced by the life-saving therapeutic value of many drugs, noted above. Furthermore, because many drugs are disease-specific, the cross-price elasticity of demand between any pair of drugs is typically low.

Supply

The supply side of pharmaceuticals is characterised by three principal features. First, it is dominated by a handful of pharmaceutical MNEs.

Second, US firms dominate this group of leading MNEs. Third, a large share of the total production of drug MNEs is generated in Western developed economies. Thus in 1985 15 drug MNEs shared about 40 per cent of global sales of drugs worth US$80 billion. Out of these fifteen firms, as many as nine were US-based and these had a 60 per cent share, followed by two firms each from West Germany and Switzerland with respectively a 16 per cent and 13 per cent share, and one firm from the UK and one from Japan with 6 per cent share each.[2] As regards the share of foreign sales to total sales, the data for 50 large drug firms with foreign operations show that in 1977 it ranged up to 29 per cent for eight firms, 30–59 per cent for 27 firms, 60–89 per cent for 12 firms, and above 90 per cent for three firms (UNCTC, 1979, p.113). So far as LDCs are concerned, in 1975 the share of national sales accounted for by foreign pharmaceutical MNEs was 100 per cent in Saudi Arabia, 97 per cent in Nigeria, 88 per cent in Venezuela, 85 per cent in Brazil, and 75 per cent in India. A large number of smaller firms account for the rest of the percentage share of sales in most of these countries. Comparable figures for industrialized countries are 60 per cent in the UK, 50 per cent in Sweden, 45 per cent in France and 35 per cent in West Germany (UNCTC, 1979, p.115). These percentages are still quite large, although significantly lower than for most LDCs.

More recent data on the pharmaceutical industry in selected LDCs is presented in Table 3.1. With only two exceptions – Egypt and Korea – foreign firms hold over half the local market. Most countries are net importers of drugs, but once again there are two exceptions. The most notable of these is India. India is second only to Argentina as a producer of drugs in spite of the fact that it has the lowest per capitum expenditure on pharmaceuticals of any of the countries in the table. The industry has an apparently impressive export performance with 40 per cent of production being exported. The large size of the Indian population, together with the export potential to East African and Other Asian markets, had encouraged 26 foreign enterprises to establish majority-owned local production units by 1980, while others had entered into licensing and cooperative arrangements with indigenous firms.

India

The pharmaceutical industry is the largest chemical-based industry in India. It is also unusually dependent on local sources of inputs because of the strict import-substituting policy pursued by the Indian

TABLE 3.1 *The pharmaceutical industry in selected LDCs*

Country	Pharmaceutical expenditure per capitum (US$)	Total drug production* (US$ million)	Total drug consumption (US$ million)	Production as percentage of consumption†	Market share of foreign firms (percentage)‡	Number of foreign production units§
Argentina (1980)	68.8	1900.0	1920.0	99	53	60
Brazil (1980)	12.7	1301.5	1544.0	84	78	71
Colombia (1980)	20.8	532.0	560.0	95	88	60
Costa Rica (1980)	13.3	21.0¶	28.0	75	82	3
Egypt (1980)	8.2	273.9	320.0	86	30	4
India (1980)	1.3	1450.0	880.0	165	70	26
Kenya (1978)	2.1	8.0	32.5	25	90	7
Korea (1980)	16.6	950.0	630.0	151	18	14
Malaysia (1980)	5.2	34.0	68.5	50	64	5
Mexico (1980)	15.7	973.9	1100.0	89	72	118
Sierra Leone (1980)	3.2	0.2	11.0	2	100	1
Thailand (1979)	7.3	250.0	335.0	75	na	14

* Production figures: Brazil (1979), Costa Rica (1977), Malaysia (1978).
† Percentages refer to finished drugs and not their imported inputs.
‡ Refers to the sales turnover of foreign subsidiaries, including locally manufactured drugs and imported products.
§ Figures refer to foreign subsidiaries wholly owned or with majority ownership by their parent companies engaged in the manufacture of drugs.
¶ Of $21 million produced in Costa Rica half was exported.
SOURCE: UNCTC (1985).

TABLE 3.2 *Time pattern of entry of foreign drug firms in India*

Time period	*Number of companies*
Up to 1947	13
1947–51	10
1951–6	6
1956–61	6
1961–6	7
1966–9	4
Total	46

SOURCE: Ministry of Petroleum, Chemicals and Fertilisers, Government of India, *Indian Drug Statistics*, various issues, and company reports.

government (Singh, 1985). After independence, the government launched a programme of planned industrialisation. This programme received a big push after the Second Plan was launched. The philosophy behind planning for industrialisation in India was one of self-reliance. Massive public-sector investment, supported by a similar effort in the private sector, would lay the foundation for self-reliant growth. This effort was deemed to require the creation of a domestic market through restriction of imports and enlargement of the services sector. Investment programmes involving complementary projects, connected by bulk intermediate product flows, were scheduled to meet physical output targets. This strategy changed the composition of domestic output so that India now produces more intermediate and basic industrial output than consumer goods.

The broad principles of policy towards foreign capital, as laid down in the Third Five Year Plan, were straightforward. Foreign capital was to be permitted 'in spheres where new lines of production are to be developed or where special types of experience and technical skill are required or where the volume of domestic production is small in relation to demand and there is no reasonable expectation that the indigenous industry can expand at a sufficiently rapid pace'.

Government policy towards foreign capital has changed little since then, although it became somewhat more liberal in the later 1980s. Government policy does not seem to have been a crucial factor in either attracting or repelling foreign firms. The dates of establishment in India of 46 foreign drug companies appear in Table 3.2. It can be seen from this table that 23, or half, the total number of companies already had a place of business in India before the First

Five Year Plan was launched. Six companies each entered the industry during the Second and Third Plans while seven companies came during the Fourth Plan and four while the annual plans (1966–9) were in progress. There are, however, no proper data available on companies which may have left India. An examination of available data from the Department of Company Affairs shows that no major pharmaceutical company has wound up its business in India. This is not surprising in view of the profitability of the Indian market caused by the high degree of protection available to both foreign and domestic firms operating in the country.

3.4 IMPORT AND EXPORT PROPENSITIES OF PHARMACEUTICAL MNEs

Foreign MNEs attracted to India by the existence of a populous and heavily protected market are likely to have a low export propensity. As a result of government policy they are likely to have a low import propensity too. On the other hand, foreign MNEs attracted to India as an export production base will have a higher export propensity. A good export performance will assist in obtaining government import licences, and so the import propensity may be higher as well. In any case, an export base may need to operate as a corporate entrepôt, taking in products from the parent firm (or other subsidiaries) for re-export, in order to provide a full range of products to neighbouring markets from a single source.

It is possible to examine this issue using data from annual company accounts. It was possible to establish the value of imported material consumed in production, the value of production, the value of exports, and payroll information relating to 45 medium and large enterprises in the Indian pharmaceutical industry for the three years, 1976–8. Twenty-four of these enterprises were foreign MNEs – 11 from the USA and 13 from Europe – and 21 were Indian. Normalising import and export values with respect to production generated import and export propensities for each firm.

The payroll information generated a skill factor, based on the proportion of highly-paid employees in the total workforce. Specifically, the skill factor measures the proportion of the wage bill accounted for by remunerating employees earning more than Rs36 000 per annum. Dummy variables were used to capture US and Indian ownership, leaving European MNEs as the control group.

TABLE 3.3 *Determinants of import and export propensities of medium- and large-size pharmaceutical enterprises, 1976–8*

(a) Imports

Year	*Constant*	*Skill factor*	*USA*	*India*	R^2	*N*
1976	0.106***	−0.032	−0.054**	−0.074***	0.30	45
	(7.15)	(0.53)	(2.66)	(4.21)		
1977	0.100***	0.171	−0.066***	−0.076***	0.37	45
	(3.97)	(0.82)	(3.09)	(3.30)		
1978	0.113***	0.050	−0.066***	−0.082***	0.25	45
	(6.76)	(1.00)	(3.01)	(4.14)		

(b) Exports

Year	*Constant*	*Skill factor*	*USA*	*India*	R^2	*N*
1976	0.066***	−0.002	−0.048**	−0.046**	0.16	45
	(4.32)	(0.03)	(2.27)	(2.52)		
1977	0.062**	0.010	−0.045*	−0.036	0.09	45
	(2.05)	(0.04)	(1.76)	(1.32)		
1978	0.033***	0.001	−0.020	−0.011	0.06	45
	(3.33)	(0.03)	(1.56)	(0.95)		

* significant at 10 per cent level.
** denotes 5 per cent significance.
*** significant at 1 per cent level.
NOTE: The absolute value of the *t*-statistic is shown in brackets.

Regression analysis of the import and export propensities is shown in Table 3.3. The results show that *both* Indian and US firms import significantly fewer materials than their European counterparts. They also export less as well, though the differences here are not so significant. The differences cannot be explained by differences in standards of quality control because these would tend to be captured by the skill factor, which in any case is insignificant. The most obvious interpretation of these results is that while MNEs in general may have a significant tendency both to import and export more than indigenous firms, it is the multinationals with the nearest home base that do this most strongly. The significant difference between US and European propensities seems to reflect the factor that US MNEs pursue a very pure import-substituting strategy while European MNEs pursue more of an internationally rationalised strategy in which they import materials from the parent firm and export to neighbouring markets. The greater prevalence of this rationalised strategy among European firms may be explained by several factors. It may be partly due to the greater proximity of Europe compared with the USA, partly to the traditional links between Europe and the Indian subcontinent which give European firms a stronger market presence in neighbouring countries, and partly to the fact that several European MNEs are more highly internationalised than their US counterparts because they are based in small countries – such as Switzerland – and have therefore been forced to pursue an internationally rationalised strategy because of their very small and compact local production base.

From a long-run standpoint it is useful to know whether import and export propensities influence the long-run profitability of the firm. The same data source also gives pre-tax profits and net fixed assets, from which a profitability measure can be constructed in ratio form. In view of the importance of advertising expenditure in long-run corporate strategy (see section 3.7) it is useful also to construct a measure of advertising intensity. This is generated by normalising advertising expenditure by total production. The results of a regression analysis of corporate profitability for the period 1976–8 are presented in Table 3.4. It is quite clear that neither the import propensity nor the export propensity have any impact on profitability, and advertising intensity has no effect either. Separate information, given later, suggests that firms differ quite significantly in the effectiveness of their advertising. Thus, while advertising strategies certainly seem to count, it is not total expenditure on advertising but the effectiveness of this expenditure which influences profitability.

While the skill factor takes the expected positive sign in each of the three years, it is significant only in 1977. This is sufficient to suggest that skill influences performance independently of its impact on import and export propensities, though the effect is neither large nor persistent.

US MNEs are, on average, more profitable than their European rivals, though significantly so only in 1978, and then only at 10 per cent significance. Indian firms are significantly less profitable than their European counterparts in 1976 and 1978, and significantly less profitable than their US counterparts in every year. If profitability is to be explained by the value of the underlying ownership or competitive advantages transferred to India, then this suggests that US firms have greater advantages than European firms, which in turn have

TABLE 3.4 *Determinants of profitability of medium- and large-size pharmaceutical enterprises, 1976–8*

	Year		
	1976	*1977*	*1978*
Constant	0.053	0.025	0.087**
	(1.23)	(0.58)	(2.31)
Material imports	0.220	0.218	0.387
	(0.43)	(0.61)	(0.86)
Exports	0.289	0.214	−0.323
	(1.21)	(1.31)	(0.81)
Advertising intensity	0.443	0.244	0.045
	(1.09)	(0.66)	(0.13)
Skill factor	0.097	0.605*	0.036
	(0.31)	(1.99)	(0.50)
USA	0.046	0.049	0.080*
	(1.55)	(1.34)	(1.75)
India	−0.071*	−0.049	−0.075**
	(1.94)	(1.42)	(2.16)
R^2	0.48	0.58	0.50
N	32	33	32

* significant at 10 per cent level.
** significant at 5 per cent level.
NOTE: The absolute value of the *t*-statistic is shown in brackets.

greater advantages than indigenous Indian firms. It could, of course, be the case that the advantages of US firms are actually no greater than those of the Europeans but that they are simply more readily transferred. This seems unlikely, however, because of the long-standing European presence in India and the greater geographical proximity involved. The evidence clearly suggests that, in spite of their greater familiarity with the local market and with indigenous business practices generally, the Indian firms remain handicapped by their inability to absorb Western technology.

3.5 COMPETITION AND MONOPOLY IN MARKET NICHES

It was noted earlier that the pharmaceutical market consists of a large number of small niches with very low cross-elasticities of demand between them. Utilising data from the Organisation of

Pharmaceutical Producers of India it was possible to identify 102 niches which are represented in the Indian pharmaceutical industry. For convenience, the niches are grouped into 15 categories. Each category represents a distinct field of medical knowledge. So far as a pharmaceutical MNEs' research is concerned, it can be said that economies of scope in the exploitation of firm-specific expertise are likely to be much smaller between categories than within them. Economies of scope in marketing may also be lower since different groups of private medical practitioners will have to be targeted where different categories are concerned.

Data were collected on the products sold by all the 41 major pharmaceutical firms operating in India in 1980 in which there was significant foreign participation. Table 3.5 profiles the sample in terms of the number of foreign firms represented in each category and the average number of firms supplying each niche in that category. The top categories in the table are those that exhibit the highest degree of monopoly power, in terms of the least number of firms in each market niche, whilst the bottom categories are the more competitive ones (although there are insufficient firms in each niche to avoid an oligopolistic structure).

By and large the categories with the largest number of niches are those where medical knowledge is well-established and products are relatively mature: for example, many firms produce antibiotics to treat infections. Conversely, the categories with the smallest number of niches tend to be those where medical research is relatively recent and products are very new, such as cancer, where only two niches exist. Both these cancer niches are monopolised, illustrating another point: it is the relatively modern categories with few niches where the niches are most likely to be monopolised. Too much should not be read into this result, however, because niches are rather difficult to define. Note, though, that if the definition of niche were quite arbitrary, there would be a tendency for the number of firms represented in each niche to decline as the number of niches in a given category were expanded, whereas what is observed is the reverse: the larger the number of niches identified within a given category, the larger tends to be the number of firms per niche. What seems to be happening is that the emergence of a product quite unlike any other necessitates the identification of a new niche, while the niche itself is sufficiently far removed from other niches that a new category must be defined as well. Hence the most modern categories are populated

TABLE 3.5 *Profile of Western MNEs in the Indian pharmaceutical industry*

Category	*Number of niches in the category*	*Number of firms represented in the category*	*Average number of firms per niche*
I *Strong monopoly*			
Cancer	2	2	1.00
Diagnostics	1	1	1.00
Surgical	7	9	1.43
II *Weak monopoly*			
Skin	6	14	1.83
Cardiovascular	8	16	2.00
Muscular skeletal	2	5	2.00
Metabolism	3	7	2.33
Genito-urinary	5	13	2.80
III *Strong oligopoly*			
Nutrition	12	25	3.67
Central nervous system	18	31	3.67
Hormones	4	13	3.75
Infectious infestations	17	33	3.88
IV *Weak oligopoly*			
Respiratory	5	17	4.60
Allergies	3	13	4.67
Alimentary	9	30	4.89

by a small number of niches, each monopolised by an innovative product.

The structure of competition is exhibited in a slightly different form in Table 3.6. Here the emphasis is on the number of rivals that each firm faces in each particular niche. Each of the 41 firms is represented, on average, in just over 9 niches, giving a total of 337 instances in which one firm may face rivalry from another. The top line of the table shows that in 47 of these cases the firm actually faces no rival; it enjoys a pure monopoly situation. The second line shows that in 36 other cases there is a duopoly between them, and so on down the table. Monopoly and duopoly between them account for 25 per cent of all the situations.

The number of such encounters faced by a firm depends on the

TABLE 3.6 *Intensity of rivalry analysed by the number of rivals and the scope of the firm*

	Scope of the producers' output (number of niches filled)				
Number of rivals	*1–5*	*6–10*	*11–15*	*16–20*	*Total*
0	9	23	3	12	47
1	2	20	6	8	36
2	3	9	5	1	18
3	8	8	10	6	32
4	4	10	4	7	25
5	2	4	0	0	6
6	7	21	9	5	42
7	2	14	6	2	24
8	3	11	1	3	18
9	3	9	4	4	20
10	0	0	0	0	0
11	3	6	3	0	12
12	0	0	0	0	0
13	0	0	0	0	0
14	0	0	0	0	0
15	2	8	4	2	16
16	0	0	0	0	0
17	0	0	0	0	0
18	0	0	0	0	0
19	5	9	3	3	20
20	6	9	3	3	21
Total	59	161	61	56	337

breadth of its product range. Table 3.7 summarises the product diversification of the firms in terms of the number of niches and the number of categories in which they are involved. It can be seen that the typical firm has a product range of 6–10, with only three firms having a range in excess of 15. The number of categories spanned is much lower. While no firm is concentrated in only a single category, no firms span more than nine categories either. Most firms belong to one of two distinct groups: 17 span a modest 3–4 categories, while 13 span a more ambitious 7–8 categories.

Table 3.6 also provides a break-down of the number of rivals in each niche by the firm's product range. The top line of the table, for example, shows that, in spite of their relatively narrow product range, firms sourcing 1–5 niches account for 9 out of 47 (or 19 per

TABLE 3.7 *Summary of the pattern of diversification*

(a) By niche

Number of niches	*Number of firms*
1–5	14
6–10	19
11–15	5
16–20	3
Total	41

(b) By category

Number of categories	*Number of firms*
1–2	1
3–4	17
5–6	8
7–8	13
9–10	2
Total	41

cent) of all monopolies, while firms sourcing 16–20 niches account for only 12 (or 26 per cent) of these. On the face of it, therefore, diversification of the product range runs into diseconomies beyond a certain point because the chance of obtaining a monopoly declines. Unfortunately, however, this interpretation of the data is complicated by the fact that there are different numbers of firms in each category. It cannot in fact be inferred from the table that well-diversified firms underperform in the quest for monopoly because, as Table 3.3 shows, there are in fact far fewer of them.

Regression analysis offers a convenient way of resolving this difficulty. Table 3.8 reports the results of linear regressions in which the frequency of encountering a particular number of rivals is related to two measures of the scope of the firm: the number of niches it is represented in, and the number of categories in which it participates. Theory implies that the independent variables impact multiplicatively on the dependent variable, so that a logarithmic transformation of variables is required to generate the linear form. Diseconomies of diversification with respect to niches are represented by a coefficient on the number of niches which is less than one. This shows that as the number of niches expands, the number of niches with a small number of rivals increases less than proportionately.

TABLE 3.8 *Regression analysis of the number of niches in which the number of rivals is less than or equal to some critical value*

		Coefficient of logarithm of:			
Critical value	*Constant*	*Number of niches*	*Number of categories*	R^2	N
0	0.15	1.02***	−1.23**	0.25	41
	(0.67)	(2.77)	(2.48)		
1	−0.39	0.90**	−0.13	0.35	41
	(1.86)	(2.51)	(0.28)		
2	−0.48**	0.89**	0.08	0.40	41
	(2.17)	(2.48)	(0.17)		

** significant at 5 per cent level.
*** significant at 1 per cent level.
NOTE: The absolute values of the *t*-statistics are shown in brackets.

Diseconomies of diversification with respect to categories are indicated by a negative coefficient on the number of categories: this implies that for a given degree of diversification by niche, the chance of encountering a small number of rivals declines as the number of categories over which the niches are spread increases.

The estimated coefficients on the number of niches are significantly positive (as indicated by the reported *t*-statistics) but are not significantly different from unity. The estimated coefficient on the number of categories is significantly negative in one case, however. This indicates that diseconomies of diversification are confined to the inclusion of new categories within the product range. These diseconomies are significant only in the quest for monopoly, moreover. The coefficient becomes less negative, and insignificant, as the chances of participating in a duopoly or more general oligopoly are considered.

The absence of diseconomies in respect of niches is confirmed by Figure 3.1, which shows the cumulative frequency distribution of the number of rivals for each of the four degrees of diversification shown in Table 3.7. It can be seen that the most highly diversified firms on average enjoy more market power than the least diversified firms, with the moderately diversified firms lying somewhere in between. Although there is some reversal in the ordering of the two moderately diversified groups, there is a slight tendency for the more diversified firms to enjoy greater market power. In respect of pure monopoly, however, the less diversified firms have the edge. Overall,

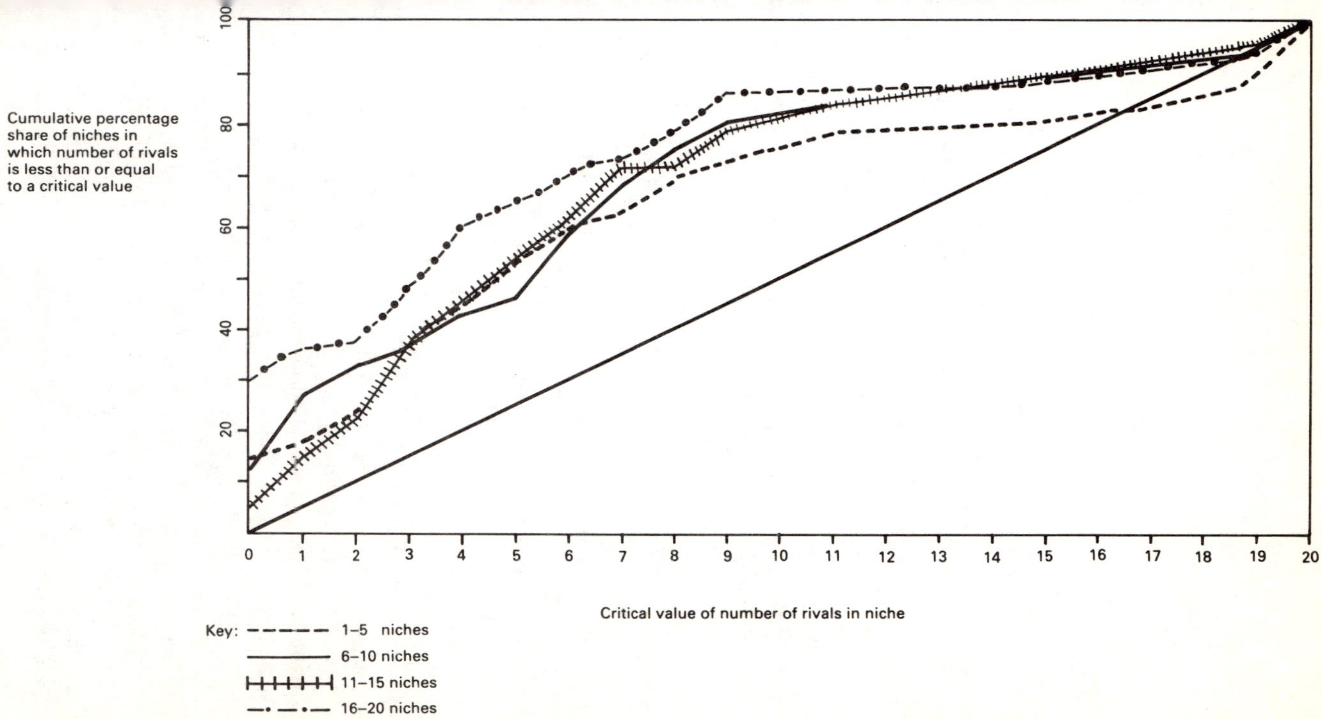

FIGURE 3.1 Indications of market power for firms with different degrees of diversification by niche

therefore, there is some slight tendency for market power to increase with diversification by niche, although the effect is neither large enough, nor consistent enough for moderately diversified firms, to appear statistically significant.

3.6 THE IMPACT OF SCOPE ON PROFITABILITY

Diversification strategies should impact on the profitability of the firm. Several theoretical effects can be distinguished. First, a firm which concentrates on a small number of monopolised niches should have higher profitability than one which dissipates its activities over more competitive niches. Second, a firm which spans several categories may well encounter diseconomies in managing very different areas of technical competence and different types of market. Thus, when controlling for the proportion of niches which are monopolised, the number of categories should impact negatively on profitability.

Diversification should affect the variability of profit, too. Operation in a large number of niches should reduce profit variability because market conditions in different niches may be subject to independent disturbances, and spill-over effects will be negligible because of low cross-price elasticities of demand. On the other hand, operations that span several categories may induce high variability because the dissipation of management attention across very different environments may reduce the speed of response to change, and impair the ability to foresee change in the first place. It could be argued that the monopolisation of niches will introduce an element of stability into profits, but the contrary view is that because of the limited patent lives of ethical drugs, and the ease of entry for generic producers once patents have expired, monopolistic profits are short-lived. Thus, while monopolies may increase average profitability, industry dynamics may mean that they also increase profit volatility.

An attempt was made to test these propositions by pooling the profitability data and the product data, but this was successful for only 19 firms. Average profitability was calculated as the ratio of pre-tax profit to net fixed assets for 1979–80 (the year for which product information was available) and the variability of profit was calculated as the standard deviation about a linear profit time trend over a ten-year period centred on this date. Both profitability and profit variability were regressed on the proportion of the firm's niches

TABLE 3.9 *Regression analysis of scope and profitability for a subset of firms monopolising at least one niche*

	Constant	*Percentage of* monopolised niches	*Number of* categories	*Number of* niches	R^2	N
Profit rate	−0.18	2.53	0.18	−0.05	0.13	11
	(0.16)	(0.85)	(1.04)	(0.73)		
Profit variability	−0.79	0.12	0.30*	−0.06	0.37	11
	(0.77)	(0.04)	(1.88)	(1.04)		

NOTES: The absolute values of the *t*-statistics are shown in brackets.
* significant at 10 per cent level.

that it monopolised, the number of categories it served, and the total number of niches involved. A logarithmic transformation of the variables, similar to that used above, produced a very poor fit in both cases, and so untransformed regression results are used for inference.

There were eight firms which had no monopolised niches and the profit behaviour of these firms appeared rather different from that of the other 11. The 11 firms with some monopoly power exhibited some interesting tendencies, as indicated by the regression results reported in Table 3.9. Although not highly significant because of the small number of observations, these results appear to be economically meaningful in the sense that they support a plausible interpretation, although not one on which a great deal of weight can be placed.

Monopoly power enhances profitability – though not significantly so – whilst a proliferation of niches reduces it, as might be expected. The main paradox is that a large number of categories increases rather than reduces profitability. If interpreted literally, this suggests that there are knowledge-based scope economies in the pharmaceutical industry.

The variability of profits is significantly increased by the number of categories, however, suggesting that knowledge-based economies are likely to be partially offset by managerial diseconomies. Monopolisation increases the variability of profitability – though not significantly so – suggesting that in the pharmaceutical industry, at least, monopoly does not provide management with a 'quiet life'. Instead, monopolisation of niches, together with a wide scope of activity, allows the firm to exploit a trade-off in which the stability of profits is reduced in order to achieve a higher average return.

TABLE 3.10 *Standard breakdown of a manufacturer's costs*

Component	*Percentage*
Production and quality control	30
Advertising and scientific information	20
Research and development	15
Distribution	7
Administration	6
Miscellaneous	7
Profit (pre-tax)	15
Total	100

SOURCE: Ciba-Geigy data reported in UNCTC (1979), Note 44, p. 36.

3.7 ADVERTISING STRATEGIES

The oligopolistic structure of many of the market niches suggests that advertising may well be an important instrument of rivalry in the pharmaceutical industry. Since drugs are relatively complex products, advertising is also required to launch new products to the medical profession.

Table 3.10 depicts a standard breakdown of pharmaceutical manufacturer's costs. It can be seen that expenditure on 'advertising and scientific information' constitutes 20 per cent of total expenditure. This expenditure ranks second highest after expenditure on production and quality control.

There is probably no other industry in which advertising campaigns are so intense, elaborate and expensive as they are in pharmaceuticals. This is in spite of the fact that ethical drugs (unlike proprietary medicines) cannot by law be advertised to the public. The expenditure is largely accounted for by medical representatives who visit doctors and organise seminars. In comparison, free samples, advertising in learned journals and mail-shots are of minor importance.

The importance of advertising in the launch of a drug suggests that advertising expenditure will tend to decline as time elapses since the launch. If the drug is successful, however, then entry by potential imitators 'inventing around' the patents is likely to be encouraged. Advertising may then be employed for defensive purposes. The return to defensive advertising is likely to vary according to the level of sales established. It is more important to defend the sales of a successful drug than an unsuccessful one. Another complication is that a firm which has only recently established itself in a country may have to spend more to achieve the same effect as its rivals because it must establish corporate credibility before it can obtain credibility for its product.

Pharmaceutical firms operate in several market niches, so the data on firms' total advertising expenditures used above cannot be employed to examine these hypotheses. Appropriate data is, however, available for the USA. Given that many of the leading firms in Indian pharmaceutical industry are US-based, it is not unreasonable to assume that advertising strategies in India will be broadly similar to those in the USA so far as the major ethical drugs are concerned. The data, derived from Schwartzman (1976), are actually taken from UNCTC (1979), Table 23, pp.143–6. They relate to 37 drugs marketed in 1973, and provide advertising expenditure on the drug, its sales and its year of introduction, together with the type of drug and its manufacturer. The aim is to explain the variation across drugs in the ratio of advertising expenditure to sales. Using a regression approach, this is related to the time elapsed since the drug's introduction, a dummy variable indicating whether or not the firm itself is a late entrant (post-1960), and a series of dummy variables identifying particular categories of drug.

Diagnostic tests indicated that a logarithmic transformation of the continuous variables produced the most satisfactory results. These are reported in Table 3.11. In the second equation the coefficients on both the age of the product and the value of sales are significant and take the expected signs. In the first equation the coefficient on the age of the product is insignificant, but it still takes the expected sign. This insignificance can be explained by the fact that part of the age effect is being captured by the product category dummies, because the products in the different categories have a different average age. Once the dummies are eliminated due to their insignificance, the age variable becomes very significant indeed.

The sign of the coefficient for the late entry dummy is positive, as expected, but insignificant. If there is a tendency for late entrants to increase their advertising budgets above early entrants' levels it is too small to appear significant in this rather limited data base. The only product category dummy to be significant takes a value of unity for members of the penicillin, tetracycline and erythromycin groups and is zero otherwise. Its positive coefficient indicates the advertising is

TABLE 3.11 *Regression analysis of advertising/sales ratio for 37 ethical drugs, 1973*

	Regression number	
	1	*2*
Constant	0.07	0.51
	(0.13)	(1.69)
Logarithm of age of product	−0.35	−0.82***
	(0.97)	(5.75)
Logarithm of sales of product	0.24**	0.26**
	(2.09)	(2.59)
Late entry dummy	0.38	
	(1.03)	
Product category dummies		
Tetracycline	−0.20	
	(−1.22)	
Erythromycin	0.01	
	(0.08)	
Pencillin, tetracycline or erythromycin	0.40**	0.35**
	(2.11)	(2.11)
Firm dummies		
Lilly (early entrant)	−0.27	
	(−1.29)	
Robins (late entrant)	0.15	
	(0.68)	
R^2	0.69	0.64
N	37	37

*** significant at 1 per cent level.
** significant at 5 per cent level.
NOTE: The figures in brackets are absolute values of *t*-statistics.

particularly intensive where antibiotics are concerned. Antibiotics is a relatively large market in which many of the major firms are represented, and so it is quite plausible that oligopolistic rivalry through advertising is particularly intense in this category.

Despite the systematic elements in advertising strategy noted above, it is interesting to observe the differences in the strategies employed by different firms in marketing similar drugs, and the quite remarkable differences in their apparent effectiveness. Table 3.12 shows the advertising expenditures and the sales achieved for three

TABLE 3.12 *Advertising strategies in 1973 for three brands of erythromycin introduced in 1972*

Drug	*Manufacturer*	*Advertising ($000)*	*Sales ($000)*	*Advertising/sale*
Ethril	Squibb	419	1137	36.8
Robimycin	Robins	648	787	82.3
SK-Erythromycin	Smithkline	133	649	20.5

different varieties of the antibiotic erythromycin, all launched in 1972. Smithkline achieved almost the same level of sales as Robins with less than one-quarter the advertising expenditure, while Squibb spent three times what Smithkline spent but still less than doubled its sales. It is, of course, difficult to evaluate the performance of post-launch advertising on the basis of just a single year's results, but nevertheless the differences are sufficiently striking that substantial underlying differences in the effectiveness of these strategies seem the most likely explanation.

3.8 SUMMARY AND CONCLUSIONS

This chapter has examined the business strategies of Western foreign investors in the Indian pharmaceutical industry. It has been shown that competition between Western firms is limited by the frequency with which particular market niches are protected by patents which confer monopoly power on the incumbent firm. The main competition process is that of entry, which involves two distinct stages: first, the transfer of technology from the laboratory and the production plants in developed countries, and second the marketing of the product. Where an entrant is breaking in to a previously monopolised niche it is advertising rather than price that is the principal competitive weapon.

European firms tend to use India as a production base within a rationalised corporate system, exporting products to neighbouring countries with which their source countries have traditional ties. US firms, by contrast, have fewer established markets in the area, and so concentrate on a more traditional form of import-substituting investment oriented to a protected domestic market. Nevertheless, US firms turn in a better profit performance than their European counterparts, probably because the competitive advantages embodied in product performance and managerial practices are correspondingly greater.

Recently Indian government policies have become more liberal (Nair, 1987), but the basic thrust of policy towards self-reliance in key sectors still remains. Thus, while the Indian economy may become more trade-oriented, it is likely to be some time before it evolves a significant indigenous technologically-oriented pharmaceutical industry.

Notes

1. *The Economist*, 7 February 1987, 'Survey on Pharmaceuticals', p.4.
2. UNCTC (1985). The nine US firms are Merck, American Home Products, Pfizer, Warner-Lambert, Abbott, Eli-Lilly, Bristol Myers, Smithkline Beckman and Upjohn. The West German firms are Hoechst and Bayer. The Swiss firms are Ciba-Geigy and Sandoz. The British and Japanese firms are respectively Glaxo and Takeda.

4 International Business Strategies in the European Service Sector: A Comparative Study

JOSE-PAULO ESPERANCA

4.1 INTRODUCTION

The ownership and control strategies of foreign subsidiaries has become one of the most fashionable topics among researchers in international business. Such interest is linked to the important role played by joint ventures and other cooperative arrangements. Several analytical works have drawn attention to the management issues raised by the internationalisation of service industries (Dunning, 1989; Segal-Horn, 1988; Casson, 1990, Chapter 8). However, empirical research is still very limited, both in variety and scope. This chapter attempts to answer questions about subsidiaries which cannot be addressed using conventional data bases or information obtained from headquarters. The focus is the ownership and control strategies of service multinational enterprises (SMNEs) in five industries: banking, insurance, car rental, advertising and hotels.

Two criteria were paramount in selecting these industries: suitable diversity between the industries, so that comparisons are interesting but not misleading, and the willing compliance of subsidiaries in supplementing published industry data. The selection includes two financial services (banking and insurance), one information service (advertising) and two travel-related capital-intensive industries (car rental and hotels). Other industries, such as auditing and management consulting, were included initially, but abandoned later because of the reluctance of managers to divulge sensitive information. From this point of view, it was found that larger incorporated firms were most cooperative, although in certain instances of intense oligopolistic rivalry they were reluctant to supply information.

The host countries were selected using similar criteria: Italy and Portugal are significantly different by market size, economic development, economic integration and history. In 1988 Italian gross domestic product (GDP) reached US$467.15 billion, against US$23.56 billion for Portugal (OECD, 1990); approximately 20 times larger for a population about 5.5 times larger. The difference is less striking in purchasing power parity terms, but it emphasises that Italy is much larger and wealthier, although recently it has been growing at a slower pace than Portugal. The difference in economic integration is equally significant: Italy is a founding member state of the EC since its creation in 1957 by the Treaty of Rome. Portugal only joined the club in 1986 and, despite early membership of EFTA, remained quite isolated until 1974.

The literature on the service sector has emphasised a number of characteristics of services, such as simultaneity of production and consumption and location-boundedness, which suggest that FDI in services is, relative to manufacturing, more important than exporting (Boddewyn, Halbrich and Perry, 1986). Important differences are also to be expected with respect to the ownership and control of the local operations. Full ownership has often been considered a necessary means to safeguard proprietary secrets from opportunistic partners. It is acknowledged that service firms may have fewer proprietary secrets than high-technology manufacturing firms, suggesting a greater willingness for cooperation with local partners. However, this view neglects the importance of brand image and, in particular, the 'follow the customer' behaviour of many SMNEs who move abroad to service the local affiliate of a home-country client firm or a travelling client.

Another interesting phenomenon specific to some service industries is the rise of management contracts which give total control without equity to SMNEs enjoying strong brand image and management expertise. The importance of management contracts highlights the fact that ownership and control should not be viewed as perfectly correlated, as ownership is not the only means to protect proprietary secrets, brand image or privileged relationship with customers. Industry-specificities and cultural differences between source countries are expected to influence the adoption of management contracts and the general attitudes to ownership and control. Local differences concerning size of market and level of economic integration are likely to be important too.

Of the five industries included in this study, banking has received the most attention from researchers. Kindleberger (1983) provides a historical review, showing that there was an early trend to internationalisation among nineteenth-century banks well before modern international communication networks were established. Tschoegl (1987) emphasises the distinction between wholesale and retail banking, while Campayne's study (this volume) distinguishes commercial and investment banking (see also Goldberg and Saunders, 1981). Casson (1989) emphasises the internalisation of correspondent relations as a factor in the growth of branch banking across borders.

The hotel industry has also been fairly well researched, with two important works by Dunning and McQueen (1981) and Dave (1984) focusing on the importance of following the customer in the establishment of multinational hotels. Advertising was the subject of an early study by Weinstein (1974), who described the move from partial (even minority) ownership to full ownership by advertising MNEs. An interesting study of advertising subsidiaries by Terpstra and Yu (1988) was hampered by lack of data on the ownership structure of subsidiaries. Finally, it is worth mentioning the study produced by the UNCTC (1988), which compiles interesting information on the country and firm distribution of FDI in services with a particular focus on US investments.

This study takes a broad view of ownership and control strategies. Following an outline of research methodology in section 4.2, four separate groups of strategic issues are examined. Section 4.3 considers the determinants of the foreign owner's equity stake in the subsidiary, and the choice of entry mode (acquisition, partnership or greenfield venture). Theory suggests that foreign stake and entry mode are related to a large number of factors, each of which is a potential influence on other strategies too. These factors include the accumulated experience of the investing firm, the nature of its customer base, capital-intensity, perceptions of political and currency risk, and many others.

Section 4.4 considers the influence of these same factors on the locus of control. The degree of autonomy of the subsidiary and the nationality of the subsidiary's general manager are both examined. The nationality of management leads on to the question of management development strategies, which is addressed in section 4.5. The motivation of managers is considered from the perspectives of both profit-sharing schemes and partnerships in the subsidiary, and the manager's prospects for promotion overseas. Finally, procedures for decision-making are considered in section 4.6. Methods of appraising entry and expansion projects are discussed, and so too is the familiar issue of unitary (U-form) versus multidivisional (M-form) organisational structure.

In each of these four sections theory is used to derive predicted signs for the impact of key explanatory variables on the strategic decisions. These predicted signs are then compared with the actual signs obtained from regression analysis. The conclusions are summarised in section 4.7, where policy implications are also discussed.

4.2 STATISTICAL METHODOLOGY

A questionnaire was mailed to 115 SMNE subsidiaries, 75 of which answered (a response rate of 65 per cent). However, only 70 gave all of the information needed for subsequent analysis. Follow-up interviews and telephone contacts were carried out to clarify issues with respondents and this helped to stimulate the high level of response. The sample is reasonably representative of the corresponding population of firms, as Table 4.1 shows. As might be expected, there are more foreign firms in Italy than in Portugal, but in several of the industries they enjoy a smaller market share in Italy because of the larger size of the indigenous sector there. It is interesting that in highly regulated industries like banking and insurance, foreign market share is relatively low, whereas with less regulated industries (such as car rental and advertising) it is quite high. This suggests that in the service sector regulation is an effective deterrent to foreign entry. International tourism explains the high foreign market share in the Portuguese hotel industry. The data sources used in the compilation of Table 4.1 are described in the appendix.

The basic model used to analyse the questionnaire responses involves 14 simultaneous linear equations of the form:

$$Y_{ik} = a_i + \sum_{j=1}^{34} b_{ij} X_{jk} + \varepsilon_{ik} \tag{4.1}$$

TABLE 4.1 *Profile of sample and population SMNEs*

	Percentage market share			*Number of firms*		
	1 Foreign firms (1)	*2 Foreign firms in sample (2)*	*3 Percentage coverage (3)*	*4 Foreign firms (4)*	*5 Foreign firms in sample (5)*	*6 Percentage coverage (6)*
Italy						
Banking	1.8	1.6	87	33	14	42
Insurance	24	16	67	21	7	33
Car rental	76	71	93	na	4	na
Advertising	53	33	63	20	10	50
Hotels	na	na	na	na	6	na
Portugal						
Banking	5	3	67	11	7	64
Insurance	33	14	42	14	9	64
Car rental	49	43	88	4	3	75
Advertising	49	30	61	10	5	50
Hotels	53	34	64	7	5	71

NOTE: na = not available.

where Y_{ik} is the ith dimension of strategy pursued by the kth firm, X_{jk} is the jth characteristic of the kth firm, and a_i, b_{ij} are fixed coefficients. As usual the stochastic variables ε_{ik} are assumed to be independently and identically normally distributed, in contrast to the X_{jk} variables which are fixed ($i = 1, \ldots, 14$; $j = 1, \ldots, 70$).

The dependent variables Y_{ik} include three variables registering ownership and the entry and expansion modes; three variables registering control; five variables for management development strategies and three organisational variables. The explanatory variables X_{jk} cover five affiliate variables, two source country dummies, seven variables relating to specific motivations, five to general motivations, three to risk perceptions, five dummies for identifying the industries of each firm, one dummy for the host country, three environmental and company variables and finally three source country dummies. (There are five industry dummies rather than four because different hypotheses require different groups of industries to act as the control group.)

Apart from the dummies, the variables included in the model are mostly of a discrete and limited nature with values ranging between 0 and 4. Some, however, are continuous. Table 4.2 gives a description

TABLE 4.2 *(a) Dependent variables and (b) Independent variables*

(a) Dependent variables

Variables	*Range*	*Dummy*	*Source*
Ownership variables			
Y_1 Ownership	1–4		Q
Y_2 Entry mode	0–1	D	Q
Y_3 Expansion mode	0–1	D	Q
Control variables			
Y_4 Centralisation of control	0–1		Q
Y_5 Nationality of general manager	0–1	D	Q
Y_6 Weighted control	0–1		Q
Management development strategies			
Y_7 Promotion opportunity abroad	0–4		Q
Y_8 Training in subsidiaries	0–4		Q
Y_9 Profit sharing in subsidiaries	0–4		Q
Y_{10} Partnership in subsidiaries	0–4		Q
Y_{11} Other fringe benefits in subsidiaries	0–4		Q
Organisation variables			
Y_{12} Entry appraisal	0–1	D	Q
Y_{13} Expansion appraisal	0–1	D	Q
Y_{14} Subsidiary U-form dummy	0–1	D	Q

(b) Independent variables

Variables	*Range*	*Dummy*	*Source*
Affiliate variables			
X_1 Age			Q
X_2 Labour intensity	0–1	D	Q
X_3 Global customers	Positive		Q
X_4 Market share	Positive		Ind.
X_5 Relative size	Positive		Ind.
Source country dummies			
X_6 Parent U-form	0–1		Q
X_7 Foreign experience			Q
Specific motivations			
X_8 Spread fixed costs	0–4		Q
X_9 Low costs	0–4		Q
X_{10} Government incentives	0–4		Q
X_{11} Overcome tariff barriers	0–4		Q

(b) Independent variables

Variables	*Range*	*Dummy*	*Source*
X_{12} Close to important markets	0–4		Q
X_{13} Follow customers	0–4		Q
X_{14} Quality of labour	0–4		Q
General Motivations			
X_{15} Profit growth	0–4		Q
X_{16} Sales growth	0–4		Q
X_{17} Market growth	0–4		Q
X_{18} Brand image improvement	0–4		Q
X_{19} Diversification	0–4		Q
Risk perceptions			
X_{20} Political risk	0–4		Q
X_{21} Currency risk	0–4		Q
X_{22} Business risk	0–4		Q
Industry dummies			
X_{23} Banking	0–1	D	
X_{24} Insurance	0–1	D	
X_{25} Car rental	0–1	D	
X_{26} Advertising	0–1	D	
X_{27} Hotels	0–1	D	
Host country dummy			
X_{28} Italy/Portugal	0–1	D	
Environmental and company variables			
X_{29} Size of the MNE	Positive		Ind.
X_{30} Industry concentration	Positive		Ind.
X_{31} Presence of MNEs of same origin	Positive		Ind.
Source country dummies			
X_{32} US parent dummy	(0–1)	D	
X_{33} European parent dummy	(0–1)	D	
X_{34} Japanese parent dummy	(0–1)	D	

NOTES: Q: questionnaire data.
Ind.: industry data (see appendix).

of the 14 dependent and 34 independent variables, together with their range of variation and the source of information. It also indicates by a D whether they are dummies or not.

Data on variables ranging from 0 to 4 are all based on the questionnaire. The 5-point scale means that a factor obtaining a value 4 is very important while O means that the item is of no importance.

The ownership question (Y_1) relates to the equity stake held by the parent MNE. The scale was built as follows: 4=100 per cent; 3=50–99 per cent; 2=25–49 per cent and 1=0–24 per cent.

The entry and expansion mode dummies (Y_2 and Y_3) receive the value 1 if a greenfield type of entry or expansion was exclusively used, and 0 in the case of association with, or acquisition of, an existing firm.

The nationality of the general manager (Y_5) equals 1 if the subsidiary's general manager is a foreigner, and O if he is a host country citizen.

The appraisal of foreign investment decisions (Y_{12} and Y_{13}) receive the value 1 if sophisticated evaluation techniques (Net Present Value or Internal Rate of Return) were preferred to any of the proposed alternatives (Accounting Rate of Return, Pay Back and Absence of Formal Analysis).

Subsidiary U-form (Y_{14}) equals 1 for all subsidiaries possessing a functional type of organisation, either exclusively or in addition to some divisionalised structure.

Parent U-form (X_6) is interpreted in the same way as subsidiary U-form, but refers to the parent company's organisational structure.

The centralisation of control (Y_4) variable was generated in two stages. First of all, four decision topic areas were identified. A value 1 was conferred if the relevant decisions were mainly centralised at headquarters. The four topic areas included are cost control, investment, personnel and operations. An index was then constructed by aggregating the values and dividing the total by 4. Weighted control (Y_6) is the simple average of Y_4 and Y_5, designed to capture the joint effect of centralisation of control and use of expatriates to manage the subsidiary. As it is a dependent rather than an independent variable, there is no multicollinearity problem.

Age of the subsidiary (X_1) was measured in the number of years elapsed since the formation or acquisition of the subsidiary.

Labour intensity (X_2) captures the relative importance of personnel expenses in the investment decision. This dummy received the value 1 if recruitment and training were the highest ranked (or equal first) cost factor in the investment appraisal process, and was zero otherwise.

Global customers (X_3) measures the percentage of sales to foreign customers to total sales by the subsidiary.

Market share (X_4) registers the market share of the subsidiary as obtained from industry rankings and other sources. The data reflect the total value of services supplied, including both national and foreign customers.

Relative size of the subsidiary (X_5) is given by the ratio of local employees to the MNE's total employees. Besides company data, *Fortune*, Forbes and the UNCTC (1988) report have provided relevant information on this (see appendix).

MNE size (X_{29}) was measured by the MNE's total number of employees. The advantage of using the number of employees rather than overall turnover or total assets is that it seems to be a fairly robust measure, given the heterogeneous nature of the service industries considered in the study.

Industry concentration (X_{30}) was given by the Herfindhal index of industry concentration.

Presence of MNEs (X_{31}) measures the share of total assets in the host country industry held by MNEs originating from the same source country. In the case of Italy, data on the number of employees by nationality of parent company was also available and was utilised as required.

Theories of international business are tested within this framework by using them to impose constraints on the values of the b_{ij} coefficients in equations (4.1). The predictions of most theories are of a qualitative nature; they predict the sign of the coefficient but not its exact value. Tests of significance are used to determine whether a sign of the correct value is statistically significant from zero. Because of the large number of independent variables, only the results of step-wise regressions are shown. The procedure involved step-wise inclusion with the cut-off criterion of 10 per cent significance. Estimation was by ordinary least squares, supplemented by the usual range of diagnostic tests.

The four sets of dependent variables are examined in turn, beginning with ownership strategies. In each case the theoretical predictions are summarised in a table, so that the regression results can be compared with them. Where theory predicts two opposing effects, a +/− is shown, whereas when theory predicts no effect at all a zero is shown.

4.3 OWNERSHIP STRATEGIES

Theory

Age of subsidiary is expected to be positively related to ownership. It has been found that, in their early stages, firms tend to overestimate foreign risks and underestimate foreign revenues (Davidson, 1980; Caves, 1982). Experience in foreign markets starts with exporting, which may be followed by licensing (Telesio, 1979) or FDI. Anecdotal observation of firms included in this study confirmed that some service MNEs may set up joint venture at an early stage and later evolve to full ownership of a subsidiary. Pure exporting or licensing are less frequent in the service sector due to problems of location-boundedness (which inhibits exporting) and client–firm relationship (which inhibits licensing). The existence of a positive correlation between age and ownership of foreign subsidiaries has also been established in the case of manufacturing firms (Gatignon and Anderson, 1988).

The expected impact of labour-intensity on ownership is mixed (see Table 4.3). On the one hand, more capital-intensive firms may possess more important proprietary secrets requiring protection through ownership. On the other hand, firms relying on strong people-embodied knowledge may also require strong ownership because, although the secrets may be less valuable, the risks of losing them may be greater.

Share of global customers is expected to be positively related to ownership, as the risks of goodwill dissipation through poor service at a single location rise with the importance of global customers, while the need to adapt to local customers with an idiosyncratic culture declines.

Market share and relative size should be positively related to ownership. Cooperation with a local partner should help an MNE with small market share to overcome what the Hymer–Kindleberger paradigm has identified as the significant barriers associated with doing business abroad. The contribution of the local partner is accumulated country-specific knowledge and the goodwill of important local customers. Subsidiaries with a large relative weight in the context of the MNE create greater risks for the overall performance of the firm. While low ownership reduces exposure to these risks, stronger ownership facilitates the management of these risks. The impact of subsidiary size on ownership has been investigated by

TABLE 4.3 *Ownership strategies: predicted impacts*

Dependent variables	*Ownership variables* Y_1 *Ownership*	Y_2 *Entry Mode*	Y_3 *Expansion Mode*
Affiliate variables			
X_1 Age	+	+/−	+
X_2 Labour intensity	+/−	+/−	+/−
X_3 Global customers	+	+	+
X_4 Market share	+	+	+
X_5 Relative size	+	+	+
Source country dummies			
X_6 Parent U-form	0	+	+
X_7 Foreign experience	+	+	+
Specific motivations			
X_8 Spread fixed costs	+/−	+/−	+/−
X_9 Low costs	−	−	−
X_{10} Government incentives	−	−	−
X_{11} Overcome tariff barriers	−	−	−
X_{12} Close to important markets	+/−	+/−	+/−
X_{13} Follow customers	+	+	+
X_{14} Quality of labour	+/−	+/−	+/−
General motivations			
X_{15} Profit growth	+/−	+/−	+/−
X_{16} Sales growth	−	−	+/−
X_{17} Market growth	−	−	+/−
X_{18} Brand image improvement	−	−	−
X_{19} Diversification	+/−	+/−	+/−
Risk perceptions			
X_{20} Political risk	−	−	−
X_{21} Currency risk	−	−	−
X_{22} Business risk	0	0	0
Industry dummies			
X_{23} Banking	+	+	+
X_{24} Insurance	+	+	+
X_{25} Car rental	+	+	+
X_{26} Advertising	−	−	−
X_{27} Hotels	−	−	−
Host country dummy			
X_{28} Italy/Portugal	+	+	+
Environmental and company variables			
X_{29} Size of the MNE	+	+	+

continued on page 98

TABLE 4.3 *continued*

Dependent variables	*Ownership variables* Y_1 *Ownership*	Y_2 *Entry Mode*	Y_3 *Expansion Mode*
X_{30} Industry/Concentration	+	+	+
X_{31} Presence of MNEs of same origin	+	+	+
Source country dummies			
X_{32} US parent dummy	–	–	–
X_{33} European parent dummy	+	+	+
X_{34} Japanese parent dummy	–	–	–

Stopford and Haberich (1978), who found a significant positive relationship within a sample of UK-based MNEs. Hennart (1990) has confirmed the existence of a positive correlation between relative size and ownership for a sample of American subsidiaries of Japanese firms.

The organisational structure of the parent (X_6) may not have a clear implication for ownership. However, predominantly functional organisations are more likely to prefer greenfield entry and expansion modes, to guarantee closer coordination with the parent. Divisionalised structures are better adapted to self-managed and more decentralised organisations, and so are more compatible with entry and expansion through merger or association.

Foreign experience (X_7) is expected to be positively related to ownership. Two main factors create this relation: first, experience with other foreign locations reduces the marginal entry costs associated with the new location and so lowers the value of a local partner's knowledge contribution; and second, the spill-overs for the global business rise with the proliferation of subsidiaries and so call for closer coordination. Although, as previously emphasised, coordination through centralised control does not necessarily imply ownership, on balance it tends to favour it.

Spreading of R & D and other fixed costs (X_8) should give mixed results. Although the perishability of superior knowledge in the service sector due to ease of replication pushes service firms to fast exploitation of their superior knowledge, this may sometimes be done best through local partners.

When the main motivation for investment is to benefit from low costs or government incentives in the host location (X_9,X_{10} and X_{11}) it is possible that the competitive advantage possessed by the MNE is fairly modest, which suggests a potential interest in joint ventures to supplement the firm's own know-how.

The follow the customer motive (X_{13}) is expected to be positively related to ownership, and also to the share of global customers (X_3).

The main growth objectives pursued by firms can be divided into two groups: profit-related factors (X_{15}) and sales-related factors (X_{16} and X_{17}). Especially in an early stage, fast growth is more easily achieved through interfirm cooperation, and so ownership should, on balance, be negatively associated with sales-related growth.

High political and currency risk are generally believed to lead to low ownership. This hypothesis is taken as valid, but it is assumed that it applies less strongly to services due to their lower capital-intensity.

Industry-specific factors are expected to be significant in several contexts. Banks face low capital requirements, especially in proportion to their size, when starting new operations. Ownership and entry mode should therefore be independent in this case. Advertising is similar, in the sense that capital requirements are very low. However, country-specific knowledge of media and cultural characteristics may require cooperation with local firms. Hotels, as previously discussed, are expected to manifest low ownership and high control. Management contracts with very strict conditions reconcile the need to maintain the reputation of the brand name with the need to access local capital.

Host country market size, per capitum income and economic development are expected to be positively correlated with ownership and level of control. Fully-owned new ventures require higher fixed costs than do weaker entry or expansion forms involving cooperation with local firms, raising the break-even point (Buckley and Casson, 1981; Root, 1987). For this reason, smaller national markets may have dimensions too reduced to sustain high-ownership, high-control entry modes. For the industries considered in this study, Italy is expected to have higher level entry modes than Portugal.

The size of the MNE (X_{29}) is expected to be positively related with ownership and control. A positive correlation between firm size and ownership of the subsidiary is to be expected on the grounds that large and successful companies possess more proprietary secrets and are more reluctant to share them. They also have better access to capital markets and greater expertise in controlling international operations. Franko (1987) considers smaller investors to be more prone to seek joint ventures, 'if only because they lack the competitive muscle to do it alone'. This view is similar to the asset-complementarity hypothesis of joint ventures literature. Buckley and Casson (1981) observe that the higher set-up costs associated with the building of a new foreign subsidiary are more difficult for small firms to resource because of capital markets imperfections.

Several empirical studies (Stopford and Wells, 1972; Davidson, 1982; Davidson and McFetridge, 1985) have confirmed the 'Wells effect' (Franko, 1989): smaller lower market-share firms within an industry tend to utilise proportionately more joint ventures than do industry leaders. However, other authors have argued in favour of the general superiority of full ownership. Stopford (1987) presents some aggregate data suggesting that smaller investors are equally anxious and equally successful in asserting unambiguous control via ownership.

US and Japanese MNEs are expected to possess lower ownership and control than their European counterparts because of the greater remoteness of the parent firm. The literature on geographic and socio-cultural distance has emphasised the strong impact of this variable on both the decision to invest abroad and the choice of the mode of entry. It is generally accepted that firms face lower entry costs when they move into more familiar markets. In the Hymer–Kindleberger tradition, it can be said that they are at a smaller disadvantage with respect to indigenous firms than in a less familiar market. Therefore it is easier to create fully owned subsidiaries in similar countries. Furthermore, the benefits of full internalisation are also higher due to the reduction of internal uncertainty (Anderson and Gatignon, 1986). Gomes-Casseres (1989, p.15) confirms that the odds that joint venture is the mode chosen by US firms are $2\frac{1}{2}$ times greater when entering Argentina than when entering Canada.

Results

The ownership regression in the first column of Table 4.4 is the most successful of the 14 stepwise regressions reported in this study. A good fit is obtained, with 62 per cent of all variation being explained by nine independent variables, five of which are significant at the 1 per cent level. The signs of the coefficients confirm the hypotheses previously formulated except in the case of three variables: low costs, political risk and MNE size. One often-mentioned form of political

TABLE 4.4 *Ownership strategies: regression results*

	Ownership variables		
Dependent variables	Y_1 *Ownership*	Y_2 *Entry Mode*	Y_3 *Expansion Mode*
X_1 Age	0.3785 (4.448)**		
X_5 Relative size	–0.4675 (–5.123)**		
X_6 Parent U-form		0.1561 (1.766)	
X_9 Low costs	0.2286 (2.694)**	0.4212 (4.472)**	0.3736 (3.517)**
X_{11} Overcome tariff barriers	–0.1491 (–1.706)		
X_{19} Diversification		0.1957 (2.147)*	
X_{20} Political risk	0.3852 (4.524)**		
X_{21} Currency risk		–0.1691 (–1.740)	
X_{22} Business risk	0.1485 (1.866)		0.2014 (1.887)
X_{23} Banking		0.4869 (5.061)**	
X_{27} Hotels	–0.3952 (–4.320)**	–0.2782 (–2.839)**	–0.4705 (–3.878)**
X_{28} Italy/Portugal	0.3872 (4.467)**		
X_{29} Size of the MNE	–0.2267 (–2.415)*		
Adjusted R^2	0.6231	0.4696	0.2520
F	13.6771**	11.1823**	8.7481**

** significant at 1 per cent level.
* significant at 5 per cent level.
All remaining values shown are significant at 10 per cent level.
NOTE: *t*-values inside parenthesis.

risk was legal restriction of management decisions, of the sort imposed by central banks on other banks, in both Portugal and Italy. The results suggest that the higher is political risk, the higher is ownership. This result might be a consequence of the generally low capital involvement of service firms. As previously mentioned, even in the case of capital-intensive industries such as hotels, SMNEs avoid direct involvement through management contracts. Unlike most manufacturing MNEs, service firms are relatively footloose and scarcely vulnerable to political threat.

The size of the MNE may be negatively related to ownership because large size can better be achieved through association. Hotel chains are possible examples of such a path to growth. The need to follow customers, even to locations of very reduced market dimension or facing demanding local requirements for the right of establishment, reinforces such willingness to accept cooperation. In some cases the cooperation is not confined to local firms but to competing MNEs. The insurance sector is the best example, possibly due to less rivalry (for example, Phoenix Soleil Italia is jointly owned by GAN Assurance and EGF, both French insurers).

What determines the entry mode choice of SMNEs? In the Y_2 regression all the coefficient signs confirm the predicted relationships except, once again, the low costs motive. It is interesting to observe that the industry effect is very high, with banks strongly choosing the greenfield and total ownership mode of entry, while hotels significantly choose cooperation.

The determinants of expansion mode are less clearly captured by this analysis. The third regression can explain only 25 per cent of the variation of the expansion mode choice, and includes only three significant variables. Comparison with the previous equation shows that the banking dummy variable is no longer significant, suggesting that banks have been more consistent in entering than in expanding. The reason, many respondents have suggested, is that entry into the retail market segment through opening new branches is extremely difficult or restricted by law. It is not the capital cost of purchasing the site and so forth that is so great, but the enormous cost of building up a local client base. Banks entering a national market are often following a major customer, but those expanding within it do not have the advantage of ready-made clients at their new locations. Acquisition of equity stake in an indigenous extensively-branched bank has been described as the best route for expansion by more retail-oriented foreign banks.

4.4 CONTROL STRATEGIES

Theory

Age is expected to show a less clear relationship with control than with ownership. The contradictory factors are the learning process which makes the subsidiary more autonomous (with the consequent savings in coordination costs) and the growing integration of global business, requiring more coordination between one subsidiary and another as well as between subsidiary and headquarters (see Table 4.5).

TABLE 4.5 *Control strategies: predicted impact*

	Control variables		
Dependent variables	Y_4 *Centralisation of control*	Y_5 *Nationality of general manager*	Y_6 *Weighted control*
Affiliate variables			
X_1 Age	+/−	+/−	+/−
X_2 Labour intensity	+/−	+/−	+/−
X_3 Global customers	+	+	+
X_4 Market share	−	−	−
X_5 Relative size	−	−	−
Source country dummies			
X_6 Parent U-form	+/−	+/−	+/−
X_7 Foreign experience	+	+	+
Specific motivations			
X_8 Spread fixed costs	+	+	+
X_9 Low costs	−	−	−
X_{10} Government incentives	−	−	−
X_{11} Overcome tariff barriers	+	+	+
X_{12} Close to important markets	+	+	+
X_{13} Follow customers	+	+	+
X_{14} Quality of labour	+	+	+
General motivations			
X_{15} Profit growth	+	+	+
X_{16} Sales growth	+/−	+/−	+/−
X_{17} Market growth	+/−	+/−	+/−
X_{18} Brand image improvement	+	+	+
X_{19} Diversification	+/−	+/−	+/−
Risk perceptions			
X_{20} Political risk	+/−	+/−	+/−
X_{21} Currency risk	+/−	+/−	+/−
X_{22} Business risk	0	0	0
Industry dummies			
X_{23} Banking	+	+	+
X_{24} Insurance	+	+	+
X_{25} Car rental	+/−	+/−	+/−
X_{26} Advertising	−	−	−
X_{27} Hotels	+	+	+

continued on page 104

TABLE 4.5 *continued*

	Control variables		
Dependent variables	Y_4 *Centralisation of control*	Y_5 *Nationality of general manager*	Y_6 *Weighted control*
Host country dummy			
X_{28} Italy/Portugal	+	+	+
Environmental and company variables			
X_{29} Size of the MNE	+	+	+
X_{30} Industry concentration	+	+	+
X_{31} Presence of MNEs of same origin	+	+	+
Source country dummies			
X_{32} US parent dummy	–	–	–
X_{33} European parent dummy	+	+	+
X_{34} Japanese parent dummy	–	–	–

Share of global customers is expected to be positively related with control. Association with or total delegation to local suppliers of the same service presents some benefits to the SMNE by diminishing the risk and costs associated with autonomous start-up in an alien location. However, it poses serious problems of goodwill dissipation, as the local partner or agent may feel tempted to free ride on the relationship established between the service MNE and the customer. This problem is similar to the difficulty of sharing other intangible assets, such as those based on advertising or R & D. Caves (1982, p. 86) and Franko (1987) have identified the lack of willingness of the local partner to invest resources in the improvement and maintenance of intangible assets as a factor reducing the likelihood of joint ventures the more important are such assets.

Market share and relative size are expected to be negatively related to the centralisation of control. The larger is the subsidiary the more compelling is the logic of delegation even where ownership gives the parent overall control. Garnier (1984) studied the relationship between relative size and centralisation of control but his results were not significant and of opposite signs for the two samples he considered. However, centralised control may be particularly important in minimising the risks of opportunism in the case where there are significant fixed costs incurred in R & D.

Political and currency risk, although expected to be negatively correlated with ownership, may have a mixed impact on control, as observed in Anderson and Gatignon (1986). The conflicting force is that the MNE may try to increase control to manage country risk more effectively.

Empirical studies on the relationship between centralisation of control and size have also generated mixed results. Garnier (1984) and Gates and Egelhoff (1986) have used organisation theory to argue that large firms demand higher decentralisation in order to avoid excessive governance costs. The results were mixed, and Gates and Egelhoff found a contradictory positive relation for the marketing function: the marketing of large firms was *more* centralised. In the light of the internalisation theory this result may be interpreted as showing that the benefits of greater integration of the marketing function outweigh the costs until a very large organisational scale is reached.

The presence of MNEs of the same origin is positively related to ownership and level of control of the subsidiary. This hypothesis derives directly from the assumption that customer-specific knowledge is a major competitive advantage of SMNEs, combined with the belief that the presence of other SMNEs proxies for the prominence of such knowledge. This type of proprietary knowledge needs even stronger protection through internalisation than typical R & D based on proprietary knowledge. The reason is that the damaging effect of opportunistic behaviour and loss of reputation can be reflected in a large number of locations, as Dunning and McQueen (1981) found in international hotels.

Industry concentration is expected to be positively related with ownership and level of control. Industries characterised by atomistic markets and perfect competition should not leave space for the appropriation of economic rents. In conditions close to perfect competition, such economic rents may be too low to cover the higher set-up costs associated with the undertaking of new ventures. Dircct investment is more frequent in more concentrated industries as tested by Buckley and Casson (1976). Pearce (1989b) has also predicted a positive correlation between industry concentration and the overseas production ratio, based on the further grounds that rivalry starts a follow-the-leader behaviour, precipitating FDI decisions. (Nevertheless his empirical test covering the 792 largest industrial firms in 1982 did not confirm the hypothesis).

TABLE 4.6 *Control strategies: regression results*

	Control variables		
Dependent variables	Y_4 *Centralisation of control*	Y_5 *Nationality general manager*	Y_6 *Weighted control*
X_3 Global customers	0.2286 (2.041)*		0.3478 (3.210)**
X_5 Relative size	–0.2802 (–2.339)*		
X_{12} Close to important markets	0.3502 3.039		0.2173 (2.066)*
X_{23} Banking	–0.2420 (–1.910)		
X_{24} Insurance		–0.3422 (–2.782)**	
X_{26} Advertising		–0.7023 (–4.682)**	–0.4199 (–3.849)**
X_{29} Size of the MNE		–0.2454 (–1.768)	
X_{30} Industry concentration		–0.2792 (–2.296)*	
Adjusted R^2	0.1838 4.8852**	0.2364 6.3399**	0.2495 8.6474**

** significant at 1 per cent level.
 * significant at 5 per cent level.
All other values are significant at 10 per cent level.
NOTE: *t*-values inside parenthesis.

Results

The three equations attempting to measure the determinants of control generate relatively poor results (see Table 4.6). However, the comparison with ownership permits some significant conclusions. The global customer variable, measuring the relative importance of global customers, has a stronger relation with centralisation of control than with ownership, showing that control is more important than ownership in safeguarding privileged relations with global customers. Curiously, the coefficient relating global customers to ownership is negative, although insignificant. This result suggests that following the customer does not preclude cooperation with local firms, and that control can be an efficient substitute for ownership. In this mode strong benefits of cooperation, such as lower set-up costs and quicker acquisition of country-specific knowledge, can be achieved without incurring unbearable risks of opportunism.

The use of expatriates has often been mentioned as an instrument to exert control. The results show that differences between industries are the most powerful determinants of the decision to use expatriates. Country-specific business conditions, regulations and culture explain the limited use of expatriates in advertising and insurance.

Weighted control – the weighted average of centralisation of control and general manager nationality – improves the fit of the control variable only marginally. It confirms the importance of control in serving global customers who require certain key locations to be serviced.

Finally the reciprocal effect of ownership on control and control on ownership has been tested by adding ownership to the right-hand side of the weighted control equation and vice versa. In neither case is a significant improvement of fit obtained.

4.5 MANAGEMENT DEVELOPMENT STRATEGIES

Theory

The five management development strategies identified in Table 4.7 represent distinct but potentially complementary ways of promoting company performance through improved managerial competence and motivation.

A significant relation is expected between the spreading of R & D and other fixed costs and the availability of promotion opportunities abroad, since the international expansion generated by the first directly promotes the second. Efficient exploitation of R & D is best achieved through frequent training of local staff, so a positive relation between training and the spreading of fixed costs is expected as well.

The larger market share enjoyed by SMNEs in Portugal than in Italy, as shown in Table 4.1, together with the greater economic development of the latter country, including large domestic firms, should lead to significant differences between Italy and Portugal. More intensive use of management development strategies is expected in Portugal because indigenous firms provide a smaller and

TABLE 4.7 *Management development strategies: predicted impacts*

		Management development strategies				
Dependent variables		Y_7 *Promotion opportunity abroad*	Y_8 *Training in subsidiaries*	Y_9 *Profit sharing in subsidiaries*	Y_{10} *Partnership in subsidiaries*	Y_{11} *Other fringe benefits in subsidiaries*
Affiliate variables						
X_1	Age	+/−	+	+/−	+/−	+/−
X_2	Labour intensity	0	+	+	+	+/−
X_3	Global customers	+	+/−	+	+/−	+/−
X_4	Market share	−	+/−	+	+/−	+/−
X_5	Relative size	−	+	+	+	+/−
Source country dummies						
X_6	Parent U-form	0	0	0	0	0
X_7	Foreign experience	+	+	0	0	0
Specific motivations						
X_8	Spread fixed costs	+	+	0	0	0
X_9	Low costs	0	0	0	−	−
X_{10}	Government incentives	0	0	0	−	−
X_{11}	Overcome tariff barriers	0	0	0	−	−
X_{12}	Close to important markets	−	0	0	+	+
X_{13}	Follow customers	+/−	+	+	0	0
X_{14}	Quality of labour	+	+	+	+/−	+/−
General motivations						
X_{15}	Profit growth	+	0	+	+	0
X_{16}	Sales growth	+	0	+	−	0
X_{17}	Market growth	+	0	+	−	−
X_{18}	Brand image improvement	+	+	+/−	+/−	−
X_{19}	Diversification	0	0	0	0	0
Risk perceptions						
X_{20}	Political risk	+	+/−	+	+	0
X_{21}	Currency risk	+	+/−	+	+	0
X_{22}	Business risk	+/−	+/−	−	−	+
Industry dummies						
X_{23}	Banking	+	+	−	−	+
X_{24}	Insurance	−	+	−	−	+
X_{25}	Car rental	−	−	+	−	0
X_{26}	Advertising	−	−	+	+	−
X_{27}	Hotels	+	+	+	−	0
Host country dummy						
X_{28}	Italy/Portugal	−	−	−	−	−
Environmental and company variables						
X_{29}	Size of the MNE	+	+	−	−	+
X_{30}	Industry concentration	+/−	+	+	−	0
X_{31}	Presence of MNEs of same origin	0	0	0	0	0

Dependent variables		Management development strategies Y_7 Promotion opportunity abroad	Y_8 Training in subsidiaries	Y_9 Profit sharing in subsidiaries	Y_{10} Partnership in subsidiaries	Y_{11} Other fringe benefits in subsidiaries
Source country dummies						
X_{32}	US parent dummy	+	0	+	+	0
X_{33}	European parent dummy	–	–	–	–	0
X_{34}	Japanese parent dummy	–	–	–	–	0

less effective source of skilled labour for the foreign entrant to recruit.

Results

Promotion abroad is explained mainly by industry dummies. In particular, interest in interchanging experiences and know-how through personnel mobility is important in banking and hotels. The predicted positive relation with the spreading of fixed costs is confirmed. The negative relation with proximity to major markets is worth noting, as it suggests that large local markets discourage mobility because they provide better local career opportunities (see Table 4.8).

The results on the frequency of training also provide useful insights. The spreading of fixed costs is again positive and significant, confirming the importance of training in firms involved in transferring know-how to subsidiaries. Portuguese subsidiaries appear to use training more intensively, confirming that less outside professional experience and lower technical skills, as compared to Italian professionals, requires higher in-firm training.

Profit sharing is negatively related to operating in Italy, to insurance, to multinational size and to Japanese ownership. The result for insurance may reflect the fact that it takes a long time after the sale of a policy for the claims experience to show up in reported profits, so that profit-sharing in insurance would encourage the overselling of high-risk policies. The result for multinational size may reflect the difficulty of accurately imputing profits to a subsidiary that is part of a large global network, and the danger that any attempt to do so would lead to excessive internal wrangling over transfer prices. The result

TABLE 4.8 *Management development strategies: regression results*

		Management development strategies				
Dependent variable		Y_7 *Promotion opportunity abroad*	Y_8 *Training in subsidiaries*	Y_9 *Profit sharing in subsidiaries*	Y_{10} *Partner-ship in subsidiaries*	Y_{11} *Other fringe benefits in subsidiaries*
X_1	Age		0.3591 (3.242)**			
X_5	Relative size		–0.2324 (–2.233)*			
X_8	Spread fixed costs	0.1577 (1.700)	0.1997 (1.851)			
X_{10}	Government incentives				–0.2702 (–2.720)**	
X_{12}	Close to important markets	–0.2545 (–2.514)*				
X_{15}	Profit growth				0.2140 (2.227)*	
X_{17}	Market growth		0.1921 (1.778)			
X_{18}	Brand image improvement	0.2006 (2.123)*				
X_{20}	Political risk		0.2749 (2.433)*			
X_{21}	Currency risk			0.1919 (1.845)	0.1926 (1.824)	

X_{22}	Business risk				−0.2089 (−2.141)*	0.2313 (1.981)
X_{23}	Banking	0.4231 (4.443)**			0.2928 (2.833)**	−0.2282 (1.955)
X_{24}	Insurance			−0.4182 (−3.967)**		
X_{25}	Car rental				0.2377 (2.396)*	
X_{26}	Advertising				0.6124 (5.904)**	
X_{27}	Hotels	0.4863 (5.142)**				
X_{28}	Italy/Portugal	−0.2278 (−2.340)*	−0.2304 (−2.206)*	−0.3334 (−3.20)**	−0.4392 (−4.69)**	
X_{29}	Size of the MNE			−0.3358 (−3.067)**		
X_{32}	US parent dummy		0.1892 (1.843)			
X_{34}	Japanese parent dummy			−0.1996 (−1.927)	−0.1708 (−1.816)	
Adjusted R^2		0.4927	0.4409	0.3035	0.4407	0.0683
F		12.1709**	6.9834**	7.0143**	7.040**	3.530*

** significant at 1 per cent level.
 * significant at 5 per cent level.
All other values are significant at the 10 per cent level.
NOTE: t-values inside parenthesis.

for Japan is consistent with the view that Japanese firms motivate their managers more by leadership and by values instilled through training than through pecuniary incentives.

Equity sharing by managers is a related strategy. Its importance in advertising is probably explained by the necessity of attracting and retaining highly-skilled professionals to sustain competitive advantage.

With the exception of fringe benefits, which are difficult to explain statistically, the remaining management development strategies appear to be related predominantly to industry and host country factors.

4.6 ORGANISATIONAL STRUCTURES AND ADMINISTRATIVE PROCEDURES

Theory

The final group of dependent variables is concerned with the sophistication of the decision-making procedures used in the subsidiary, and the organisational structure of the subsidiary. Decision-making is evaluated with respect to two issues: the way management appraises the costs and benefits of initial entry into the foreign market, and the way it appraises the returns to subsequent expansion. Both these issues are amenable to various techniques of investment appraisal. SMNEs were asked what method of appraisal had been used to decide on entry, and what method would be used to evaluate further expansion (see Table 4.9 and 4.10).

The sophistication of investment appraisal is expected to be negatively associated with the relative weight of labour costs: 'manufacturing like' capital-intensive projects such as hotels are more easily appraised with conventional evaluation techniques than human-intensive activities such as advertising. It is important to note that MNEs in the hotel industry concentrating on management contracts or franchising are generally not involved with the initial investment associated with the construction phase.

Share of global customers is expected to be negatively related to the sophistication of investment appraisal in the subsidiary. Company-wide considerations are dominant due to stronger global strategic implications. Most of the sophisticated decisions will therefore be taken at headquarters. Several companies reported that they have started

TABLE 4.9 *Organisational structure and administrative procedures: predicted impacts*

Dependent variables		*Organisation variables* Y_{12} *Entry Appraisal*	Y_{13} *Expansion Appraisal*	Y_{14} *Subsidiary U-form*
Affiliate variables				
X_1	Age	–	–	+
X_2	Labour intensity	–	–	0
X_3	Global customers	–	–	+
X_4	Market share	+	+	+
X_5	Relative size	+	+	+
Source country dummies				
X_6	Parent U-form	–	–	+
X_7	Foreign experience	+	+	+
Specific motivations				
X_8	Spread fixed costs	+/–	+/–	+
X_9	Low costs	+	+	+
X_{10}	Government incentives	+	+	–
X_{11}	Overcome tariff barriers	+	+	+
X_{12}	Close to important markets	+	+	+
X_{13}	Follow customers	–	–	+
X_{14}	Quality of labour	+	+	+
General motivations				
X_{15}	Profit growth	+	+	+
X_{16}	Sales growth	+/–	+/–	+/–
X_{17}	Market growth	+/–	+/–	+/–
X_{18}	Brand image improvement	+	+	+
X_{19}	Diversification	+	+	–
Risk perceptions				
X_{20}	Political risk	+	+	–
X_{21}	Currency risk	+	+	–
X_{22}	Business risk	+/–	+/–	+
Industry dummies				
X_{23}	Banking	+	+	–
X_{24}	Insurance	+	+	0
X_{25}	Car rental	+/–	+/–	0
X_{26}	Advertising	–	–	0
X_{27}	Hotels	+	+	0

continued on page 114

TABLE 4.9 *continued*

Dependent variables		*Organisation variables* Y_{12} *Entry Appraisal*	Y_{13} *Expansion Appraisal*	Y_{14} *Subsidiary U-form*
Host country dummy				
X_{28}	Italy/Portugal	+	+	+
Environmental and company variables				
X_{29}	Size of the MNE	+	+	+
X_{30}	Industry concentration	+	+	+
X_{31}	Presence of MNEs of same origin	+/−	+/−	+/−
Source country dummies				
X_{32}	US parent dummy	+	+	+
X_{33}	European parent dummy	−	+	−
X_{34}	Japanese parent dummy	−	−	−

operations in countries with domestic markets too small to break even. The local presence of global customers led the SMNE to follow them, to preserve a good relationship with the customer and to avoid the customer switching to a rival SMNE already established in that market.

Parent U-form is expected to be related to subsidiary U-form as the organisational structure of the parent tends to be transplanted to the subsidiary, after taking into account differences of size and scope. A second significant relationship, but negative, is expected between subsidiary U-form and the sophistication of project appraisal in the subsidiary, due to the greater integration of decision-making in U-form firms around the headquarters.

Market share, relative size, foreign experience, size of MNE and industry concentration are all expected to be positively related to the organisational variables considered here. Greater experience, market power and the relative importance of the subsidiary should lead to more careful investment appraisal as well as stricter coordination on account of the interactions with the world-wide activity of the firm. It should be noted, though, that similar research carried out with manufacturing industries (Kelly and Philippatos, 1982) found no association between MNE size and the sophistication of evaluation techniques.

TABLE 4.10 *Organisational structures and administrative procedures: predicted impacts*

		Organisation variables		
Dependent variables		Y_{12} *Entry appraisal*	Y_{13} *Expansion appraisal*	Y_{14} *Subsidiary U-form*
X_1	Age	–0.3417 (–3.061)**	–0.2701 (–2.243)*	
X_6	Parent U-form			0.3028 (2.953)**
X_8	Spread fixed costs			0.3095 (2.682)**
X_{10}	Government incentives			–0.3204 (–2.864)**
X_{13}	Follow customers		–0.2181 (–1.837)	
X_{14}	Quality of labour	–0.2317 (2.076)*		
X_{20}	Political risk		0.2736 (2.406)*	
X_{22}	Business risk			0.3050 (2.918)**
X_{30}	Industry concentration			0.2960 (2.938)**
Adjusted R^2		0.1811	0.1544	0.3428
F		8.628**	5.198**	8.197**

** significant at 1 per cent level.
 * significant at 5 per cent level.
All other values shown are significant at the 10 per cent level.
NOTE: *t*-values inside parenthesis.

Results

The results relating to entry appraisal were scarcely significant. However, the significant negative relationship with age shows that more recently arrived SMNEs have made far more use of sophisticated project appraisal techniques.

The results relating to expansion appraisal are even poorer, with only 15 per cent of the variance being explained. Sensitivity to political risk acts as an incentive to sophisticated evaluation practices – which is obviously plausible – while the follow the customer motive acts as a deterrent. The negative association between following the customer and the sophistication of project appraisal confirms the limited importance of local considerations, *vis-à-vis* the broader world-wide interests of the SMNE, in regard to its relationship with global customers.

The choice of organisational form confirms previous hypotheses: parent U-form promotes subsidiary U-form, which suggests that not only do companies like to maintain uniformity in organisational structure but that the U-form intrinsically demands it. The positive association with spreading fixed costs and with industry concentration indicates that the subsidiary U-form is favoured where strong firm-specific assets are exploited in an oligopolistic environment.

4.7 CONCLUSIONS

This study has provided a wide-ranging analysis of the determinants of SMNEs' international strategies. Two major investment decisions, setting up a subsidiary in a new country and expanding the existing capacity, have been taken into account.

A strong significance has been found for the trend to higher ownership as the subsidiary ages and acquires country-specific knowledge. Control, however, does not follow the same path. This could be interpreted in the following way. The initial activities of a typical SMNEs' subsidiaries are oriented exclusively to customers (MNEs and travelling individuals) originating in the home country. A relatively small wholly-owned subsidiary is generally the initial organisation in the new location. After obtaining more familiarity with the host country, the SMNE becomes interested in exploiting further economic rents by servicing domestic customers. Given a still insufficient country-specific knowledge, the creation of a joint venture with local service firms is generally the most efficient mode for reaching the new market segment.

Later, as the country-specific learning process expands further, the subsidiary reabsorbs the joint venture and the original ownership pattern is restored. After this, relations between the subsidiary and its parent evolve according to two opposite forces. One leads to declining contact between the parent and the host country and to less parent–subsidiary cooperation. This reflects the subsidiary's growing confidence and its declining need to rely on the parent's expertise. The opposite force is the expansion abroad of local customers, giving

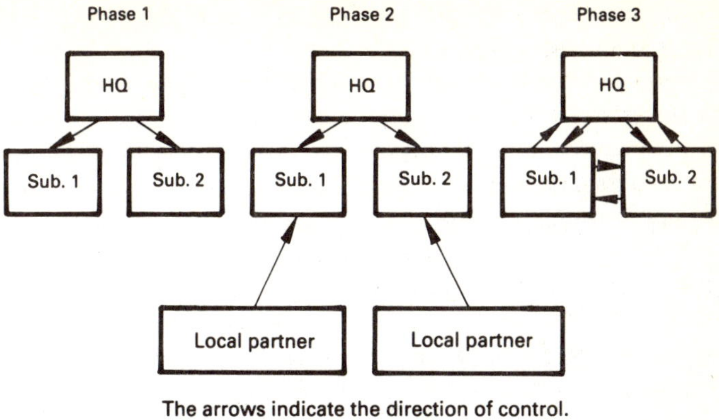

FIGURE 4.1 Three phases in the evolution of a subsidiary of an SMNE

the subsidiary a more important role in the international network and leading to the need for greater internal coordination and control. However, in this phase information and guidance concerning client-specific information moves in new directions, from subsidiary to subsidiary or even from subsidiary to parent: for example, the case of the Italian subsidiary of an American service company whose Italian client has become a MNE with operations in the USA. Figure 4.1 summarises this process schematically in terms of three phases.

Another second general conclusion is that political and currency risk play a smaller role in ownership and control decisions than expected given previous studies on manufacturing MNEs. It was observed that SMNEs are less sensitive to political risk. The same applies to currency risk because of the limited need for capital disbursement at the initial investment stage, and the low importance of exports. Income and capital flows are not very relevant except for the payment of royalties and transfer of profits. However, they are important in the case of insurance companies whose subsidiaries reinsure risks with the parent.

Size of MNE was scarcely significant. However, an interesting result was found with the relative size of the subsidiary compared to the MNE as a whole. As in Hennart's (1990) study of Japanese manufacturing subsidiaries in the USA, relative size was found to be negatively related with ownership. The same relationship was found with control, but to a smaller extent. This suggests that parent firms economise on capital investments by taking a smaller proportional stake in the larger subsidiaries, and as a consequence give those subsidiaries greater autonomy.

The cultural background of the SMNE seems to be of some importance in explaining foreign investment behaviour, especially among Japanese firms. Contrary to Garnier's (1984) findings, the Japanese delegate less than their Western counterparts. Japanese firms offer subsidiary managers a very limited financial stake in the subsidiary. This may be because elaborate career-planning within the lifetime employment system makes the prospect of promotion back to headquarters the main incentive for Japanese nationals employed in the subsidiary. So far as non-Japanese employees are concerned, the failure to involve them in profit-sharing may reflect a Japanese view that such pecuniary rewards are incidental to employee motivation.

It was also found that SMNEs not only transfer technological know-how and spread fixed costs through foreign expansion, as do their manufacturing counterparts, but are also particularly influenced by the follow-the-customer motive. This confirms the results obtained in previous empirical work.

It was found that SMNEs are reluctant to share technology and reputation with local firms. Full ownership is possibly lower in advertising and hotels than, on average, in manufacturing, but alternative and significant means to exert control were exploited in hotels (namely, the management contract). Advertising follows a typical pattern of country-specific, people-embodied knowledge. However, as Weinstein (1977) discovered, advertising MNEs show a clear trend to higher levels of equity ownership by the parent.

The policy implications of this study stem from the recent attention given to trade in services, which may normally be interpreted as FDI in services. Recent GATT negotiations and the growing understanding by Eastern European countries of the importance of services as infrastructure have brought FDI in services on to the agenda of many nations. Some relevant policy implications may be drawn from this study. While services are generally less sensitive to government incentives than footloose manufacturing, FDI in services can be deterred by hostile internal regulation, as happened with banking in Portugal and Italy. The most important incentive, however, is the presence of home-country business clients or travelling individuals.

Appendix

Several sources have complemented information supplied by the questionnaire, especially at industry level. A list is given below, organised by industry and type of data:

Banking
Il Mondo, July 1989, p.29. Gives a ranking of banks operating in Italy. Data on total volume of credit allowed the calculation of concentration indexes for the Italian market and each bank's market share.

Caixa Geral de Depositos annual report on the banking industry, 1989. *Idem*, for Portugal. Age of foreign banks also contained in the report was cross-checked with data available from the questionnaires.

ABI, the Italian banking association, has prepared a specific report with information on foreign banks in Italy, including year of establishment.

Fortune, June 1989, contains a ranking of the largest banks world-wide by total assets. It includes total number of employees, information used for estimating the size of banks.

Insurance
Il Mondo, October 1989, p.41. Gives a ranking of insurance companies operating in Italy. This information was complemented by data obtained from the Annual Report, 1989, of ISVAP, the Italian insurance regulatory body. Market shares and industry concentration were estimated from these sources.

The Annual Report for 1989 of ISP, the Portuguese insurance regulatory body, has been the source of equivalent data for Portugal. APS, the Portuguese association of insurance companies, has been the source of information on the year of establishment of each firm.

UNCTC (1988) includes information on total number of employees of the largest world-wide insurance companies.

Car Rental
Data on number of employees, and on the market shares of the Italian and Portuguese subsidiaries, were based exclusively on company reports and specific estimates. However, cross-checking between different sources was used.

Advertising
Total billings by agency was the basis for calculating market shares and industry concentration. This information was available from *Pubblicita Domani*, June 1989, for Italy and from data collected by APAP, the Portuguese association of advertising agencies, for Portugal.

For the world-wide level, *Advertising Age*, March 1989, provided information on number of employees.

Hotels
Italian market shares and concentration measures were calculated from

company and ISTAT (Italian statistics office) data, published in 1989. Data from the Portuguese Secretaria de Estado do Turismo was used to estimate these values for the Portuguese case.

The global size (number of employees) of hotel MNEs has been estimated from data published in *Hotels and Restaurants International*, July 1989.

5 The Impact of Multinational Banks on International Financial Centres

PAUL CAMPAYNE

5.1 INTRODUCTION

The theories of international production have traditionally viewed the locational decisions of multinational banks (MNBs)[1] as a choice between FDI and exports. However, this traditional choice may be of less relevance today as the reduced segmentation of financial markets has made possible a more globally optimal locational pattern of banking activities. The post-war period has been one in which many dramatic changes have occurred in the banking industry and the environment in which it operates, due to technological progress, deregulation and financial innovations. These have facilitated the creation of global financial markets. Individual markets, with their own unique rules and regulations, traditions and dominant institutions, have become increasingly integrated with the supranational Euromarket and with each other. Although barriers to integration still remain and segment parts of the market, there is still a strong trend towards globalisation, drawing together investors and borrowers from around the world. This increased integration of product and geographical markets more readily permits an international division of banking activities across a global hierarchy of financial centres.

In response to the changing environment the competitive strategies of banks have been adapted. Their multinational operations have increased in size, geographical spread and importance, as can be seen in Table 5.1. The data reveal the dramatic increase in the foreign networks of the world's largest banks between 1968 and 1987. There were 18 banks for which complete data were available and which were in the top 50 in both years. Their total network grew from 284 branches and representative offices to 787: that is, from an average per bank of nearly 16 to 44. It has not only been the size of the largest banks' networks that has grown, however. The number of countries in which they operate has also increased. In 1968 the Japanese banks in the top 50 had branches in 3.5 countries, on average, and representative offices in 2.9. By 1987 these averages had grown to 6.4 and 10.3 respectively. For the European banks in the sample, the respective figures were 1.4 and 5.2 in 1968, and 9.7 and 13.1 in 1987. So the spread of activities of the world's largest banks has clearly increased substantially.

The increase in foreign operations has facilitated the interpenetration of national and international markets. Once started, this growing interpenetration was perceived as a prerequisite for maintaining market shares and keeping up volume growth in highly competitive markets (Pecchioli, 1983). The interpenetration of markets by MNBs was to lead to competition in which the activities of banks in one market had a direct bearing on their position in another. As a result many banks have moved from individual market servicing strategies, which Porter (1986) terms a 'multidomestic strategy', to a 'rationalised investment or global strategy', in order to deal with the competition.[2] This means that they offer financial products to whomever demonstrates a need and can be profitably served, wherever they may be located. But while the overall strategy is designed to provide a full range of services to multinational and other domestic clients (Rybcynski, 1988), the locational strategy to provide these services differs. With the reduction in much of the segmentation of financial markets, and increased international competition, a more globally optimal locational pattern of activities is made possible.

This chapter undertakes an analysis of the optimal locational pattern of MNBs' activities and its determinants, and examines the extent to which the locational structure of the banks' activities corresponds to the theoretical pattern. The next section provides a brief review of the literature relating to MNBs. Section 5.3 then develops a theoretical framework that examines the optimal location pattern, and explains the relationship between the structure of the MNB's operations and the hierarchy of financial centres. It brings together theories of the optimal location of economic activity and the

TABLE 5.1 *The foreign networks of the world's largest 50 banks*

(a) 1968

Bank	*Branches*	*Number of countries*	*Representative offices*	*Number of countries*	*Total network*
Bank of America	72	35	11	11	83
Citibank	nsa	52	2	2	nsa
Chase Manhattan	47	24	7	7	54
Barclays	nsa	nsa	nsa	nsa	nsa
Manufactures Hanover	3	2	15	15	18
JP Morgan	8	6	5	5	13
National Westminster	nsa	nsa	nsa	nsa	nsa
Western Bancorp	0	0	4	4	4
B. Nazionale de Lavoro	2	2	8	7	10
Chemical	2	1	9	9	11
Bankers Trust	2	2	11	11	13
Royal Bank of Canada*	106	22	9	7	115
Fuji	2	2	3	3	5
Westdeutsche	0	0	0	0	0
BNP	nsa	nsa	nsa	nsa	nsa
Mitsubishi	2	2	0	0	2
Sumitomo	2	2	2	2	4
Sanwa	4	3	0	0	4
CIBC	51	11	5	3	56
Midland	nsa	nsa	nsa	nsa	nsa
Credit Lyonnais	nsa	7	8	7	nsa
Continental Illinois	7	5	10	10	17
B. of Montreal	6	2	7	6	13
Deutsche	0	0	13	12	13
B. Commerciale Italiano	3	2	4	4	7
B. of Tokyo	34	18	18	16	52
First Chicago	4	3	2	2	6
Nippon Kogyo (IBJ)	0	0	3	3	3
Mitsui	5	4	0	0	5
B. do Brasil	7	6	0	0	7
Cassa Risparmio Lombarde	0	0	1	1	1
Security Pacific	1	1	1	1	2
Lloyds	nsa	nsa	nsa	nsa	nsa

continued on page 124

TABLE 5.1 *continued*

(a) 1968

Bank	*Branches*	*Number of countries*	*Representative offices*	*Number of countries*	*Total network*
Sociéte Générale	4	2	9	8	13
Marine Midland	2	2	7	7	9
Tokai	1	1	1	1	2
Dresdner	0	0	9	9	9
Dai Ichi	1	1	2	2	3
Irving Trust	1	1	3	3	4
Credito Italiano	0	0	7	7	7
B. di Roma	14	4	4	4	18
Wells Fargo	1	1	4	4	5
Standard Chartered	nsa	nsa	nsa	nsa	nsa
Nippon Kangyo	2	2	0	0	2
Monte Paschi Siena	0	0	0	0	0
Union B. Switzerland	1	1	11	9	12
B. Nova Scotia	50	13	0	0	50
Crocker National	0	0	4	4	4
Commonwealth B.	33	4	0	0	33
Hessiche Landesbank	0	0	0	0	0

* Branches and sub-branches.
NOTE: nsa = not separately available.
SOURCE: *Bankers Almanac and Yearbook* (1970).

(b) 1987

Bank	*Branches*	*Number of countries*	*Representative offices*	*Number of countries*	*Total network*
Dai Ichi Kangyo	11	9	23	17	34
Sumitomo	15	11	25	20	40
Fuji	7	7	15	13	22
Mitsubishi	7	6	17	16	24
Sanwa	13	8	2	2	15
Industrial B. Japan	6	5	22	13	28
Credit Agricole	5	4	8	7	13
Citicorp	135	65	12	8	150
Norinchukin	1	1	1	1	2
BNP	95	26	25	21	120
Deutsche	14	11	18	16	32
Credit Lyonnais	nsa	16	25	22	nsa

Bank	*Branches*	*Number of countries*	*Representative offices*	*Number of countries*	*Total network*
Mitsubishi T & B	5	5	6	5	11
Barclays	nsa	nsa	nsa	nsa	nsa
National Westminster	nsa	nsa	nsa	nsa	nsa
Tokai	9	7	21	16	30
Sumitomo T & B	5	5	7	7	12
Mitsui	13	11	23	14	36
Société Générale	30	18	29	25	59
LongTermCredit	4	4	19	14	23
Taiyo Kobe	8	6	15	13	23
B. Tokyo	52	23	27	19	79
Mitsui T & B	5	4	7	6	12
Dresdner	10	8	21	18	31
Yasuda T & B	4	4	11	9	15
Daiwa	6	5	15	14	21
Union B. Switzerland	8	5	19	19	27
Paribas	25	17	19	14	44
Swiss B. Corp.	12	6	26	21	38
Toyo T & B	4	4	6	4	10
Hong Kong Bank	nsa	nsa	nsa	nsa	nsa
Commerzbank	11	9	14	14	25
Chase Manhattan	119	34	15	15	134
Westdeutsche	4	4	7	7	11
B. Nazionale de Lavoro	11	6	17	14	28
Bay. Vereinsbank	17	14	12	11	29
Nippon Credit	5	5	5	5	10
Bank America	78	37	13	12	91
Midland	nsa	nsa	nsa	nsa	nsa
Kyowa	6	3	9	8	15
ABN	74	23	8	8	82
Lloyds	nsa	nsa	nsa	nsa	nsa
Credit Suisse	13	10	24	18	37
Shoko Chukin	1	1	1	1	2
Rabobank	5	4	3	3	8
B. of China	46	10	0	0	46
AMRO	10	10	7	5	17
Deutsche GB	7	6	4	3	11
Bay. Hypo und Wechsel	3	3	5	5	8
Chemical	20	16	16	16	36

NOTE: nsa = not separately available.
SOURCE: *Bankers Almanac and Yearbook* (1989).

organisational structure of MNEs. The next two sections empirically examine the hierarchy of financial centres (section 5.4), and the structure of the international division of banking activities across this hierarchy (section 5.5). The final section provides a summary of the chapter and its main conclusions.

5.2 A REVIEW OF THE LITERATURE

The Eclectic Approach

The existing theoretical work on MNBs has been adapted from the more general theories of FDI which were developed for manufacturing MNEs. A general framework to explain international production has been developed by Dunning (1977, 1980, 1981, 1988a, 1988b). The gist of the eclectic paradigm is the 'juxtaposition of the ownership specific advantages of firms contemplating foreign production, or an increase in foreign production, the propensity to internalise the cross-border markets for these, and the attractions of a foreign location for production' (Dunning, 1988b, p.5).

Yannopoulos (1983) and Cho (1985) argued that the eclectic paradigm can successfully explain the growth and pattern of multinational banking. Four main sources of location advantage are identified:

(a) different national regulatory frameworks;
(b) different economic situations, such as the size and structure of the host economy, and the level of trade between host and home countries;
(c) the presence of individuals and firms from the bank's home country, especially those that were already its clients;
(d) agglomeration factors such as the proximity to sources of information, and the availability of a large pool of skilled labour.

Four broad groups of ownership advantages are also identified:

(a) managerial resources, expertise, knowledge, and experience;
(b) the banker–customer relationship established in the home market with companies that have become multinational, and the proprietary information the bank has as a result;
(c) the size and multinationality of the bank;
(d) the nationality of the bank.

Internalisation refers to the benefits the bank acquires from using the hierarchical rather than market route to exploit its ownership advantages (Cho, 1985). Cho suggests five areas in which internalisation advantages arise:

(a) the availability and lower costs of intrabank fund transfers;
(b) efficient and extensive customer contact;
(c) transfer pricing manipulation;
(d) larger and improved networks of market information and commercial intelligence;
(e) the potential for reduced earnings variability.

Another reason for internalisation in banking is that it permits banks to reap the benefits of maturity transformation when dealing with their MNE clients (Yannopoulos, 1983).

Cho concludes that 'Dunning's eclectic approach is expandable to a service industry and provides a general model from which the emergence of different modes of multinational business involvement can be explained and predicted as special cases' (Cho, 1985). The eclectic paradigm does indeed seem the most appropriate framework to explain the existence of MNBs and the reason for FDI in banking.

A Business Strategy Approach

The main criticism of the traditional multinational literature, given the present changing economic environment, is that it is best suited to explaining why firms become multinational, rather than to explaining the operations of established ones. However, it must be said that it was not derived with such questions in mind. As the competitive conditions facing firms are very different today from the time at which the theories were established, there is an increasing emphasis on global competition and strategies (Doz, 1986; Porter, 1986; Dunning, 1988b). The focus is on the ability of MNEs to rationalise their investments, and compete across many national markets simultaneously. There is also a continuing emphasis on the firm-specific advantages that stem from multinationality *per se* (Kogut, 1983; Doz, 1986; Dunning, 1988b). Many banks active today have been operating internationally for a number of decades, and could be expected to have developed the administrative technologies to conduct their international operations at minimum cost (Tschoegl, 1987). Today, as most large banks already have a foreign network, it is the world-wide configuration of their activities and the systemic advantages of multinationality that are most important.

Studies of Financial Centres

The literature on FDI in banking has paid little attention to financial centres. Most use aggregate data at the national level, such as Goldberg and Saunders (1981), Khoury (1980) and Terrell (1979). The more microeconomic study of Ball and Tschoegl (1982) deals with Japan and California, where foreign bank entry motivation might include a desire to participate in the financial centres. But the authors' focus is on the extension of the activities of existing entrants in the market as a whole (Choi, Tschoegl and Yu, 1986).

Two major studies of financial centres have been undertaken that are of relevance to this analysis. Kindleberger (1974) provides a comparative analysis of the evolution and development of a number of financial centres. He suggests that the primary purpose of a financial centre is to provide a central clearing place where investors and borrowers can engage in transactions that result in realistic market-determined prices. The nature and location of the banking industry in particular cities are determined by the extent and nature of local economic activity. He suggests that there are economies of agglomeration inherent in the organisation of financial markets which produce a single dominant financial centre within the country. The same process of concentration that produces a single dominant financial centre within a country tends to result in the emergence of a single world-wide centre that acts as an international clearing house. Although the process is similar to that within a country, barriers of exchange risk and higher international transaction costs prevent it from being carried as far. The formation of different ranked or sized centres is the result of diseconomies that work against centralisation. The primary diseconomy is the cost of information, which gives local institutions an advantage in dealing with the regions' firms. Others are the difference in time between centres, and discrimination in favour of compatriots, as well as the costs of transportation and communication.

Reed's (1981, 1983) studies emphasise the international dimensions of financial centres. He examines the organisational structure of the global network of international financial centres. The technique that Reed uses to determine the structure of financial centres over time is hierarchical cluster analysis. His results suggest that in 1980 the hierarchical structure of centres was determined by the number of large internationally active commercial banks headquartered in the centre, the total amount of foreign financial liabilities and foreign financial assets held in the centre, the amount of international currency clearings, and the size of the Eurocurrency market. Reed also concluded that not only are financial centres organised in a hierarchical structure for finance, but also for communications and management activities. Overall, Reed's study revealed the hierarchy of financial centres and the factors that have accompanied its development over time. The aim of this chapter is to analyse further the locational element of the eclectic paradigm and the concept of interdependence between location and ownership advantages by focusing on the interaction between the international hierarchy of financial centres and the activities of MNBs.

5.3 THE DETERMINANTS OF THE INTERNATIONAL PATTERN OF BANKING ACTIVITY

The Attractiveness of the Location

The initial question that needs to be addressed is what makes a particular location attractive to an MNB. The least-cost location theories of Weber (1929), Isard (1960), Smith (1966, 1981) and others suggest that cost-minimising considerations are an important factor in the locational decisions of firms, and thus the pattern of economic activities. The importance of the cost factor then varies between industries, and between activities. For example, the product cycle model distinguishes between the location of innovative products near R & D sites, and the location of mature products at cost-minimising locations.

The largest cost element in banking is labour. Consequently, firms may seek out sites with the most attractive set of labour market conditions for the activities they intend to carry out. Variations in actual wage levels, however, may be partly compensated for by variations in productivity levels; hence it is the marginal revenue product relative to costs that is the important factor, not the cost itself (Davis, 1990). The capacity to transfer resources and labour internally, however, gives MNBs an added margin of flexibility in locating activities. It has also been suggested that MNBs will tend to seek locations in which they gain access to cheap deposits. In the 1950s and 1960s this is thought to have led many banks to set up operations in the USA, and in New York in particular. The 1970s saw many foreign banks locate in London to get direct access to 'Petrodollars' through the Euromarkets. However, the increased interdependence and linkages between markets, in part brought about through MNBs, means that the cost of funds is slowly being equalised.

Communication costs are another locational factor in banking. The need for simultaneous interaction between the producer and consumer of banking services often necessitates either locating activities abroad or being part of a correspondent network which would then take care of the foreign business. Where telecommunication and data storage are not available or costs are high, this tends to reduce service trade and at the same time encourage foreign investments. However, in the past few decades trade in financial services has grown substantially because technological improvements have lowered the cost and time of undertaking an international transaction, and brought a wider geographic market within the range of a financial office location. At the same time technological developments have facilitated FDI because they have strengthened the capacity of MNEs to increase the coherence of their world-wide corporate systems, and to manage and allocate corporate resources more efficiently and effectively (Sauvant and Zbigniew, 1985). Hence access to cheap modern telecommunication facilities is an important locational attraction (Dunning and Norman, 1987). New York, London, Tokyo and Hong Kong have all benefited as key international financial centres from the hubbing of communication networks around them (Reed, 1981).

Another important determinant of the location of banking activity is the regulatory environment. Indeed, it is impossible to account for either the international organisation or the level of foreign bank activity without reference to bank legislation (Tschoegl, 1987). First, there are the direct costs arising from regulations relating to taxation, interest rates, reserve requirements, foreign exchange, and so on. The response of many MNBs is to set up operations in less tightly regulated locations, although the safety of their investments is a crucial factor. (Political stability is an important factor here: MNBs always have to trade off the advantages of direct investment in a given location against the political risk of expropriation.) Second, there are indirect costs that arise out of regulations relating to what kinds of banking activities foreign banks are permitted to undertake. The expansion of foreign bank establishments has been favoured by the opening-up of domestic markets to foreign banks, the gradual relaxation of exchange controls, and the lessening of provisions discriminating against foreign bank entities in some host countries (Pecchioli, 1983). A further lowering of restrictions would serve to reduce the international variations in regulatory costs for an MNB. The experience of the industrial sector when trade barriers have been lowered would suggest that deregulation could then further reinforce the incentives for MNBs to organise an international division of activities.

A major criticism of least-cost location theory is its abstraction from demand (Smith, 1981). Optimal location is seen largely as a result of spatial cost differences, with variations from place to place in sales potential virtually ignored. The relative attractiveness of a location to a bank is therefore also a function of the level and nature of demand that is served from that location. The first consideration is that of the time zone. The leading MNBs tend to want to set up the full range of activities in each of the three time zones in order to service their demand. Consideration of the particular financial centres chosen would then reflect other factors.

It is not just the level of demand that is important, though, but the type of customer too. The greater the number and the larger the size of foreign MNEs in a particular country, the more attractive is the location, and the more extensive the range of activities undertaken by MNBs (Reed, 1981; Nigh, Cho and Krishnan, 1986). As more banks locate in the particular centre, agglomeration economies are generated. Moreover, the requirements of the banks themselves increase demand for specialist banking services. For both these reasons more banks are attracted to the location. A process of cumulative growth then gets under way.

The Nature of the Activity as a Determining Factor

The market area location theories of Losch (1954) and Christaller (1933) suggest that economic activities will tend to cluster together into a hierarchy of central places. The key reason for a hierarchy emerging is that the minimum 'threshold level' of demand needed to ensure the survival of a producer varies by the type of product being produced. It differs due to many variables, such as price elasticity and frequency of demand. Lower-order goods only need a small market area and therefore are available at a large number of locations. As the order of a good increases, its locational frequency will become less, so that high-order goods are produced at only a few locations. Hence it is in a sense the very nature of the activity that determines its locational pattern.

In banking, as in services in general, the ease with which the product can be traded is a crucial influence on clustering. Delivery of a service normally requires the simultaneous interaction of the producer and consumer (Hirsch, 1987, refers to the 'factor of simultaneity'). At an international level the need for simultaneity acts as a trade-retarding element in the service sector. When the cost disadvantage of the simultaneity factor exceeds the cost advantages ascribed to the more intensive use of the factors abundant at the location, the service becomes non-tradable (Hirsch, 1987). Some activities have very low simultaneity costs because the same product may be transmitted to other locations via various modes of communication (Coffey and Polese, 1987). These are what Boddewyn, Halbrich and Perry (1986) call 'foreign tradeable services', and Bhagwati (1986) calls 'long distance services'. They are service activities that generate a product separable from the production process, and transferable across national boundaries by means of modern microelectronics technology and telecommunications equipment (such as bond sales).

However, not all financial activities are tradable. Some are what Boddewyn, Halbrich and Perry (1986) call 'location bound'. They have very high simultaneity costs, perhaps because local information is of great importance. All else being equal, banking activities sensitive to such costs are likely to be produced at local offices close to the client, and exhibit a dispersed pattern. Examples could include retail banking, most mergers and acquisition services, and underwriting. Generally they are activities that are necessarily tailored and specialised, and require familiarity with, and contacts in, particular locations.

In between the two extremes are what Boddewyn, Halbrich and Perry (1986) call 'combination services', where part of the production process is tradable and the rest location bound. An example is where the product has to be traded on an exchange, but the provision of the service to the client can take place elsewhere (for example, financial futures and traded options). These are services in which the interaction can be achieved by some low-level presence, such as an agent or representative office, allowing the main facilities to be located elsewhere. There would appear to be a process at work encouraging both the centralisation and decentralisation of these activities.

Agglomeration Economies

The spatial ordering of industry, and thus optimal locations, has been viewed by most location theorists as being pre-ordained. However, some theorists argue that the location of an activity is historically dependent on previous locational formulations, in which chance may play a role. In particular they emphasise the role of external economies of scale and the broader agglomeration economies. The most recent justification of a historically-dependent approach to locational patterns, and of the role of agglomeration economies, is that of Arthur, Ermoliev and Kanioviski (1987). They show statistically that, rather than a pre-ordained optimal location pattern, there may be a multiplicity of possible structures, with early random fluctuations influencing which structure is selected.

In the specific case of financial services agglomeration economies are quite substantial. In particular, producers find it desirable to be in close touch with each other, with market trends and with the expertise to predict these trends, so as to anticipate the price changes in the products they are selling. For the consumers there is convenience in their suppliers being located close to one another so that price comparisons are easy and competition is fostered. There is a further tendency towards agglomeration due to a liquidity effect. Liquidity derives from the homogeneity of financial products, and is promoted by the existence of a centralised marketplace. If buyers and sellers both go to the same place to trade, search time is reduced, and so is the discount or premium demanded by the market maker. This means that trading and secondary transactions tend to be concentrated in a small number of locations. Once liquidity is established at a market place it is relatively difficult to lure trading activities away (Anderson and Harris, 1986).

The linkages promoting agglomeration can be broken down into two types. The first type involves interdependence between financial activities: for example, it is unlikely that bond underwriting activities would be undertaken in a location in which there were no bond sales. The second involves trade between financial and non-financial activities: for example, syndication work requires a large number of lawyers, while money market activities do not. Indeed, Hewson (1986) suggests that Hong Kong has an advantage over Singapore in syndication due to its better legal skills.

All banking activities would seem to benefit from agglomeration economies of one kind or another. However, one would then expect that those activities that benefited the least – that could, in a sense, 'stand alone' – would be more dispersed. In the pre-eminent financial centres there would therefore be a system of interlocking activities, each closely dependent on the others both for its spatial 'raison d'être' and its economic success (Dunning, 1969). Overall, agglomeration economies not only make a centre generally more attractive for banks, but also particularly attractive for those activities which can benefit the most from them.

The Role of the MNB in the International Division of Banking Activities

Hymer (1971) used the ideas of Chandler and Redlich (1961) to show how the behaviour of MNEs serves to reinforce the hierarchical organisation of economic activities on a global scale. His model combined the business organisation approach of Chandler with location theories. He argued that there was a correspondence principle relating centralisation of control within the MNE to centralisation of control within the international economy. An international hierarchy of corporate activities emerges, with a hierarchical division of labour between geographical regions corresponding to the spatial division of activities within the firm.

At Level Three – the lowest – activities are sensitive to traditional cost and demand factors. These activities are spread world-wide according to the pull of labour supply, market access and raw materials. Level Two – the regional management level – coordinates the activities of Level Three. It includes some higher-order production and research activities. This level tends to concentrate in large cities, because of its need for white-collar workers, good communications systems and a highly educated workforce. Since their demands are similar, corporations from different industries tend to place their coordinating offices in the same cities. Level Two activities are consequently far more geographically concentrated than Level Three activities. At the top of the hierarchy are the Level One control functions, and the highest level production and research facilities.

This is the top management level, concerned with goal determination and planning. Such activities operate within narrow spatial margins, for they must be located close to the seats of governments, the large capital markets and the best centres of learning. They are highly concentrated in the major metropolitan areas.

Hymer's model thus supports the idea of a hierarchical organisation of economic activities. However, whereas with Losch and Christaller this was due to the nature of the activity, Hymer suggested that the behaviour of the MNE would, in a sense, institutionalise and reinforce the hierarchy.[3] The particular form of global strategy pursued by the firm is important in shaping the locational pattern of its activities. A bank could have a strategy of specialising in a few activities internationally, and concentrating their production in a few centres. This is what Germidis and Michalet (1984) term the 'strategy of international financing'. They suggest that this is essentially a strategy of participating in the Euromarkets and international money markets. Some banks, however, may undertake a wide range of activities but concentrate them in a few centres. This is one strategy that Germidis and Michalet did not develop. It could be termed an 'international financial centre strategy'. Alternatively, a bank may disperse the few activities in which it has specialised internationally. This is a 'supportive strategy', to use Germidis and Michalet's terminology. The strategy is one in which the international network is used to service the requirements of MNE clients. For Hymer's model to hold, and for there be an international division of activities as he envisaged, the majority of banks would need to follow a combination of these three strategies.

However, Germidis and Michalet also suggest that banks may undertake a wide range of activities internationally, and disperse them throughout many financial centres. This they term the 'strategy of delocation' of banking activities. A full range of normal banking services are provided in a large number of locations. It is similar to what Porter (1986) terms a 'multidomestic strategy'. If it was the case that most banks were pursuing such a strategy, the international division of activities as envisaged by Hymer is likely to be weaker.

The Synthesised Framework

The model suggested for this study is one in which there is an international division of banking activities across financial centres.

This overall system corresponds to the spatial division of activities within the MNB. It is one in which progressively more of the higher-order activities are undertaken the further up the location hierarchy, until in its home and other top centres the MNB undertakes the full range of activities. The model comprises a hierarchical system of financial centres consisting of functionally coordinated levels, each of which has common properties in terms of facility cost, types of activities, size of market area, regulations and types of firms located therein. The model assumes that the MNB is multifunctional by nature. Thus the different activities of the bank are subject to different locational forces and constraints (Dicken, 1986). The highest-level functions operate within narrow spatial margins from the world's major financial centres. The lowest level activities are more sensitive to traditional cost and demand factors of location, and are therefore dispersed. The point to note is that these factors draw them to many centres, including the top ones. The intermediate activities are subject to both centripetal and centrifugal forces. The rest of the chapter is an empirical examination of this model and some of the hypotheses suggested by the framework.

5.4 THE HIERARCHIES OF FINANCIAL CENTRES AND BANKING ACTIVITIES

Introduction

This section examines empirical evidence on hierarchies of centres and of banking activities. As published data were not readily available at the disaggregated level required, a questionnaire survey was carried out to provide the necessary data base. The survey population of banks consisted of the world's 200 largest commercial banks in 1987, as shown in *The Banker*, March 1987, together with 50 of the largest investment banks in the world, being mainly from the USA, Japan, UK, Canada, Australia and Switzerland. The postal questionnaires were sent to the senior officer of each bank in the survey population located in London. Ideally it should have been sent to the banks' offices in each location, but given the constraints in the timetable and the financing of the research this was an unrealistic proposition. However, if the bank had no office in London, or if it was very small, then the questionnaire was sent to its headquarters. It was also sent to the headquarters for a small number of banks to cross-check the results from the London office. Those that were returned confirmed the response given by the London office. Sixty-one correctly completed questionnaires were returned: a response rate of 24.4 per cent.

The questionnaire consisted of a table with 26 activities across one axis and 33 financial centres along the other. It asked the bank to indicate which activities it undertook in each of the centres specified. The 33 centres were chosen by consulting Reed's (1981) study, which had previously placed financial centres into a hierarchy. One of the aims of the analysis was not only to show that the hierarchy of centres still exists, but also to see if there have been any significant changes since 1980. The centres selected are shown below. The 26 activities were selected to be representative of the range of activities undertaken by MNBs: they are also shown below.

There were two parts to the analysis. First, the centres and activities were ranked according to their size (Tables 5.2 and 5.3). The ranking of the centres was based on the sum (TS) of the number of

TABLE 5.2 *The hierarchy of financial centres for all banks*

Location	*TS**	*NA*†	*NB*‡
LN	864	26	61
NY	635	26	57
TK	497	26	44
ZH	388	26	28
HK	351	26	40
SG	289	26	35
TO	247	26	23
FT	243	26	27
PS	212	26	31
SY	190	26	21
AM	157	26	15
CH	144	24	20
LUX	141	26	17
MN	100	25	17
MD	76	23	14
BH	76	20	17
SF	70	23	14
BA	44	21	10
RIO	41	24	8
BM	40	13	8

continued on page 138

TABLE 5.2 *continued*

Location	*TS**	*NA†*	*NB‡*
AN	35	20	6
JK	32	11	10
CP	28	24	3
CY	22	7	7
SK	19	14	4
LG	14	10	5
MC	14	7	6
BAH	13	6	4
SH	12	8	5
CR	7	5	3
CO	3	3	2
BG	2	2	1
JH	0	0	0

* Sum of number of activities undertaken by all banks in the location.
† Number of activities undertaken by at least one bank in the location.
‡ Number of banks undertaking at least one activity in the location.

TABLE 5.3 *The hierarchy of financial centres by type of bank*

Commercial banks			*Investment banks*		
Location	*TS*	*NA*	*Location*	*TS*	*NA*
LN	594	26	LN	270	26
NY	432	26	NY	203	26
TK	355	26	TK	142	25
ZH	289	26	TO	114	23
SG	264	26	ZH	99	26
HK	262	26	HK	89	25
FT	201	26	PS	45	15
PS	167	26	FT	42	20
SY	157	26	SY	33	20
TO	133	26	AM	29	15
AM	128	26	SF	28	17
LUX	122	25	SG	25	19
CH	120	17	CH	24	13
MN	82	25	LUX	19	13
BH	67	19	MN	16	12
MD	61	16	BA	16	12
SF	42	12	MD	15	12

Commercial banks			Investment banks		
Location	TS	NA	Location	TS	NA
BM	40	13	AN	12	12
RIO	37	24	BH	9	6
JK	32	11	CY	4	4
BA	28	10	RIO	5	5
CP	27	24	CR	3	3
AN	23	10	CP	1	1
SK	19	14	BAH	0	0
CY	18	6	BM	0	0
LG	14	10	BG	0	0
MC	14	7	CO	0	0
BAH	13	6	JK	0	0
SH	12	8	JH	0	0
CR	4	2	LG	0	0
CO	3	3	MC	0	0
BG	2	2	SH	0	0
JH	0	0	SK	0	0

activities (NA) undertaken by all banks in the financial centre. It therefore encompasses the number of banks (NB) and the range of activities (NA). A ranking of activities is more difficult and less commonly derived. The activities at the top of the hierarchy are the ones that banks are unwilling to do in many locations because of agglomeration economies (Tables 5.4 and 5.5). High-order activities are undertaken by fewer banks, and in fewer financial centres, and their total size is smaller than lower-order activities. The size of an activity is measured as the sum (TS) over all banks of the number of financial centres (NL) in which the activity was undertaken. Whereas for financial centres, the larger the centre the further up the hierarchy it was, for activities the smaller the activity the higher was its ranking.

The ranking of centres and activities based on their size forms just one part of the analysis. In itself the ranking is not, however, sufficient to indicate the shape the hierarchy takes. The theoretical framework is quite specific in suggesting distinct groupings of centres and of activities. In order to place similar activities or similar centres into hierarchical groups, 'cluster analysis' was used. Essentially, a cluster analysis starts with a data set containing information about a

TABLE 5.4 *The hierarchy of banking activities for all banks*

Activities	*TS**	*NL*†	*NB*‡
TT	69	25	29
EEU	79	15	33
FEU	98	21	31
DEU	105	16	35
GFM	114	19	39
DBU	132	19	41
FBU	132	20	40
EBU	138	22	49
DES	147	21	41
MA	148	20	36
EES	157	22	36
TO	173	21	46
FES	181	21	38
RT	182	27	42
DBS	192	22	53
IR	199	30	47
FBS	199	21	51
ECS	205	26	51
FF	213	22	56
SW	225	24	56
EBS	237	20	53
DR	256	30	52
TR	318	28	46
CM	349	28	51
MM	373	29	52
FX	385	29	57

* The sum over all banks of the number of locations in which they are represented, for each activity.
† Number of locations in which at least one bank undertakes the activity.
‡ Number of banks undertaking the activity in at least one location.

sample of objects, and attempts to reorganise it in such a way that objects within a cluster have great similarity to each other, but show little similarity with objects outside that cluster. Since the number and nature of the groups are not known in advance the clustering process is essentially pre-classificatory. To undertake the cluster analysis the individual bank tables collected from the questionnaire were summed together to provide the raw data matrix. The cluster analysis was then carried out in two parts: (a) the clustering pro-

TABLE 5.5 *The hierarchy of banking activities by type of bank*

	Commercial banks			*Investment banks*	
Activity	*TS*	*NL*	*Activity*	*TS*	*NL*
FEU	45	15	TT	5	4
EEU	50	15	TR	9	5
DEU	60	16	RT	9	6
TT	64	24	CM	16	10
EES	72	15	ECS	21	7
FBU	73	15	MM	23	11
DES	77	17	GFM	26	9
FES	77	16			
EBU	84	17	EEU	29	8
DBU	85	19	DR	37	11
GFM	88	19	IR	38	11
			MA	40	11
MA	108	20	SW	41	11
FBS	116	18	DEU	45	10
DBS	119	20	DBU	47	8
TO	120	17	TO	53	18
EBS	130	18	FEU	53	18
FF	156	19	EBU	54	18
IR	161	30	FF	57	18
RT	173	28	FBU	59	18
ECS	184	27	FX	60	18
SW	184	24			
DR	219	30	DBS	70	18
			DBS	73	18
TR	309	28	FBS	83	19
FX	325	29	EES	85	21
CM	333	29	FES	104	21
MM	350	30	EBS	107	21

Group 1	*Group 2*	*Group 3*
London (LN)	New York (NY)	Amsterdam (AM)
	Tokyo (TK)	Chicago (CH)
		Frankfurt (FT)
		Hong Kong (HK)
		Paris (PS)
		San Francisco (SF)
		Zurich (ZH)

Group 4	*Group 5*	*Extra*
Bogotá (BG)	Antwerp (AN)	Bahamas (BAH)
Buenos Aires (BA)	Bombay (BM)	Bahrain (BH)
Caracas (CR)	Cairo (CO)	Cayman (CY)
Jakarta (JK)	Copenhagen (CP)	Lagos (LG)
Johannesburg (JH)	Shanghai (SH)	
Luxemburg (LUX)	Stockholm (SK)	
Madrid (MD)		
Mexico City (MC)		
Milan (MN)		
Rio de Janeiro (RIO)		
Singapore (SG)		
Sydney (SY)		
Toronto (TO)		

NOTE: Groups are based on Reed's ranking of financial centres in 1980 (Reed, 1981).

Domestic Bond Underwriting (DBU)	Domestic Equity Underwriting (DEU)
Foreign Bond Underwriting (FBU)	Foreign Equity Underwriting (FEU)
Eurobond Underwriting (EBU)	Euro Equity Underwriting (EEU)
Domestic Bond Sales (DBS)	Domestic Equity Sales (DES)
Foreign Bond Sales (FBS)	Foreign Equity Sales (FES)
Eurobond Sales (EBS)	Euro Equity Sales (EES)
Domestic Market Research (DR)	International Market Research (IR)
Retail Deposit/Lending (RT)	Eurocurrency Syndication (ECS)
Trade Finance (TR)	Money Market Deposit/Lending (MM)
Foreign Exchange Dealing (FX)	Currency Market Deposit/Lending (CM)
Mergers and Acquisitions (MA)	Trust Banking (TT)
Financial Futures (FF)	Traded Options (TO)
Global Fund Management (GFM)	Swaps (SW)

cedures were undertaken with the 33 centres as the objects to be clustered; and (b) the raw data matrix was then transposed and the same procedures were used on the 26 activities.

Four different hierarchical agglomerative techniques were applied to the matrix to produce the cluster solution: Average Linkage, Ward's Method, Complete Linkage and Centroid Method. Four methods were used in order to check the accuracy of the results, and confirm that the underlying population cluster is being recovered. It is a form of validation procedure, with the obvious weakness that, as all are part of the same programme, they could still be imposing a false structure. Nevertheless, should all four methods produce identical or very similar solutions then one can accept the results with a degree of confidence.

The Hierarchy of Financial Centres

The four cluster techniques produced reasonably consistent results. The composition of the clusters and the ranking of the centres are shown in Table 5.2. London, New York and Tokyo are at the top of the hierarchy, both individually and as a group. This was a similar result to Choi, Tschoegl and Yu (1986) and Reed (1981, 1983). These three centres are commonly recognised as being at the apex of the international hierarchy of financial centres across a wide range of activities. For example, in 1987 New York accounted for 37 per cent of the total world stock market capitalisation, Japan (mainly Tokyo) 35 per cent and London 10 per cent. Their share of the international banking market at the end of 1989, as measured by the Bank for International Settlements, was: UK, 19.3 per cent; Japan, 21.4 per cent; and the USA, 9.7 per cent.

All ten second-tier centres could be termed 'regional centres'. This means that they are centres which on average, across all activities, mainly service the requirements of customers located within their time zone. This is reflected in their smaller average total size compared to the top three, and the fact that fewer banks on average are located in them. Within the cluster it is possible to discern a subgroup of three centres: Zurich, Hong Kong and Singapore. Zurich has been involved in international banking for centuries. As a result it has developed the infrastructure and expertise to make it a leading centre today (Khambata, 1986). Perhaps most important to its success has been the favourable regulatory environment it offers both banks and their customers. Hong Kong also owes its high position in the hierarchy to a favourable regulatory environment. As Tan and Kapur (1986) observed, it is a larger centre than Singapore, with more international financial institutions operating from it. It is an integrated centre, where domestic and foreign banks are intermixed, deposits can be shifted flexibly between domestic currency and foreign exchange, and government regulations do not distinguish between domestic and off-shore banking (Khambata, 1986). Singapore, by contrast, is a more segregated centre. Much of its growth can be attributed to a conscious policy on the part of its government to develop the banking sector, especially its international role. It is also helped by its central location in the Far East, and a time zone that enables it to participate in the business days of the European, American and Japanese markets.

The remaining bottom-tier centres could be termed 'host international financial centres' (Reed, 1981). Foreign banks operate in these centres mainly to service the requirements of their MNE customers in these markets. The two exceptions are the Bahamas and the Cayman Islands, which are 'off-shore centres'. It is interesting to note that many of the bottom-tier centres are located in countries which since 1982 have experienced severe economic difficulties, especially high levels of debt. Relative to Reed's 1981 study this suggests a retreat on the part of the banks from, or at least a lack of expansion in, centres with severe economic problems.

The cluster analysis was also undertaken by type of bank. It produced distinct hierarchical groups for investment banks, but less clear-cut groups for commercial banks. Overall the results revealed that slightly different hierarchies of financial centres exist for investment and commercial banks, although essentially it is a difference of emphasis among the same centres (see Table 5.3). It is interesting to note that Tokyo is not a first-rank centre for the investment banks or the commercial banks, yet it is in the 'all bank' analysis. This may reflect the separation of activities in Japan. Across all banks Tokyo is a very large diversified centre, and hence is most similar to the top two centres. However, by type of bank the separation of activities by institution means it is not as evenly diversified as in the 'all bank' case. Although the same could be said for New York, the greater number of foreign banks located in New York means that it is of a much larger size and nearer to London in structure. Hence, Tokyo ends up in the second cluster at this subgroup level of analysis.

It is also interesting to note that Hong Kong is included among the second tier for investment banks, but Singapore is not. Both, as has been argued, may be regional alternatives to Tokyo. These results tentatively suggest that Singapore may be more specialised towards commercial banks and their activities, while Hong Kong may have a broader base of activities, perhaps leaning more towards investment banking. This is also reflected in the size of their stock markets. The market value of Hong Kong in 1986 was US$53.7 billion, and its capitalisation was 0.91 per cent of the world total in 1987, while the respective figures for Singapore were US$39.2 billion, and 0.16 per cent.

The results also suggest that the differences between the financial centres may be relatively less for commercial banks, or the activities they dominate, than for investment banks, as the latter have much sharper distinctions between the clusters. This would seem to be because the top centres are relatively more dominant for investment banks than for commercial banks. This suggests that the locational strategies of investment banks may differ from that of commercial banks, and that the factors that make a location attractive to them may also therefore differ. Even though investment banks, just like commercial ones, may follow their customers abroad, they would seem to have a more locationally concentrated international pattern of activities than do commercial banks.

The Hierarchy of Banking Activities

The four cluster methods produce slightly different cluster groupings. However, the degree of overlap between the methods is sufficient to suggest a three-cluster hierarchy. The highest-order activities are for the most part concentrated in a few centres and on average undertaken by a few banks (see Table 5.4). The group consists mainly of underwriting activities. These tend to be heavily regulated activities, not easily accessible to foreign institutions. Generally they need to be close to the equity and bond markets for sources of information, and they benefit from agglomeration economies. Although they require close contact between the producer and consumer of the service, and hence are relatively location bound, the extent to which they are concentrated suggests that it is the customer that travels to the producer rather than the other way round.

The bottom cluster consists of foreign exchange services, trade finance, money and currency market activities. These are undertaken in a large number of locations by a large number of banks. They are recognised as the first type of activity that a commercial bank undertakes on implementing FDI: money markets to raise funds, trade finance and foreign exchange as the first services provided (see Germidis and Michalet, 1984). They are activities which banks find relatively easy to break into abroad, and in which MNBs can have a definite competitive advantage over indigenous banks and over banks with a smaller foreign network. The activities that comprise the middle cluster have characteristics that on average fall in between the other two clusters. For example, bond sales and financial futures could be characterised as activities which generate internationally tradable products, but which still benefit from agglomeration economies.

The activities in the bottom cluster – with the exception of trade finance – result in the transfer of paper products. It could be expected that these would be more concentrated, but in fact the location-bound activities are most concentrated. This means that the agglomeration economies they benefit from are so strong as to override the need for banks to disperse to the location of their customers. Rather it is the customer that comes to the centres in which these activities are concentrated. The benefits of agglomeration would seem to outweigh the costs of simultaneity. So, whereas commercial banks can follow their customers around the world precisely because the activities in which they are specialised are footloose and tradable, investment banks cannot do so as readily and have to concentrate their activities in far fewer centres.

The cluster analysis was also conducted by type of bank. The methods did not produce distinct groupings for commercial banks. The hierarchy shown in Table 5.7 is based on the Average Linkage method. Overall, no firm conclusions can really be drawn. However, the results of the cluster analysis for investment banks are more conclusive. All four methods indicate three distinct clusters as the optimum.

Summary

The results of the cluster analysis confirm that there is a distinct hierarchy of financial centres. A hierarchy of activities also exists, but the cluster groups of activities are not so clear as they were for the centres. In other words, there is a much greater degree of similarity in the activities than in the centres.

The results support the view that regulations have a significant impact on the international pattern of activities. For example, while London and New York emerge as the highest-ranked centres for investment and commercial banks, with Tokyo downgraded to the second rank, yet in the all-bank analysis Tokyo is in the top cluster. It is suggested that this is a function of the separation of activities in Tokyo, and the relatively fewer foreign banks operating across a wide number of activities in it, which may itself be a function of a less open regulatory environment. Another result is that investment banks have followed a more concentrated locational strategy than commercial banks. At this stage it is difficult to show whether this is because of the activity of specialisation of the banks or the particular strategy they chose to follow.

Finally, the importance of agglomeration economies in shaping the locational pattern of activities is revealed. Hirsch's (1987) argument – that if an activity is tradable then it will be more concentrated, while if it is location bound it will be more dispersed – is not supported by these results. The reason for this is that in addition to the simultaneity costs implicit in all services there are other factors that influence their locational pattern, in particular agglomeration economies. It is suggested that for banking activities this is a much stronger influence than are simultaneity costs. So the need for agglomeration to facilitate linkages between activities means that some of them will be concentrated, with the consumer needing to travel to the producer. In other words, they are bound to the location of the producer rather than the consumer.

5.5 THE INTERNATIONAL DIVISION OF BANKING ACTIVITIES ACROSS FINANCIAL CENTRES

Introduction

This section examines the relationship between the activities and centres. Hypothesis I is that the locational pattern for an individual activity is not random, but is a similar hierarchy to that of all other activities. This is an assumption that underlies the theories of Christaller, Losch and Hymer. Hypothesis II is that a higher-order activity is concentrated in the leading financial centres, while a lower-order activity is dispersed throughout. This could be termed the 'geographical composition hypothesis'. To be even more specific, the particular cluster of centres in which the higher-order activities are concentrated is expected to be the top one (Hypothesis III). This is because not only are the leading centres generally more attractive locations, in terms of regulations, agglomeration economies, level of demand, and so on, but also the higher-order activities are the ones that benefit the most from these factors. As more of a higher-order activity is undertaken in the top centres, it follows that they are the activities that are the most concentrated, while the lower-order activities are the ones that are the most dispersed. This is the 'degree of concentration hypothesis' (Hypothesis IV).

Hypothesis V tests the inference drawn from the cluster analysis: when the benefits of agglomeration are combined with high simultaneity costs then the activity is concentrated in a few centres with the consumer travelling to the producer location. The test concentrates on a comparison of underwriting and retail banking. Both implicitly have high simultaneity costs but, because underwriting has greater economies of agglomeration, it is more likely to be concentrated than retail banking. Moreover, within underwriting, Euromarket activities are more likely to be concentrated than domestic ones.

Hypothesis VI asserts that in a centre at the top of the hierarchy a more diversified range of activities is undertaken, while lower-order centres are more specialised in the range of activities undertaken. In this context diversification means that many of the banks operate in the particular centre, undertaking most of the activities, and all to a similar extent. On the other hand, specialisation means that very few banks operate in the centre and each undertakes very few activities. A specialised centre, however, is different from a 'specialist centre'; the latter is one in which many banks operate, but a few activities dominate the rest.

A lower-order centre is not only expected to be more specialised than a higher-order centre, but it is hypothesised that it is so in the lower-order activities (Hypothesis VII), and specifically in the bottom cluster of activities (Hypothesis VIII). This is because it is the lower-order activities that the MNE clients of the banks are most likely to demand in these centres (Germidis and Michalet, 1984). Also, the local customers' demand for the higher-order services may be too low or infrequent to attract foreign banks, regulations may prevent them from providing the services, and the communication links necessary to service demand located elsewhere may not be of the required breadth.

The impact that regulations can have on the specialisation of centres at the top of the hierarchy can best be observed through the analysis by type of bank. Across the hierarchy as a whole it is hypothesised that, for both types of bank, a lower-order centre is more specialised than is a higher-order centre, and that it is specialised in the lower-order activities (Hypothesis IX). However, Tokyo and New York have regulations that prohibit or restrict investment banks from undertaking commercial banking activities, and commercial banks from underwriting shares and corporate bonds.[4] It is therefore hypothesised that for each type of bank their degree of specialisation is higher than in the 'all bank' analysis (Hypothesis X), and that this specialisation is in the activities which each type is permitted to undertake, thereby cutting across the cluster hierarchy (Hypothesis XI).

Statistical Methodology

Hypotheses I–V were examined using the Galtonian regression model. Following Cantwell (1987), the correlation between the hierarchical distribution index of an individual activity and the corresponding index for the rest of the activities was estimated through a simple cross-centre regression:

$$Y_{ji} = \alpha + \beta X_{ji} + \varepsilon_{ji} \tag{5.1}$$

where Y_{ji} is the share of centre i for activity j, and X_{ji} is the share of centre i for the rest of the activities, and α, β are fixed parameters. The residual term ε_{ji} is assumed to be stochastic and independent of X_{ji}.

The estimated slope coefficient b is a measure of the similarity between the hierarchical configuration of centres for the individual activity and that for the rest of the activities. Where $b > 0$ there is a degree of similarity in the hierarchical pattern of the activities across the centres. What this shows is that where the cluster analysis revealed a hierarchical pattern for all activities, a similar pattern exists for the individual activity. It means that the hierarchical pattern for the activities was not just a random one. If $b = 1$ then on average the financial centres that are important for the particular activity are equally important for the rest of activities. If $b > 1$ then on average the largest centres for the individual activity are more important than for the rest of the activities.

In order to measure the mobility of centres up and down the activity hierarchy, the Pearson correlation coefficient, R, was estimated. A high value of R indicates that the relative position of centres for the individual activity was very similar in comparison to their position for the rest of the activities. A low value for R indicates that the ranking of centres for the individual activity was different from that for the rest of activities. The magnitude of $1 - R$ thus measured what Cantwell (1987) calls the 'mobility effect'.

The degree of concentration of an activity is measured by b/R. It balances out both the mobility and regression effects. The two need to be balanced out as b is just a measure of the slope of the regression line and reveals the average distribution of the activities across the centres, while R, on the other hand, indicates whether the ranking of the centres is the same. On their own neither fully encapsulates the level of concentration.

A similar methodology is used to examine the specialisation of centres by activity. The percentage share that each activity accounts for in a particular centre is simply regressed against that for the rest of the centres:

$$Y_{ij} = \alpha + \beta X_{ij} + \varepsilon_{ij} \tag{5.2}$$

where Y_{ij} is the share of activity j for centre i, X_{ij} is the share of activity j for the rest of centres, and α, β are fixed parameters as before. When the estimated β coefficient is unity, $b = 1$, the most important activities in the particular centre are on average also the most important for the rest of the centres. If $b > 1$ then the share of the lower-order activities is higher in the individual centre than in the rest of the centres. If $b < 1$ then the share of the lower-order activities is less in the individual centre than in the rest of the centres, and the share of the higher-order activities is correspondingly greater. Where $b/R > 1$ the centre is specialised, and where $b/R < 1$ it is diversified.

Empirical Tests of Hypotheses on Concentration

The results of regression 5.1 are reported in Table 5.6. There is a significant positive correlation between the hierarchy of centres for a

TABLE 5.6 *Estimates of regression (5.1) for all banks*

	a	t_a	b	$t_{b=0}$	$t_{b=1}$	R	b/R
TT	–0.9119	–2.471***	1.3009	17.482***	4.044***	0.9068	1.4346
EEU	–1.1751	–2.086**	1.3878	12.236***	3.420***	0.9102	1.5247
FEU	–0.5416	–2.102*	1.1787	22.760***	3.450***	0.9713	1.2135
DEU	–0.8582	–2.993***	1.2832	22.232***	4.908***	0.9701	1.3228
GFM	–0.5791	–1.849*	1.1911	18.909***	3.033***	0.9593	1.2416
DBU	–0.4305	–1.160	1.1421	15.310***	1.905**	0.9398	1.2153
FBU	–0.6207	–2.069**	1.2048	19.958***	3.391***	0.9632	1.2508
EBU	–0.6956	–1.259	1.2296	11.049***	2.063**	0.8930	1.3769
DES	–0.1715	0.692	1.0566	21.235***	1.136	0.9673	1.0923
MA	–0.9119	–2.471**	1.3009	17.482***	4.044***	0.9528	1.3653
EES	–0.0941	–0.461	1.0311	25.162***	0.759	0.9764	1.0560
TO	–0.6229	–2.092**	1.2055	20.103***	3.428***	0.9637	1.2509
FES	0.0026	0.014	0.9991	26.772***	0.024	0.9790	1.0205
RT	1.0725	4.184***	0.6461	12.671***	–6.939***	0.9155	0.7057
DBS	–0.2412	–0.992	1.0796	22.094***	1.629	0.9697	1.1133
IR	0.3770	2.254**	0.8756	26.184***	–3.725***	0.9781	0.8952
FBS	–0.4053	–2.045**	1.1337	28.439***	3.351***	0.9814	1.1552
ECS	–0.3021	–1.211	1.0997	21.921***	1.986**	0.9692	1.1346
FF	–0.6667	–2.149**	1.2200	19.497***	3.514***	0.9616	1.2687
SW	–0.7604	–2.606**	1.2509	21.230***	4.260***	0.9673	1.2932
EBS	–0.1810	–0.894	1.0597	26.051***	1.467	0.9779	1.0836
DR	0.8991	4.482***	0.7033	17.653***	–7.455***	0.9537	0.7374
TR	0.7997	3.169***	0.7361	14.704***	–5.267***	0.9352	0.7871
CM	0.6932	3.037***	0.7712	17.021***	–5.051***	0.9504	0.8114
MM	0.7529	3.515***	0.7515	17.703***	–5.847***	0.9539	0.7907
FX	0.3992	2.201**	0.8683	24.026***	–3.642***	0.9742	0.8913

*** significant at the 1 per cent level.
** significant at the 5 per cent level.
* significant at the 10 per cent level.

given activity and that for the rest of the activities for all the 26 activities. This means that each activity exhibits a similar hierarchical pattern across the centres to that for the rest of the activities. This suggests that the different aspects of the nature of an activity influence only the specific locational pattern that the hierarchical structure takes, not the existence of a hierarchy itself.

All the activities at the top of the hierarchy have $b > 1$. Indeed, there are only two for which the positive regression effect is not significant. Conversely, all the lower-order activities have $b < 1$. The results for the middle group of activities were a mixture of the two. These results support the geographical composition hypothesis II. The higher-order activities are more concentrated in the leading financial centres, relative to the rest of activities, while the relative importance of the centres at the bottom of the hierarchy was greater for the lower-order activities.

The degree of concentration hypothesis, IV, is also supported by the regression results. The high-order activities at the top of the hierarchy are more concentrated than the lower-order activities. The degree of concentration of traded options, and of financial futures and swaps, is quite interesting given their position in the middle cluster of activities. Futures and options are perhaps the best examples of 'combination services' (Boddewyn, Halbrich and Perry, 1986): activities which may be initiated in many centres, but in which the actual transactions are concentrated in just a few. It is perhaps their relative newness, fairly 'knowledge-intensive nature' and trading regulations that contribute to their high level of concentration.

The role of agglomeration economies is also implicit in the results. Even though they are location bound, Euro-underwriting activities are the most concentrated activities because they benefit the most from agglomeration economies. Domestic retail banking, on the other hand, is the most dispersed of all the activities. This is partly because it is an activity that is carried out by many banks in the sample, but mainly in their home centre, so across all banks it was concentrated in different locations. When the total for all banks is derived it therefore appears very dispersed. However, the dispersion could also be because retail banking is a location-bound activity that does not benefit from agglomeration economies, but incurs high simultaneity costs. Thus a bank would have to locate in the particular foreign centre in order to undertake the activity. Hypothesis V is therefore supported.

The disaggregated results by type of bank also support hypotheses I–V (see Tables 5.7 and 5.8). It is interesting that for the commercial banks the mobility effect, as measured by $1 - R$, is highest for underwriting activities. This suggests that even though these activities are concentrated, they are concentrated in slightly different centres from the other concentrated activities. This conclusion is supported by the analysis of the specific cluster of centres in which the activities were concentrated. Although most of the slope coefficients are insignificant, their signs are still quite interesting. They suggest that the top activities undertaken by commercial banks are not concentrated in the higher-order centres, but in the middle cluster. The actual shares of Zurich and Hong Kong for underwriting activities are particularly high, given their positions in the hierarchy. This may be

TABLE 5.7 *Estimates of regression (5.1) for commercial banks*

	a	t_a	b	$t_{b=0}$	$t_{b=1}$	R	b/R
FEU	–0.5063	–0.918	1.1671	10.110***	1.448	0.8760	1.3323
EEU	–0.7574	–1.126	1.2499	8.864***	1.772*	0.8468	1.4760
DEU	–0.5283	–1.238	1.1744	13.138***	1.951*	0.9208	1.2754
TT	–0.0360	–0.077	1.0119	10.361***	0.122	0.8809	1.1487
EES	–0.7072	–2.038**	1.2334	16.948***	3.207***	0.9501	1.2982
FBU	–0.5978	–0.987	1.1973	9.428***	1.554	0.8610	1.3906
DES	–0.2931	–0.654	1.0967	11.693***	1.031	0.9029	1.2146
FES	–0.5097	–1.362	1.1682	14.910***	2.148**	0.9368	1.2470
EBU	–0.7383	–1.030	1.2436	8.267***	1.620*	0.8294	1.4994
DBU	–0.0757	–0.158	1.0250	10.208***	0.249	0.8779	1.1676
GFM	–0.5236	–1.338	1.1728	14.292***	2.105**	0.9318	1.2586
MA	–0.7953	–2.210**	1.2625	16.698***	3.472***	0.9486	1.3309
FBS	–0.6778	–2.103**	1.2237	18.075***	3.304***	0.9557	1.2804
DBS	–0.3824	–1.064	1.1262	14.944***	1.674	0.9371	1.2018
TO	–0.9068	–2.273**	1.2992	15.485***	3.566***	0.9410	1.3807
EBS	–0.7510	–2.273**	1.2478	17.962***	3.566***	0.9551	1.3065
FF	–1.0220	–2.655**	1.3373	16.470***	4.154***	0.9473	1.4117
IR	0.6134	3.162***	0.7976	19.759***	–5.100***	0.9625	0.8287
RT	1.0530	3.703***	0.6525	11.077***	–5.900***	0.8935	0.7303
ECS	–0.3255	–1.388	1.1074	22.504***	2.183**	0.9707	1.1408
SW	–0.9227	–2.742**	1.3045	18.371***	4.289***	0.9570	1.3631
DR	1.0907	5.141***	0.6401	14.611***	-8.2169***	0.9345	0.6850
TR	0.7228	2.846***	0.7615	14.506***	–4.543***	0.9336	0.8157
FX	0.3144	1.500	0.8962	20.551***	–2.381**	0.9652	0.9285
CM	0.5519	2.611**	0.8171	18.679***	–4.158***	0.9583	0.8535
MM	0.6498	3.038***	0.7856	17.773***	–4.851***	0.9543	0.8232

*** significant at the 1 per cent level.
** significant at the 5 per cent level.
* significant at the 10 per cent level.

because most of the higher-order activities are investment banking activities. As London's share of the activities is high, this suggests that regulations in New York may have driven the commercial banks to undertake these activities elsewhere. Hence the locational pattern of these activities when undertaken by commercial banks is particularly influenced by regulations. Nevertheless, as they are still concentrated in a few locations, this suggests that although regulations may influence the particular locational pattern for an activity, other features of the activity, such as agglomeration economies, may cause them to be concentrated anyway; it is just that the particular centres change.

TABLE 5.8 *Estimates of regression (5.1) for investment banks*

	a	t_a	b	$t_{b=0}$	$t_{b=1}$	R	b/R
TT	-0.8534	-0.688	1.2816	6.028***	1.325	0.7346	1.7446
TR	-1.6187	-2.300**	1.5342	12.695***	4.422***	0.9158	1.6753
RT	-0.3957	-0.396	1.1306	6.598***	0.762	0.7643	1.4793
CM	0.0975	0.167	0.9678	9.691***	-0.322	0.8671	1.1161
ECS	-1.2374	-1.488	1.4084	9.838***	2.852***	0.8703	1.6183
MM	-0.0536	-0.098	1.0177	10.803***	0.188	0.8889	1.1449
GFM	-0.6445	-1.794*	1.2127	19.647***	3.447***	0.9621	1.2605
EEU	-1.4694	-2.450**	1.4849	14.340***	4.681***	0.9322	1.5929
DR	-0.3006	-0.710	1.0992	15.117***	1.365	0.9383	1.1715
IR	-0.5650	-1.511	1.1864	18.457***	2.899***	0.9574	1.2392
MA	-1.0460	-1.935*	1.3452	14.412***	3.699***	0.9328	1.4421
SW	-0.4435	-1.104	1.1463	16.609***	2.120**	0.9482	1.2089
DEU	-0.8551	-3.842***	1.2822	33.392***	7.349***	0.9864	1.2999
DBU	-0.8156	-1.755*	1.2692	15.829***	3.357***	0.9433	1.3455
TO	0.1140	0.491	0.9624	24.253***	-0.947	0.9746	0.9875
FEU	-0.1285	-0.950	1.0424	44.922***	1.827*	0.9924	1.0504
EBU	-0.2417	-0.593	1.0798	15.431***	1.141	0.9406	1.1480
FF	0.1951	0.776	0.9356	21.788***	-1.501	0.9689	0.9656
FBU	-0.2612	-1.291	1.0862	31.252***	2.477**	0.9845	1.1033
FX	0.2702	1.068	0.9108	21.090***	-2.065**	0.9669	0.9420
DES	0.2943	1.276	0.9029	22.955***	-2.469**	0.9718	0.9291
DBS	0.2272	0.939	0.9250	22.401***	-1.816	0.9705	0.9531
FBS	0.2769	1.313	0.9086	25.273***	-2.539**	0.9766	0.9304
EES	0.8121	3.470***	0.7320	18.514***	-6.785***	0.9577	0.7643
FES	0.8229	3.316***	0.7284	17.427***	-6.498***	0.9526	0.7646
EBS	0.8018	8.364***	0.7354	18.320***	-6.599***	0.9568	0.7686

*** significant at the 1 per cent level.
** significant at the 5 per cent level.
* significant at the 10 per cent level.

Empirical Tests of Hypotheses on Specialisation

In each of the 32 centres in which the banks undertook activities the shares of the various activities are positively correlated with their shares in the rest of the centres, although for three centres the slope coefficient of the regression, b, is insignificant, as shown in Table 5.9. This means that in almost every centre there is a hierarchical structure to the activities undertaken, which is similar to that for the rest of the centres. The top three centres are all diversified into higher-order activities, with b, $b/R < 1$. By contrast, almost all the bottom centres have $b > 1$, as predicted. They were also the most specialised centres.

TABLE 5.9 *Estimates of regression (5.2) for all banks*

	a	t_a	b	$t_{b=0}$	$t_{b=1}$	R	b/R
LN	2.0589	5.277***	0.4647	5.082***	5.854*	0.7199	0.6455
NY	0.8947	1.864*	0.7674	6.742***	–2.044***	0.8090	0.9486
TK	1.0558	2.997***	0.7255	8.685***	–3.287***	0.8710	0.8330
ZH	2.8016	5.369***	0.2716	2.206**	–5.917***	0.4106	0.5261
HK	–0.4026	–1.385*	1.1047	15.944***	1.511	0.9559	1.1557
SG	–2.9377	–5.605***	1.7638	14.034***	6.076***	0.9441	1.8682
TO	0.4907	1.550	0.8724	11.582***	–1.695	0.9210	0.9472
FT	0.4180	0.880	0.8913	7.888***	–0.962	0.8495	1.0492
PS	–1.4515	–3.192***	1.3774	12.683***	3.475***	0.9328	1.4766
SY	–0.1110	–0.281	1.0289	10.919***	0.307	0.9123	1.1278
AM	0.9970	1.815***	0.7408	5.668***	–1.983**	0.7566	0.9791
CH	–8.4033	3.375***	1.8849	7.816***	3.669***	0.8473	2.2246
LUX	–1.6453	–2.387**	1.4278	8.681***	2.601**	0.8709	1.6395
MN	–2.2043	–2.797**	1.5731	8.364***	3.047***	0.8629	1.8230
MD	–2.6671	–2.435**	1.6934	6.479***	2.653**	0.7977	2.1229
BH	–4.5276	–3.970***	2.1772	7.993***	4.322***	0.8526	2.5536
SF	–1.9075	–2.056	1.4960	6.762***	2.242**	0.8098	1.8474
BA	–1.0459	–0.782	1.2719	3.994***	0.853	0.6318	2.0131
RIO	0.6413	0.566	0.8333	3.087***	–0.617	0.5331	1.5631
BM	–2.0878	–0.961	1.5410	2.986***	1.048	0.5205	2.9606
AN	–1.9021	–1.492*	1.4945	4.920***	1.628	0.7086	2.1091
JK	–6.2365	3.141***	2.6215	5.534***	3.421***	0.7487	3.5014
CP	1.7938	2.463**	0.5336	3.077***	–2.690**	0.5319	1.0032
CY	–8.7732	–2.899***	3.2810	4.544***	3.159***	0.6801	4.8243
SK	–3.9161	–2.946***	2.0182	6.370***	3.214***	0.7927	2.5460
LG	–3.3796	1.402	1.8787	3.270***	1.530	0.5552	3.3838
MC	–1.8748	–0.419	1.4875	1.396	0.457	0.2740	5.4288
BAH	–0.9025	–3.585**	3.5746	5.428***	3.909***	0.7424	4.8149
SH	–4.2165	–1.471	2.0963	3.069***	1.605	0.5308	3.9393
CR	1.9384	0.453	0.4960	0.486	–0.494	0.0990	5.0101
CO	–2.8603	–0.549	1.7437	1.404*	0.599	0.2755	6.3292
BG	0.2963	0.044	0.9228	0.575	–0.048	0.1166	7.9142

*** significant at the 1 per cent level.
** significant at the 5 per cent level.
* significant at the 10 per cent level.

Among the middle tier of centres only three are diversified: Zurich, Toronto and Amsterdam. Indeed Zurich is the most diversified of all the centres. However, an examination of the breakdown of actual activities undertaken in Zurich suggests a different emphasis in comparison to London and the other top centres. Generally, it is activities such as swaps and futures which are the largest in the top three centres, plus the Euro-activities for London, while for Zurich it is chiefly investment banking activities. The results also suggest that Frankfurt, Chicago, Hong Kong and Singapore are specialist centres in which many banks operate, many activities are undertaken, but just a few of these activities are undertaken on a far larger scale than the rest. An examination of the actual breakdown of activities suggests that in the case of Singapore and Chicago specialisation may be broadly in commercial banking activities, together with futures and options, while in the case of Frankfurt and Hong Kong it is in investment banking activities.

The hypothesis (VIII) concerning the particular cluster of activities in which centres are specialised is not fully supported by the results, as most of the coefficients are insignificant. The results suggest that the mix of activities undertaken in London is slightly different from that in New York and Tokyo. London is more evenly diversified than either of the other two, reflecting its more universal and open banking regulations. The emphasis on the middle cluster of activities in Tokyo may once again reflect its regulations, as these are the activities that both types of banks can undertake.

The results by type of bank broadly support hypotheses VI–XI as can be seen from Tables 5.10 and 5.11. The main contribution of these results it to demonstrate the effect of regulations on the relationship between the hierarchy of financial centres and their specialisation. For the commercial banks New York is specialised ($b/R > 1$) rather than diversified, as would be expected given its position, while Tokyo has a higher b/R value than in the 'all bank' case. This supports hypothesis XI, that regulations can affect the relationship between the hierarchy of financial centres and their specialisation. The range of activities which most of the commercial banks are permitted to undertake is restricted in these centres. The high degree of diversification of some other centres, by contrast, may reflect their universal banking regulations. Thus Sydney, Frankfurt and Amsterdam, for example, are diversified centres even though they are in the bottom cluster. This result is also reflected in the particular cluster of activities in which the centres are specialised. Sydney, Frankfurt, Amsterdam, London and Zurich tend to be diversified into the top cluster of activities. New York and Tokyo are more specialised in the middle cluster of activities, which contain no underwriting activities. Singapore and Chicago are specialised in the lower and middle

TABLE 5.10 *Estimates of regression (5.2) for commercial banks*

	a	t_a	b	$t_{b=0}$	$t_{b=1}$	R	b/R
LN	1.7292	4.896***	0.5504	7.222***	–5.900***	0.8276	0.6651
NY	0.1832	0.384	0.9524	9.073***	–0.453	0.8799	1.0824
TK	0.6622	1.921*	0.8278	10.944***	–2.278**	0.9127	0.9070
ZH	2.8757	7.987	0.2523	3.235***	–9.586***	0.5510	0.4579
SG	–1.3253	–3.812***	1.3446	17.429***	4.467***	0.9627	1.3967
HK	–0.0161	–0.078	1.0042	21.964***	0.912	0.9760	1.0289
FT	0.8675	2.229**	0.7744	9.060***	–2.639***	0.8797	0.8803
PS	–1.3889	–3.343***	1.3611	14.798***	3.925***	0.9493	1.4338
SY	0.5322	1.850	0.8616	13.614***	–2.186**	0.9410	0.9156
TO	–1.0518	–3.319***	1.2735	18.182***	3.907***	0.9656	1.3189
AM	1.4681	3.389***	0.6183	6.500**	–4.014***	0.7986	0.7742
LX	–0.2802	–0.475	1.0729	8.240***	0.559	0.8596	1.2481
CH	–2.9834	–4.008***	1.7757	10.751***	4.696***	0.9100	1.9513
MN	–1.7785	–2.684**	1.4624	9.986***	3.159***	0.8978	1.6289
BH	–3.2587	–4.502***	1.8473	11.531***	5.289***	0.9204	2.0071
MD	–2.4341	–2.414**	1.6329	7.325***	2.839***	0.8313	1.9643
SF	–3.7835	–3.591***	1.9837	8.517***	4.224***	0.8668	2.2885
BM	–1.3961	–0.969	1.3630	4.286***	1.142	0.6585	2.0699
RIO	1.2415	1.487	0.6772	3.6184***	–1.756*	0.6011	1.1266
JK	–4.1631	–3.512***	2.0824	7.950***	4.133***	0.8514	2.4459
BA	–2.9411	1.775*	1.7647	4.825***	2.091**	0.7017	2.5149
CP	2.1350	4.603***	0.4449	4.357***	–5.437***	0.6646	0.6694
AN	–3.7225	–2.651**	1.9678	6.349***	3.123***	0.7917	2.4855
SK	–1.7207	–1.800*	1.4474	6.866***	2.122***	0.8141	1.7779
CY	–6.7759	–3.217***	2.7617	5.936***	3.787***	0.7713	3.5806
LG	–2.6327	–1.710	1.6845	4.962***	2.016*	0.7116	2.3672
MC	–0.3604	–0.107	1.0937	1.475	0.126	0.2883	3.7936
BAH	–6.7015	–3.714***	2.7424	6.884***	4.373***	0.8147	3.3661
SH	–2.5592	–1.256	1.6654	3.706***	1.481	0.6033	1.7605
CR	0.8950	0.176	0.7673	0.686	–0.208	0.1386	5.5361
CO	–1.8693	–0.484	1.4860	1.746*		0.3357	4.4266
BG	0.8332	0.164	0.7834	0.700	–0.194	0.1414	5.5403

*** significant at the 1 per cent level.
** significant at the 5 per cent level.
* significant at the 10 per cent level.

cluster of activities, reinforcing the conclusion that they are specialist centres.

These conclusions are also reflected in the results for investment banks. There are ten centres in which the investment banks did not undertake any activities, and these are therefore excluded from the

TABLE 5.11 *Estimates of regression (5.2) for investment banks*

	a	t_a	b	$t_{b=0}$	$t_{b=1}$	R	b/R
LN	1.9099	5.666***	0.5034	6.802***	–6.711***	0.8114	0.6204
NY	1.2632	2.755**	0.6716	6.565***	–3.210***	0.8014	0.8380
TK	0.1169	0.284	0.9696	10.429***	–0.327	0.9051	1.0713
TO	0.6854	1.587	0.8218	8.448***	–1.831*	0.8651	0.9499
ZH	0.4903	1.147	0.8725	9.052***	–1.323	0.8795	0.9920
HK	–0.8152	–1.659	1.2119	10.871***	1.901*	0.9117	1.3293
PS	–3.7735	–4.060***	1.9811	9.349***	4.630***	0.8858	2.2365
FT	–0.9710	–1.725*	1.2525	9.821***	1.980*	0.8949	1.3996
SY	1.1507	1.243	0.7008	3.355***	–1.432	0.5650	1.2404
AM	–2.6864	–2.798**	1.6985	7.794***	3.206***	0.8466	2.0063
SF	–1.0826	–1.071	1.2815	5.599***	1.230	0.7526	1.7028
SG	0.0979	0.110	0.9745	4.829***	–0.126	0.7020	1.3882
CH	–3.2481	–3.784***	1.8445	9.468***	4.335***	0.8881	2.0769
LX	–3.4588	–3.456***	1.8993	8.368***	3.962***	0.8630	2.2008
MN	–4.3539	–4.870***	2.1320	10.508***	5.579***	0.9064	2.3522
BA	–3.3183	–3.538***	1.8627	8.763***	4.058***	0.8729	2.1339
MD	–3.4350	–3.949***	1.8931	9.601***	4.529***	0.8907	2.1254
AN	–2.0274	–1.957*	1.5271	6.511***	2.248**	0.7991	1.9110
BH	–3.5153	–1.352	1.9140	3.251***	1.553	0.5529	3.4617
CY	12.5191	4.060***	–2.2550	–3.243***	–4.681***	0.5520	–4.0850
RIO	–3.9672	–1.218	2.0315	2.757**	1.400	0.4904	4.1425
CR	–8.7601	–2.666***	3.2776	4.407***	3.062***	0.6686	4.9022
CP	6.0363	0.762	–0.5694	–0.318	–0.877	0.0648	–8.7870

*** significant at the 1 per cent level.
** significant at the 5 per cent level.
* significant at the 10 per cent level.

analysis. The ten were among the smallest centres of all, and this confirms the extent to which investment banks have greater locational concentration. More detailed analysis shows that New York, Tokyo and Toronto are all specialised in the middle cluster of activities. This is because the top cluster contains mainly commercial banking activities which the investment banks were prohibited from undertaking in these centres at the time of the survey. It also suggests that Singapore is used as a regional alternative to Tokyo mainly in commercial banking activities.

Summary of Empirical Results

The results broadly support the hypotheses concerning the international division of activities. The focus of the cluster analysis has been mainly on the number of centres in which an activity is undertaken. This represents the broad hierarchy. A fuller, more accurate picture of the international division of activities is revealed by examining the level of concentration, and the particular centres in which activities are concentrated.

Across all the centres an international division of activities emerges. The top activities are the most concentrated ones, and they are concentrated in the leading centres. These higher-order activities seem to be the ones that require a large market area, benefit most from agglomeration economies and/or are restricted to a few locations because of regulations. The centres in which they were concentrated were generally more liberal and open to foreign banks, had historically developed as centres of international finance, served a large local demand that was sophisticated in terms of product requirements, and had other locationally attractive features. The lower-order activities, on the other hand, were more dispersed, and exhibited a more positive relationship with the bottom-ranked centres.

The structure of this international division of activities differed by type of bank. There was, for example, a different emphasis within the top centres according to the type of bank. Underwriting was generally concentrated in London, New York, Tokyo and Toronto for investment banks, but in London, Zurich, Hong Kong and Frankfurt for commercial banks. This shows how the attractiveness of a centre varies by type of bank, even for the same activity. The most important reason for this was the regulatory environment, especially restrictions on the activities that various types of bank can undertake. The most restricted activities end up being concentrated in a few of the more open centres.

On the other hand, a comparison of the b/R values for underwriting activities in commercial and investment banks reveals that in both cases the activities are concentrated. This implies that the results were due in part to features fundamental to the nature of these activities. MNBs must take account of this when devising a global configuration of their activities. If some activities by their very nature need to be locationally concentrated then it is important for MNBs to understand the factors that determine this. For example, commercial banks entering investment-banking-type activities may find that only a few locations can be chosen to undertake certain activities from which they must then serve the wider geographical area. Conversely, an investment bank wishing to compete strongly in certain commercial banking activities may find it necessary to have a global network of offices. It should be recognised that the locational choice that the banks make can be tightly constrained by the interaction between the nature of the activities they wish to undertake, their field of expertise, and the attractiveness of the different centres.

Overall the analysis suggests a configuration of activities in line with the model outlined in section 5.3, involving four main levels of financial centre:

(a) local centres in which a few lower-order activities are undertaken by MNBs, directed towards the local market, primarily to service the needs of their home-country clients;
(b) regional centres in which a much wider range of activities are undertaken, to serve the needs not only of the local but regional markets (for example, Zurich, Toronto, Hong Kong and Frankfurt);
(c) a few specialist centres, in lower- and higher-order activities, that serve their regional market and possibly the global market as well (for example, Chicago and Singapore);
(d) the global centres, London, New York and Tokyo, undertaking the full range of activities, but in which the higher-order activities are concentrated, servicing the local, regional and global market.

5.6 CONCLUSIONS

The results focus attention on the attractiveness of different centres. Although the banks in the sample were multinational by virtue of the size of their networks, in many cases they were still dependent on their home centres. Therefore centres with a large domestic market, and where many of the world's largest banks are headquartered, could be expected (all else being equal) to be at or near the top of the hierarchy. This was shown to be the case of Reed (1981, 1983) and Choi, Tschoegl and Yu (1986). Indeed, it could be argued that centres such as New York, Tokyo, Frankfurt, and Paris owe their position in the hierarchy to the size of their domestic markets and the number of large banks headquartered in them. Their very size and importance then attracts other banks to locate in them, and a cumulative growth process then gets under way.

Centres without this natural advantage must therefore rely on other competitive advantages for their growth. These could be history, geographic location, expertise and, most importantly, regulations and political stability. Such advantages are crucial for Hong

Kong, Singapore, Zurich and Luxemburg. In London's case all these factors have encouraged its development over the last 30 years, most significantly by stimulating the growth of the Euromarkets. In the event of centres with larger domestic markets establishing a significantly more attractive regulatory and technological environment, a cumulative relocation of activities could be encouraged. The main agent in this relocation would be the MNB, especially if it already has a network of facilities established in the major centres. This would seem of particular relevance in a European context, given the moves towards a uniform regulatory environment.

Overall, the results indicate that the internal geographical hierarchy of banks does, by and large, correspond to the international hierarchy of centres. This perhaps reflects the nature of the banking industry today. Across a range of activities, the organisation of the multinational banking network supersedes considerations of operations in national markets by its focus on the overall international competitive position of the bank. The concentration of activities in particular groups of centres, for whatever reasons, suggests a particular type of market servicing strategy, in which a choice between exporting or FDI in serving particular national markets has been displaced by a need to locate in the most appropriate centre from which to service a wider regional market. Although barriers to integration still remain and segment parts of the banking market, there is a strong trend towards a global financial market, which would more readily permit a globally optimal locational pattern.

An important policy issue which arises from a study of this nature is the future international pattern of banking activities. The theoretical framework suggested that a hierarchy of financial centres is the basic international structural pattern for banking activities. This hierarchy is primarily based on the benefits arising from external and agglomeration economies. The particular locations at the top depend on the features outlined in section 5.3, including the advantage of cumulative growth. However, this hierarchical structure assumes a differential regulatory environment and a technological environment in which the production and transfer of information and banking services/products is neither timeless nor cost-free. *The question is, in a world of uniform regulations and no technological or distance costs, what structure would emerge, a hierarchy or a network of co-equal centres?*

In favour of a hierarchy continuing is the argument that the benefits of external economies, both for the higher-order activities and for established pre-eminent centres, would still be the overriding factors. *The reduced technological and regulatory costs could then stimulate a consolidation of the present hierarchical clustering of activities, with essentially a large number of local sales/retail outlets plugged into the centre.* Alternatively, a reduction in these costs could reduce these advantages of external economies, and encourage a dispersion of activities. *It then becomes possible to envisage a system of co-equal centres, all electronically linked, with information and products flowing across the network.* One could even then have specialised locations providing the support services. This issue is still open to debate. In a European context that debate is not necessarily hypothetical. It is not inconceivable that a relatively uniform regulatory environment could emerge in Europe. Moreover, the relatively small distances between the major centres and the increasing pace of technological innovations make it possible to conceive of an environment of relatively timeless, cheap transfers of information and products.

Notes

1. An MNB can be defined as an enterprise that owns or controls banking activities in more than one country (Casson, 1989).
2. For example *The Economist*, March 1989, cites the shift towards a rationalised investment strategy on the part of Barclays Bank.
3. Campayne (1990) suggests that it is not the degree of multinationality *per se* that influences performance, but the particular geographical configuration.
4. Recently the US Federal Reserve Bank has granted US commercial banks permission to underwrite corporate bonds. However, in 1987 when the data was collected, commercial banks were still barred from underwriting bonds.

6 Global Integration through the Decentralisation of R & D

MARK CASSON, ROBERT D. PEARCE AND SATWINDER SINGH

6.1 INTRODUCTION

It is often assumed that MNEs are structured as spatial hierarchies, in which key functions are centralised and only routine activities are dispersed. There is certainly a tendency towards centralisation in areas such as finance and personnel (Brooke, 1984), but in other respects the hierarchical view is misleading. This is definitely the case with R & D. In large firms R & D is not necessarily concentrated in a single headquarters laboratory. Some major firms decentralise research activities, creating a network of laboratories in different countries. Overseas laboratories may enjoy considerable autonomy; they are not necessarily subordinated to a single central facility.

This chapter aims to provide an informed assessment of the determinants of the internationalisation of corporate R & D. It suggests that the economic forces promoting internationalisation are similar to those that have promoted the internationalisation of production in the past, although in the case of R & D they manifest themselves in a somewhat different way. The policies of both individual firms and nation states are crucial in determining how the costs and benefits of this development are distributed. The coordination of intracorporate networks of R & D requires considerable management skill (Bartlett and Ghoshal, 1990; Hakanson, 1990): successful coordination of R & D, it is argued, depends crucially on the quality of corporate culture.

Section 6.2 provides a brief historical perspective on the evolution of corporate R & D. It shows that the emergence of the international decentralisation of research is a relatively recent phenomenon. Section 6.3 draws upon a set of interviews with R & D directors in 27 major multinationals (both North American and European) to report recent trends in the organisation of corporate R & D. The interviews, carried out in 1989, reveal the 1980s as a decade of considerable trauma for Western corporations committed to more basic types of research, as they struggle to reorganise in response to the Japanese challenge. A model of the international division of labour in R & D is presented in section 6.4. The model considers not only the division of labour *between* R & D and production and marketing but also the division of labour *within* R & D between generic and adaptive research, basic research and reverse engineering, quality control and capital equipment design, and so on.

This model provides a conceptual framework for the main part of the chapter (sections 6.5–9) which analyses the results of a major questionnaire to which almost 300 corporate research laboratories responded. The geographical distribution of laboratories is profiled in section 6.5, while the nature of the research they undertake is examined in section 6.6. Factors influencing the choice of location for overseas laboratories are considered in section 6.7, whilst the choice of organisational structure for the coordination of international R & D is examined in section 6.8. The parent's perception of overall R & D strategy is related to other corporate characteristics in section 6.9.

The final part of the chapter considers policy-related issues. Section 6.10 looks at the impact of host government policies on overseas laboratories. It shows, in particular, that managers of foreign-owned laboratories in the USA sometimes perceive the local regulatory environment as quite a hostile one. Section 6.11 considers the impact of education and domestic infrastructure on international R & D strategies. It argues that the 'invisible infrastructure' of indigenous business culture is important not only in respect of attracting foreign-owned R & D facilities but, above all, in creating technological capability in locally-headquartered firms, so that they can successfully manage overseas R & D activities of their own. It suggests that some countries have a business culture far more supportive of R & D than do others, and argues that despite their relatively high degree of internationalisation, major UK firms have failed to give technology the corporate status it deserves. Section 6.12 concludes.

6.2 HISTORICAL BACKGROUND

In historical terms the decentralisation of corporate R & D is quite a recent phenomenon. Until the turn of the century there was very little corporate R & D of any kind. Branch plant research laboratories began to emerge in the interwar period, but it was really only in the period of consolidation that followed the early post-war multinational expansion that a coherent strategy of decentralisation was evolved.

In the early companies that were geared to R & D the influence of a single individual was often paramount. This individual was usually a member of the family that owned the firm: perhaps the founder's son who was enthused by the progressive scientific spirit of the Victorian age. Thus young William Siemens was the driving force in Siemens' London telecommunications laboratory (established in the 1860s), whilst Tom Vickers was largely responsible, from the age of 22, for the transition of Vickers from a steel firm to the world's leading armament manufacturer by 1900 (Scott, 1962; Trebilcock, 1977; von Weiher, 1980).

These individuals did not usually run the entire company single-handed, however. They were part of an informal intrafamily division of labour, vividly illustrated in the Vickers case, where Tom's brother Eric had a quite different personality and concentrated almost entirely on the commercial side of the firm's operations. This entrepreneurial partnership between the introverted scientist and the extroverted market opportunist proved highly successful.

The reform and extension of the patent system in the 1870s and 1880s encouraged speculative financing of patent-driven research, particularly in the USA, where the most notable example was Edison's Menlo Park laboratory. Patents, however, proved costly to enforce, for reasons which transaction cost theory makes very clear: namely, the ease of 'inventing around' a patent and the difficulty of monitoring covert use. The initiative in innovative industries gradually passed to firms which integrated forward into the production activities which utilised their ideas.

The scientific approach was well adapted to factories which were making the transition from small-scale batch production to large-scale continuous flow. As the division of labour within the factory increased, individual tasks became sufficiently simple that they could be mechanised, and carried out routinely by machine tools powered from a common source. The capital goods industries played a crucial role in these innovations, with the capital good producer designing the machinery in close collaboration with the users.

Nowhere was the harnessing of basic science to commercial innovation so systematically applied as in Germany. The Prussian elite, bent on modernising Germany through rapid industrialisation and the expansion of the internal market, financed the development of polytechnics in which some brilliant chemists were employed. These chemists addressed themselves to practical issues, such as recycling waste products to reduce pollution, increasing thermal efficiency, and expanding the supply of useful intermediate inputs to other industries. The strong emphasis on practical study at the laboratory bench generated a stream of highly professional inventors (Wrigley, 1986).

The rest of the world benefited enormously from this. Foreigners came to Germany to be trained in the polytechnics. Young Germans left for England and the USA to set up plants to work their patents, to gain access to new sources of funds, to avoid conscription and, in some cases, to escape anti-Semitism (Cohen, 1956).

The first fully-fledged industrial research laboratory was established by the German pharmaceutical company Bayer in 1886 to develop new synthetic dyestuffs from a coal-tar base (Kaku, 1980). The Bayer example was followed in the USA by General Electric (Edison's successor) in 1900 and Du Pont in 1902. The German influence was very strong, with many recent immigrants being employed in the new chemical research laboratories (M. Wilkins, 1989).

Two main factors gave the impetus to the formal organisation of research (James, 1989). The first was the need to synthesise knowledge from different scientific disciplines by adopting a team approach. The photographic industry affords an excellent example (Edgerton, 1988). The optical properties of lenses needed to be understood for camera design. The properties of synthetic dyes were crucial in the formulation of the film emulsion. Precision machine tools were required to produce reliable cameras on a sufficient scale to make photography an affordable hobby for the masses. The ability of the Eastman Kodak laboratory to synthesise the relevant skills was crucial to the company's enduring success in this field.

The second was the trust movement, which is a landmark in the development of managerial control. The financial requirements of a trust could rarely be satisfied by a single family. A single family could not easily staff all the key management positions, either. A formal structure therefore replaced informal family arrangements. Nevertheless some wealthy families with large numbers of children managed to maintain control even in rationalised organisations: a family member still controlled R & D policy in Du Pont at the time the general laboratory was established in 1902 (Hounshell and Smith, 1988). The increasing availability of academic specialists with a practical orientation in the land-grant universities provided an important source of salaried research managers (Lazonick, 1986). General Electric was one of the first US companies to appoint an 'outsider' to head its research department: Willis R. Whitney, recruited from MIT (Reich, 1985).

In the climate of political uncertainty after the First World War, the international exploitation of technology was effected mainly through cartel agreements which involved cross-licensing of patents and the division of the world market into European and American spheres of influence. This division was facilitated by high tariffs, which made it difficult for the licensee to invade the licensor's market. Each major industrial market for a product was therefore normally reserved for one of the cartel members, with *ad hoc* arrangements being made in the smaller, less significant markets (Reader, 1975). Cartel agreements tended to inhibit radical innovation as they were costly to renegotiate in the light of new developments.

After the Second World War, foreign direct investment replaced the international cartel as the main contractual arrangement through which technology was transferred. US hegemony meant that the political risks of foreign investment were lower – at least for US firms – whilst trade liberalisation increased the strategic risks of market invasion by licensees. There was a growing perception of the need to adapt products to the local market environment. Small laboratories were created for quality testing and for the 'reverse engineering' of competitors' products, and these gradually evolved a capacity for adaptive work, often under the influence of an enterprising indigenous manager who was sensitive to local requirements (Pearce, 1989a).

Dependence on a headquarters laboratory often remained significant, however. It was only when the larger multinationals began to rationalise their international operations in the 1960s that the idea of devolving major research responsibilities to an overseas laboratory gained momentum. Until then only a few firms, such as the Anglo–Dutch food firm Unilever, had employed this approach (Wilson, 1954, 1968; Fieldhouse, 1978). The reduced costs of international communication – both remote communication utilising information technology and face-to-face communication by jet travel – have encouraged the proliferation of this strategy. Even so, it is still confined mainly to the very large firms which are the focus of this study.

A major advantage of rationalisation is that it avoids unnecessary replication, and so reduces the fixed costs of R & D required to sustain a given market share in an innovative industry. Intrafirm rationalisation may not go far enough, however. Costs of research have recently escalated quite significantly in many industries. It has been estimated by a large UK MNE that R & D costs have risen consistently at a few percentage points above the retail price index during the 1980s. Rationalisation *between* firms is required to cope with this. Unless the proliferation of products is reduced, no product will have sufficient market share (on average) to reimburse its costs of development. This has provided a major impetus to the development of joint venture arrangements in the 1980s (Hladik, 1988).

6.3 RECENT TRENDS

Western firms have undergone a good deal of self-examination by management – and external examination by institutional shareholders – during the 1980s. Corporate self-diagnosis has mainly concentrated on the problem of poor value for money in basic research. Interviews with research managers in 27 major companies identified three related problems.

First, basic research is easily 'hijacked' by scientists who are more concerned with academic approval than with financial returns. By striving to please their academic peers, they duplicate the kind of work that is best left to universities, and neglect the kind of work that industry requires. Central laboratories, divorced from operating divisions, are particularly prone to 'pure' research of this kind.

Next, basic research too easily gets stuck on the drawing board because of an interest in technical perfection for its own sake. Basic researchers are too interested in quantum leaps in the state of the art, and too little concerned with continuous incremental improvement within existing paradigms. Senior managers often lack the technical expertise to determine which high-risk projects need to be killed off before they reach the very expensive development stage.

Finally, many post-war growth industries have now matured technologically, and basic research is no longer as financially rewarding as it used to be.

Thus during the 1980s there has been a significant trend for corporate R & D to become more applied. Headquarters laboratories of US firms have undergone major changes as a result. In the 1950s and 1960s some of these laboratories became major institutions for fundamental research. In the 1980s their roles have often been redefined to encourage more active support of product development in the companies' operating divisions.

Resources saved on basic research are now devoted to 'getting closer to the customer' instead. The customer is perceived as increasingly sophisticated and demanding. In some consumer goods industries these demands express themselves directly in the marketplace, through increased awareness of the brands that offer high performance and reliability. In other cases they are mediated by governments through safety regulations, pollution standards, and so on. Customers in capital goods industries such as engineering, or intermediate product industries such as aircraft or office equipment, are in any case more sophisticated, but because they too are subject to new competitive pressures they have passed these pressures on to their suppliers through the procurement process.

There is also a trend for corporate R & D to become more diversified, especially in laboratories located in the USA and UK. On the face of it this is somewhat surprising. Current thinking in corporate strategy suggests that firms would have become more focused instead, but only a small number of respondents indicated that such was the case.

Part of the answer seems to lie in the new cross-disciplinary linkages being invoked to solve research problems: for example, the synthesis of biochemistry and advanced computing in molecular modelling. The fact that *line of business* is becoming increasingly focused is perfectly compatible with the fact that *research competence* is becoming more broadly based. This trend to broader research competence is also linked to the emergence of more loosely coordinated teams within the 'network firm' (Chesnais, 1988, 1990).

Another part of the explanation for the diversification of research competence may be the need to redeploy researchers in mature industries such as steel and heavy chemicals. In a declining industry the firm's laboratory may well lose internal custom for product development and so be forced to sell its services outside if it is to survive. This may involve the firm in a wider range of applications than usual, and hence require its competence to be diversified.

Finally, diversification of research may be a consequence of greater internalisation in production and distribution. In some industries there is a need to integrate backwards into new sources of supply: for example, to investigate the use of wood in place of oil within the energy sector. In other industries the drive to get closer to the customer implies integrating downstream, even to the extent of placing R & D personnel within the customer's own firm.

Any discussion of recent trends must recognise the growing importance of Japanese competition over the last two decades. Japanese competition has reduced profitability in many Western industries and so dried up internal corporate funding for R & D. At a time when Japanese firms are investing a steadily increasing proportion of their resources in R & D, their Western rivals are doing less; certainly at the basic level, though in some countries more is being done in product development than before.

The effects of this are all too clear from the patent statistics, which show that the Japanese have wrested technological leadership from the West in engines and motor vehicles, and now pose a serious challenge in office equipment and scientific instruments too (Cantwell, 1991).

The Japanese are noted for their incremental approach to innovation, in which successive small improvements are made as a result of bottom-up suggestions from the factory floor. The Japanese have overthrown conventional Western ideas of the product life-cycle by tooling up for mass production at the outset and using 'learning by doing' to improve the product in the course of production. This has encouraged Western imitators to shorten their own product life-cycles and invest in continuous product and process improvement.

Part of the price paid for this has been the downgrading of basic research. There is evidence, however, that the Japanese are now moving strongly towards basic long-term research and are establishing laboratories in the West not only to support product and process adaptation but to carry out more fundamental research as well. Although apparently averse to formal contracting out of research, the Japanese appear to be developing informal links with Western universities and independent research institutions. By contrast, Western firms in Japan are more inclined to seek out Japanese corporate partners. Partly this is because that is where much Japanese technology resides. By repute, corporate partnerships also help in getting official approval for new products and in locating suitable production premises. The cross-flows of R & D investments are therefore slightly different, but the net effect is to produce a convergence of R & D practice in

Japan and the West, at least so far as the balance between basic research and development work is concerned.

6.4 A MODEL OF THE INTERNATIONAL DIVISION OF LABOUR IN R & D

This section outlines a formal model of R & D which encompasses a number of the features of corporate R & D mentioned above. It also provides a useful transition from the informal discursive treatment of historical trends to the more formal statistical analysis presented in subsequent sections.

Figure 6.1 illustrates schematically the close interaction between production, marketing and R & D within a profit-maximising firm. The thin lines indicate information flows and the thick lines the flows of physical product moving downstream. Note that each activity is linked to two or more other activities. Although the physical linkages are rather sparse, they are supplemented by the dense network of

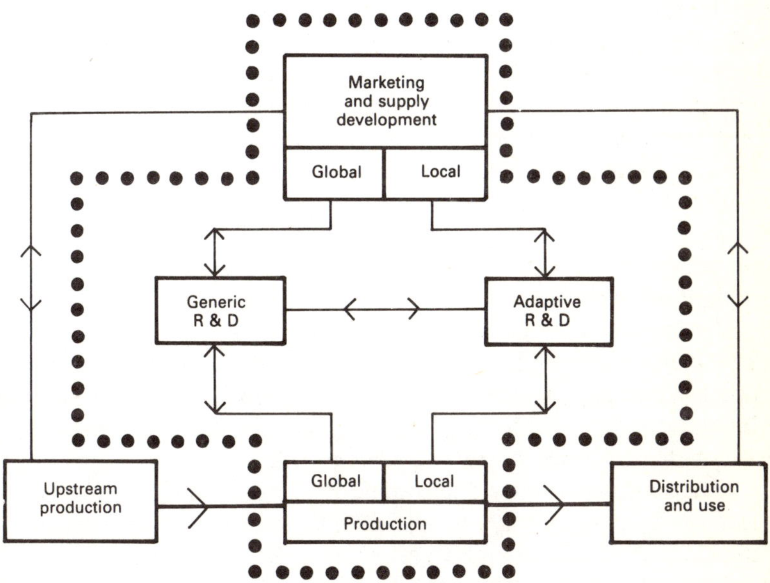

FIGURE 6.1 The division of labour between generic and adaptive R & D

information linkages. Whilst the physical linkages are one-directional, the information linkages are all two-way.

The figure illustrates not only a division of labour between production, marketing and R & D but also a simple division of labour *within* R & D. Two types of R & D are differentiated: *generic* and *adaptive*. Generic R & D develops a new product or process concept, such as a medicinal drug, or power-generating unit. Generic R & D also includes major functional applications. The typical concept can be embodied in various forms, all of which are of potentially global application. Thus a drug may be incorporated into a tablet, a bottled liquid, an injection, and so on, while a new power unit may be configured either for vehicular or stationary use, and amongst stationary uses for pumping, compressing air, generating electricity, and so on.

Adaptive R & D modifies the applications with a specific local environment in mind. Like generic R & D, both products and processes are included in it. Tablets, for example, may be given tastes or colours according to local preferences, and power units may be adapted to run under different climatic conditions, or to cope with local impurities in fuels. In some cases local conditions may turn out to be less idiosyncratic than first thought, so that what commences as adaptive R & D may turn into application-centred generic R & D. Generic and adaptive R & D are linked by a two-way flow of information, as indicated in the figure. Global applications flow from generic to adaptive R & D, whilst information on local opportunities for new types of application flows in the opposite direction.

The specialised activities created by a division of labour do not all have to be owned by the same firm. If different firms operate different activities then the links between these activities are externalised; information and products must be traded between the firms. The scope for activities undertaken by the same firm is determined by economies of internalising these links. A typical pattern of internalisation is illustrated by the dotted line in the figure. All activities within the dotted perimeter line are owned and controlled by the same firm, whilst those outside it are independent of it.

The case illustrated is one commonly discussed in the MNE literature. Production, marketing and R & D are integrated, internalising the dense network of information flows between them. Upstream production, however, is conducted by independent suppliers, whilst downstream distribution relies on independent wholesalers and retailers, though in both cases the marketing and purchasing departments will maintain a staff to monitor these activities, as far as they

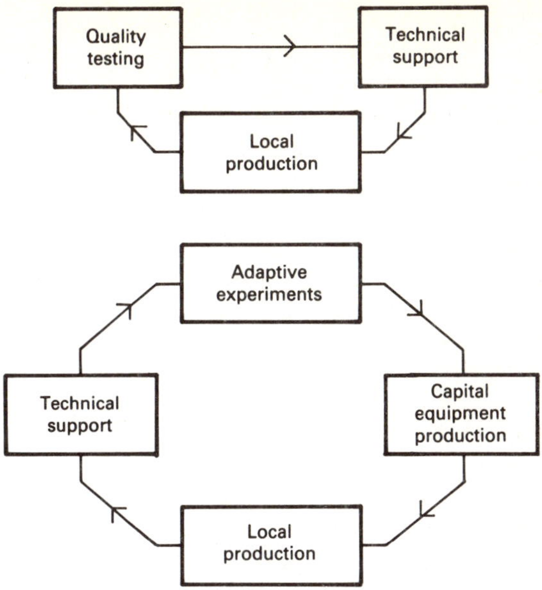

FIGURE 6.2 The cyclical view of R & D

are able, by visits to the independents' premises. Notice that the two stages of R & D are vertically integrated whereas the three stages of the production sequence are not. This reflects the importance attached by conventional theory to the internalisation of proprietary information flow.

Figure 6.1 exemplifies the linear view of R & D, in which innovation proceeds smoothly from basic science through various stages of R & D to final embodiment in the product. An alternative is the cyclic view, which emphasises the feedback of information from later stages of this process. The linear view encourages the perception of innovation as a discrete and intermittent process, whilst the cyclic view emphasises incremental and continuous aspects instead.

Two key elements of the cyclical view are illustrated in Figure 6.2, namely the role of technical support in mediating the feedback of operating experience from production to R & D, and the role of capital equipment manufacture in the 'embodiment' of new technology derived from adaptive R & D.

The linear and cyclic views are synthesised in Figure 6.3. The left-hand side of the figure highlights the role of *global scanning* and *reverse engineering* in generating information inputs to generic R & D.

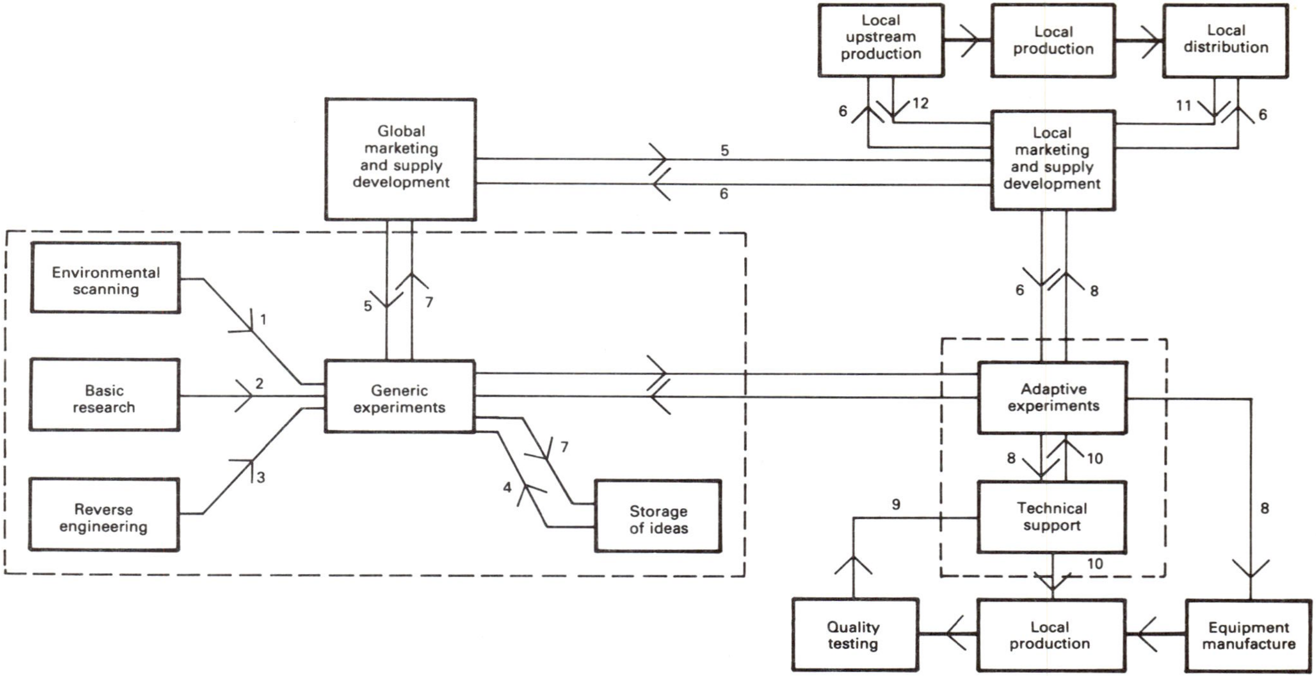

FIGURE 6.3 A synthetic view of the R & D system

Global scanning includes monitoring public opinion and government policies on matters such as health and safety, conservation, strategic self-sufficiency and so on. Reverse engineering is particularly important in non-collusive differentiated-product oligopolies, where it not only helps to prevent rivals from gaining a major technical lead, but also supports the development of low-cost 'me-too' products, which can starve rivals of monopoly profits on their recent innovations (and thereby reduce their internal sources of finance for future R & D). The figure also recognises the role of marketing in guiding generic R & D, and the role of corporate memory in storing ideas that are peripheral to current problems but may have a useful role in the future.

The figure identifies a total of 12 different types of information generated within the R & D system. The advantages of internalising each of these flows depend mainly on the interplay between problems of quality control on the one hand, and the availability of economies of scope on the other. Low quality-assurance implies a high propensity to internalise, because if quality cannot be assured then the user's risks are high, and need to be reduced by gaining the additional information and power of control that internalisation provides.

Economies of scope, on the other hand, favour an arm's length arrangement because the costs of internalising different uses begin to escalate as diseconomies of bureaucracy set in. Typical externalisation policies include licensing concepts to other firms for application, licensing other firms' concepts for in-house application, renting out quality control facilities to other firms or doing subcontracted research for them, renting other people's facilities or getting them to act as subcontractors, and so on.

Overall estimates of the incentive to internalise are presented in Table 6.1. Each type of information flow is identified by a number which refers to Figure 6.3. A combination of large economies of scope and high quality assurance favours externalisation.

When a facility is involved in several linkages, some of which are best internalised and others not, the integration of the facility into the firm is determined by a trade-off between the benefit to one linkage and the cost to another. Global scanning and basic research are the most likely candidates for externalisation. They have just a single linkage to the rest of the system, and their economies of scope are quite high. Externalisation is therefore appropriate, despite the problems of quality assurance involved. These problems are typically

TABLE 6.1 *Internalisation strategies for the information markets created by a division of labour in R & D*

Reference	*Market*	*Degree of quality assurance*	*Economies of scope and scale*	*Strategy*
1	General knowledge	Moderate	High	Externalise
2	Basic scientific results	Moderate	High	Externalise
3	Intelligence on rival products	Moderate	Low	internalise
4	Ideas not required for immediate use	Low	High	Marginal
5	Global marketing requirements	Low	High	Marginal
6	Local marketing requirements	Moderate	Low	Internalise
7	New concept	Low	Moderate	Internalise
8	Adapted design	Low	Low	Internalise
9	Quality measurements	Moderate	Moderate	Marginal
10	Technical advice	Moderate	Low	Internalise
11	Local customer intelligence	Low	Low	Internalise
12	Local supply intelligence	Low	Low	Internalise

overcome by reliance on the reputation of the source and, where appropriate, on the use of multiple sources to provide checks on each other.

In principle each R & D activity can be located on a different site. Different activities require different types of immobile input, as indicated in Table 6.2, and so there may be locational specialisation according to comparative advantage within R & D.

The greater the distance between the sites, however, the greater are the difficulties of communication. This may prove a significant constraint on specialisation because of the importance of face-to-face communication in R & D. Information of an ambiguous and controversial character is best communicated face-to-face. Ambiguities can be minimised by supplementing verbal comments with gestures. Doubts about reliability can be settled through conversational traps, and through cross-examination which spontaneously elicits corroborative (or conflicting) evidence. Emotional bonds can also be built up to encourage integrity in the first place. Some of these effects can also be achieved by 'ear-to-ear' telephone conversation, but this is by no means a perfect substitute.

The more frequently face-to-face meetings are needed, the stronger is

TABLE 6.2 *Availability of local inputs as an influence on the location of activities*

Activity	*Major factor*
Environmental scanning	Information hub
Basic research	Access to academic labour
Reverse engineering	Access to scientific labour
Storage of ideas	
Generic experiments	
Adaptive experiments	
Technical support	
Quality testing	
Global marketing	Access to managerial labour
Local marketing	
Equipment manufacture	Access to skilled labour
Local production	Access to skilled and unskilled labour
Local upstream production	Access to raw material deposits and energy sources
Local distribution	Proximity to customers' residences

the incentive to locate the activities close together. It seems likely, for example, that generic experiments will be pulled towards universities and research institutions where basic science is going on, whilst adaptive research will be pulled towards local markets. This could create locational tension by pulling apart generic and adaptive research. The problem should not be exaggerated, however. Adaptive research is likely to be focused on the largest and wealthiest markets where product demand is strong at an early stage of the life-cycle. Such markets may well be based in metropolitan centres within industrialised countries where many basic research institutions can be found. The overall effect, therefore, may be to pull both stages of R & D towards major regional agglomerations of sophisticated activity.

These results need to be qualified in three ways, however. First, the spatial division of labour must be efficient not only with respect to the communication of information but with respect to the transport of physical products as well. Thus difficulties in transporting product samples could pull adaptive R & D towards production sites which (because of access to raw materials) are remote from major markets. Similarly, difficulties in transporting bulky equipment may tie production, and hence adaptive R & D, to major agglomerations of capital goods industries. Neither of these cases is of major practical importance, though.

Second, the political risks associated with a multinational R & D system must be taken into account. An R & D facility is probably less vulnerable to expropriation than a production facility since there is usually a smaller degree of irreversible commitment to the site: brains and software are more portable than factory equipment. On the other hand, the expropriation of an R & D facility could have serious consequences for the long run viability of the firm.

The third qualification – differential threats of espionage – is much more important than the other two. The threat may come from the host-country government (this is one reason why Western firms do not carry out major R & D in the CMEA countries even though scientific labour is very cheap there). More significantly, the threat may come from the firm's own rivals, either through clandestine operations or the overt poaching of key personnel. In oligopolistic industries firms wishing to catch up on a leader's technology may wish to site their own R & D facilities close to his, whilst the leader may wish to locate well away, if he can, from his follower's facilities.

6.5 THE DISTRIBUTION OF OVERSEAS RESEARCH LABORATORIES

In 1989 a questionnaire was sent to a sample of 560 major enterprises. Separate questionnaires were addressed to the parent laboratory and the subsidiary laboratories in each case. A parent laboratory was defined as either a corporate-level R & D unit (physically located at headquarters, or distinguished as the corporate unit) or, with a diversified enterprise, as the main R & D facility of a major division. Overseas laboratories were defined as non-parent laboratories located outside the headquarters country. Some respondents denied that the distinction between parent and subsidiary laboratory was relevant to them because all major laboratories were of equal status. Closer examination often suggested, however, that where influence on corporate policy was concerned 'some were more equal than others'. Since the main reason for the distinction was simply to match the questionnaire as closely as possible to the respondent's experience, the issue is of little importance for the interpretation of the results.

The sample comprises three distinct subsets of firms.

Sample A: the 500 companies in sample A are the 500 largest industrial enterprises in the world in 1986 as derived from the *Fortune* listings. A number of the leading directories of R & D facilities were scrutinised to find the parent and overseas subsidiaries of sample A companies (Bowker, 1987; Longman, 1987, 1988a, 1988b). Since, as noted above, large divisionalised companies were often considered to have more than one parent R & D facility, more than 500 parent laboratories were found for sample A companies. On the other hand, not all had overseas facilities and the total of these came to less than 500. To cover cases with no overseas R & D, a section of the parent questionnaire was directed at such enterprises, seeking elucidation of the lack of such decentralisation. In a small number of cases the R & D directories did not even produce addresses for parent facilities. For these companies parent questionnaires were sent to corporate headquarters, using addresses from *Dun and Bradstreet Principal International Businesses*.

Sample B: in reviewing the directories to locate facilities for the 500 enterprises of sample A a number of companies outside this sample were discovered which seemed to constitute relevant cases of international decentralisation of R & D. A sample of 30 of these companies was distinguished (as sample B) and parent and subsidiary units surveyed as for sample A.

Sample C: since sample B is a self-selecting sample of companies with some commitment to international R & D, sample C was assembled from 30 companies with no apparent overseas R & D operations. The firms in sample C were selected to match those in sample B by industry and home country as closely as possible. The results reported in this section refer to sample A only, whilst those in the rest of the chapter refer to the consolidated sample of A, B and C.

Each parent firm and each laboratory was associated with a particular industry and a particular country (binational firms were arbitrarily allocated to one country: Unilever to the Netherlands and Shell to the UK). For the purposes of statistical analysis 20 industry groups were used, and these were further aggregated into eight groups for the regression analysis (see below). A total of 1028 questionnaires was sent out, and 296 usable replies were received (an overall response rate of 28.8 per cent). Parents supplied 163 of the responses, and subsidiaries 133. The response rate was slightly higher for subsidiaries than for parents: 32.8 per cent compared to 26.2 per cent. The response rate was particularly good for foreign laboratories in the UK, and notably poor for laboratories in France. Results pertaining to Japan need to be treated with caution because although the coverage of Japanese-owned laboratories is quite satisfactory

TABLE 6.3 *Percentage size distribution of laboratories located*

	USA		*UK*	
Size range	*Parent*	*Subsidiary*	*Parent*	*Subsidiary*
1–24	0	32	4	18
25–49	1	18	7	35
50–99	17	16	21	18
100–249	24	20	21	18
250–499	25	2	18	6
500–999	11	11	18	4
1000–4999	20	0	11	0
5000–	1	0	0	0
Column total	100	100	100	100
Average size	1061	137	498	196
Number sampled	66	44	28	28

(at least in respect of home laboratories), there are only a small number of responses from foreign laboratories in Japan.

Table 6.3 presents a frequency distribution of size of laboratory, showing that in both the US and the UK the parent laboratories of local firms are on average much larger than the overseas laboratories of foreign firms. The difference is particularly marked in the USA because the parent laboratories are much larger, whilst the foreign laboratories are somewhat smaller, than in the UK.

A simple cross-tabulation by ownership and location of the laboratories associated with the parent firms in sample A affords a useful overview of global R & D. Table 6.4 shows the number of laboratories owned by parents of a given nationality in a given country. There are only 12 countries that are involved in overseas research by the leading 500 firms, and these are listed in the table. The Rest of the world simply refers to countries where some of these leading firms are domiciled but which do not source overseas research. The most obvious point is the dominance of the USA in terms of large-firm R & D. This is hardly surprising, of course, since the USA is not only the world's major economy, with a major technological orientation, but it is also the home of many of the world's largest MNEs. It is still notable, though, that 51 per cent of all laboratories in the sample are located in the USA, whilst 47 per cent are owned by US firms.

The discrepancy between these two percentages arises because the USA actually hosts more foreign laboratories than it owns overseas.

TABLE 6.4 *International distribution of the laboratories owned by 500 major firms*

	Locations													*Totals*		*International*
Ownership	*USA*	*CN*	*UK*	*FR*	*GR*	*IT*	*NL*	*SW*	*SZ*	*OE*	*JP*	*AL*	*RW*	*O/S*	*All*	*ratio*
USA	*282*	17	41	12	14	7	3	1	6	11	1	6	5	124	406	31
Canada		*11*	1									1		2	13	15
UK	68	1	*55*	1	3		2			1	1	4		81	136	60
France	12		1	*25*		1			1					15	40	37
W. Germany	50		4		*29*					2		1		57	86	66
Italy	3		1			*5*		1						5	10	50
Netherlands	12		4	2	2		*5*		1					21	26	81
Sweden	1						1	*11*						2	13	15
Switzerland	26		2	1	3			1	*10*	1	1	1		36	46	78
Other Europe	2									*7*				2	9	22
Japan	7		1								*96*			8	104	8
Australia												*4*		0	4	0
Rest of world													*11*	0	11	0
Total foreign	181	18	55	16	22	8	6	3	8	15	3	13	5	353		
Grand total	463	29	110	41	51	13	11	14	18	22	99	17	16		904	
Foreign domination ratio	39	62	50	39	43	62	55	21	44	68	3	76	31			

NOTE: The key to the locations at the head of the table is given by the listing in the ownership column.
SOURCE: Authors' investigations.

The difference is captured, more generally, by the distinction between the foreign dependence ratio, which measures the percentage of all domestic laboratories that are foreign-owned, and the internationalisation ratio, which measures the proportion of all domestically-owned laboratories that are located overseas. The relation between foreign dependence and internationalisation is illustrated in Figure 6.4. Three main groups of countries can be identified by dividing up the square with two parallel lines. The countries in the central division are those which are equally 'open' in the two respects. Countries such as Japan and Sweden, which lie close to the origin, are relatively closed, while a country such as Italy, which is remote from the origin, is relatively open in both respects. The USA, together with France, occupies a middle position, having a modest and balanced openness compared with other countries.

Four countries – Switzerland, Netherlands, West Germany and the UK – are significantly more open in terms of internationalisation than they are in terms of foreign dependence. Four other units – Australia, Canada, Other Europe and the Rest of the world – exhibit the

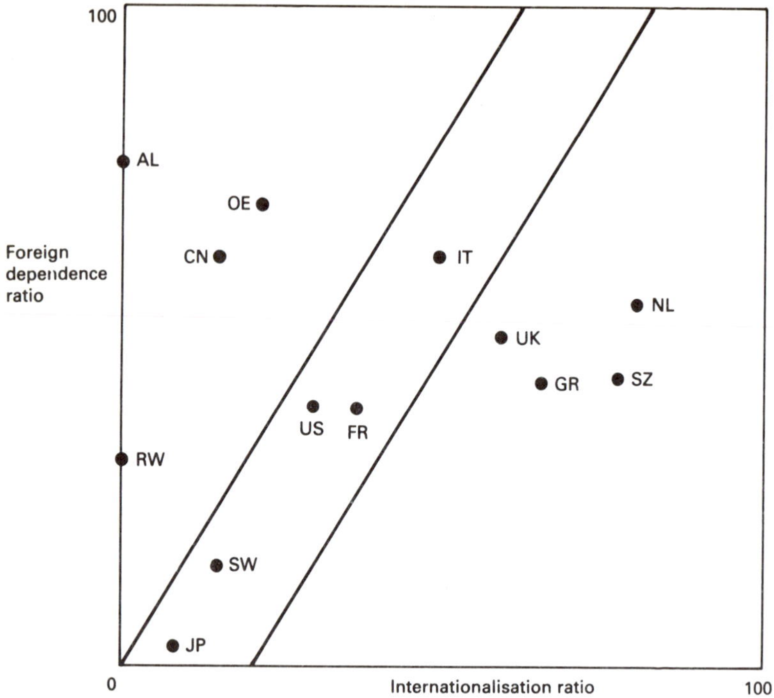

SOURCE: Table 6.4.
KEY: See Table 6.4.

FIGURE 6.4 Foreign dependence and internationalisation, based on the frequency distribution of laboratories

reverse situation, where foreign dependence is high relative to internationalisation. Firms based in these countries have made only limited attempts to exploit the potential of overseas R & D, even though their home countries host R & D themselves.

6.6 THE NATURE OF OVERSEAS R & D

This section analyses the type of R & D done in overseas laboratories. The technique used is ordinary least squares regression analysis. The dependent variables are categorical variables, ranging in value from one (no research of a given type) to three (regular participation in research of that type). The categorical nature of the dependent variable does not bias the regression results, but it means that significance tests must be interpreted with caution, as the usual assumption of normality is violated. While the *t*-tests of significance are fairly robust to such deviations, the *F*-tests are not. It is possible to decompose a categorical regression into a set of regressions with zero–one dependent variables and apply a logit transformation to each, but the results obtained from this more sophisticated approach only lead to inferences similar to the ones indicated here.

Location, ownership and industry effects are captured using dummy variables. To avoid losing too many degrees of freedom, and having too many categories with only a small number of members, countries were consolidated into eight groups: USA, Canada, Japan, UK, EC (excluding UK), Scandinavia (Sweden, Norway, Finland), Other Europe (Switzerland and Austria) and the Rest of the world (mainly Australia, India and Brazil). The Rest of the world is used as a control group. As there are no responses from foreign-owned laboratories in Scandinavia, Scandinavia appears only in the ownership and not the location category.

Seven industrial groups are used. Four high-technology industries are separately identified: pharmaceuticals, office equipment, motor vehicles, and professional and scientific equipment. Chemicals, coal and petroleum products and pulp and paper are consolidated into a 'process industry' category in which technology-intensity is medium-high. Chemical firms dominate this category. Mechanical and electrical engineering firms are similarly combined into a single 'engineering' category. The remaining industries – represented in the sample mainly by food and metals firms – form a 'low-technology' control group.

The figures in brackets in Table 6.5 represent the absolute values of the *t*-statistics. Significance is reported at three levels: 10 per cent (one asterisk), 5 per cent (two asterisks) and 1 per cent (three asterisks). The overall significance of location, ownership and industry effects is indicated by the three *F*-statistics near the bottom of each column. The *F*-statistic for the regression as a whole is also shown. Because some questions achieved a better response rate than others, the number of observations, together with the overall goodness of fit, R^2, is shown at the foot of each column.

Five categories of research are identified in the table, out of the seven identified in the questionnaire. Results relating to local adaptation of the product and local adaptation of the process have been

TABLE 6.5 *Location, ownership and industry factors influencing the nature of overseas R & D*

Dependent variable	*Basic research*	*Product development*	*Process development*	*Diversification*	*Technical support*
Intercept	1.72***	2.16***	2.51***	1.68***	2.34***
	(5.03)	(6.23)	(10.73)	(5.42)	(5.76)
Locations					
USA	0.24	0.72**	0.37*	0.12	0.08
	(0.76)	(2.27)	(1.72)	(0.44)	(0.21)
Japan	–0.04	0.13	–0.29	–0.02	0.17
	(0.07)	(0.22)	(0.72)	(0.04)	(0.25)
EC	0.32	0.63*	0.43*	–0.07	0.14
	(0.99)	(1.93)	(1.93)	(0.24)	(0.36)
UK	0.02	0.45	0.66***	0.08	–0.21
	(0.07)	(1.41)	(3.10)	(0.28)	(0.58)
Canada	1.26**	1.02*	0.73**	0.02	0.15
	(2.42)	(1.93)	(2.02)	(0.05)	(0.24)
Other Europe	–0.06	–0.09	0.29	–0.63	–0.51
	(0.15)	(0.22)	(1.01)	(1.54)	(0.95)
Ownership					
USA	–0.35	0.27	–0.24	0.36	0.12
	(1.46)	(1.12)	(1.47)	(1.58)	(0.42)
Japan	–0.24	–0.55	–0.11	–0.26	–0.37
	(0.60)	(1.38)	(0.42)	(0.73)	(0.80)
EC	–0.31	–0.11	–0.27*	0.39*	0.06
	(1.40)	(0.49)	(1.73)	(1.83)	(0.22)
UK	–0.40*	0.08	0.07	0.32	0.37
	(1.74)	(0.34)	(0.44)	(1.49)	(1.36)
Scandinavia	–0.68	–1.08**	–0.14	0.56	–0.68
	(1.50)	(2.36)	(0.43)	(1.36)	(1.27)
Canada	–0.47	0.30	–0.07	1.22***	–0.22
	(1.02)	(0.63)	(0.23)	(2.90)	(0.40)
Industry					
Pharmaceuticals	0.52**	–0.83***	–0.26*	0.18	–0.69***
	(2.51)	(3.82)	(1.83)	(0.95)	(2.81)
Office equipment	0.05	–0.68**	0.01	–0.11	–0.91**
	(0.18)	(2.26)	(0.04)	(0.40)	(2.49)
Motor vehicles	0.12	–0.59	–0.01	0.16	0.56
	(0.32)	(1.46)	(0.03)	(0.47)	(1.22)
Professional and scientific equipment	0.62	0.34	–0.60	–0.59	0.65
	(1.17)	(0.63)	(1.64)	(1.23)	(1.03)
Chemicals, etc.	0.17	–0.41**	0.06	0.56***	–0.24
	(0.93)	(2.12)	(0.48)	(3.27)	(1.08)
Engineering	0.09	–0.70***	–0.12	0.44**	–0.10
	(0.23)	(2.90)	(0.79)	(2.09)	(0.37)
F-location	1.80	2.02*	2.55**	0.89	0.74
F-ownership	0.77	1.84*	1.38	2.19**	1.09
F-industry	1.43	3.25***	1.68	3.05***	3.22***

Dependent variable	*Basic research*	*Product development*	*Process development*	*Diversification*	*Technical support*
F-total	1.37	2.83***	1.89**	2.39***	1.84**
Number of observations	131	126	131	126	131
R^2	0.18	0.32	0.23	0.29	0.23
Mean	1.80	2.30	2.77	2.32	2.14

*** significant at 1 per cent level.
** significant at 5 per cent level.
* significant at 10 per cent level.

suppressed because in almost all cases they are simply an average of those pertaining to product development or process development on the one hand, and technical support on the other.

The results indicate that the conduct of basic research is a minority interest so far as the overseas respondents are concerned. The sample mean of 1.80 is below the mid-point of the measurement scale; indeed, this figure is the lowest of the five mean responses shown in the table. None of the three major R & D centres – USA, Japan and EC – is significantly oriented to basic R & D carried out by foreign firms, compared to the Rest of the world control group. This is because the control group is responsible for quite a lot of overseas basic research, much of it in Australia. Only Canada has a significant bias towards foreign-owned basic research. Canadian firms themselves, on the other hand, are less inclined than the control group to carry out their basic research overseas. The importance of basic research in Canada seems to be mainly a consequence of US firms taking advantage of tax incentives to Canadian affiliates.

Amongst the industries, pharmaceuticals is notable for its emphasis on basic research. The results show that this emphasis on overseas basic research is coupled with a significant bias against overseas research in product and process development and technical support. The sample means show that overseas product and process development are much more common, but although pharmaceutical firms carry out such activities overseas they do so to a significantly lesser extent than firms in the control group.

Both the USA and EC are biased towards product and process development, whilst the UK is biased towards process development only. Canada is biased towards product and process development as well as basic research, which leads to an impressive overall performance in terms of foreign-owned R & D.

So far as ownership is concerned, UK firms are biased against conducting basic research overseas. Scandinavian firms are biased against carrying out product development overseas, the EC firms against overseas process development.

Office equipment, like pharmaceuticals, is biased against overseas product development and overseas technical support. Chemicals and engineering are also biased against overseas product development. Overall, it is interesting that the propensity to undertake product development overseas is lower than the propensity to undertake new process development. When product development is undertaken overseas, there is a strong tendency for it to be based in North America. Access to a large market seems to be an important factor here. The results are also compatible with the view that product development is a more secret and sensitive area than process development, and is consequently carried out closer to home.

Location and ownership effects are totally insignificant in respect of technical support. This is perhaps not surprising, given that technical support activities tend to be based close to production sites, but have few other strategic implications.

In process industries, such as chemicals, there is a strong propensity for overseas R & D to be concerned with diversification. Such diversification may simply reflect the derivation of new products within an existing area of competence. Research in process industries tends to be geared to exploiting the potential of a particular type of raw material, although if supplies are approaching exhaustion it may be geared to the discovery of substitutes as well. The link between raw materials and diversification is corroborated by the importance of Canadian ownership in diversification (Canadian multinationals are well known for their technological leadership in the resources sector: see Rugman, 1987).

It is, however, difficult to explain why engineering research and EC-ownership should promote diversification as well. A more general explanation is that diversification is a major motive in mature industries using well-proven technologies – such as chemicals and engineering – and in countries such as Canada and the EC where mature industries tend to dominate.

6.7 LOCATION FACTORS

It is possible to analyse the attractiveness of locations by examining how responses to questions about the importance of environmental factors vary between locations. R & D managers were asked to rate on a scale from one (irrelevant) to three (a major factor) the following influences on the development of the laboratory:

(a) a distinctive local scientific, educational or technological tradition conducive to certain types of research project;
(b) the presence of a helpful local scientific environment and adequate technological infrastructure;
(c) the availability of research professionals;
(d) favourable wage rates for research professionals.

The results in Table 6.6 are somewhat surprising. To begin with, no location emerges as particularly favourable. Canada scores highly on the availability of research professionals, as do Switzerland and Austria to a slightly lesser extent. The USA comes out as a somewhat unhelpful environment (an explanation for this is suggested in section 6.10).

One way to interpret these results is in terms of a 'selection and survival' principle. Firms differ in their requirements according to the nature of the research they do. Firms that do not perceive a location to be attractive will not go there, and if they find later that they have made a mistake then they will leave. Most of the firms found at a given location at a given time will therefore be the ones that find the conditions tolerable there. But, equally, it seems that few firms find their locations ideal: some are just no worse than the alternatives.

The influence of the nature of the research on the evaluation of a location can be discerned from the industry-specific factors. Thus pharmaceuticals – which is more heavily oriented to basic research than most – is the only industry to attach greater weight than the control group to all the characteristics identified in the table. Professional and scientific equipment, and chemicals, also weight local traditions and the availability of research professionals higher than the control group. This suggests that it may not be basic research *per se* which makes these factors important, but rather the demand for highly specialised professionals such as chemists, biochemists and electronic engineers. The important thing in these industries, it may be suggested, is not so much the general scientific background of researchers but the existence of highly specific competences produced by a high level of specialisation in education and training.

It is interesting to note that the wages of research professionals are of much less concern than their availability. This suggests that in many locations the wages of scientists may be low relative to market

TABLE 6.6 *Location/ownership and industry factors influencing the importance of environment to the overseas laboratory*

Dependent variable	*Local traditions*	*Helpful environment*	*Availability of professionals*	*Diversification*
Intercept	1.96***	2.15***	1.53***	1.58***
	(5.05)	(6.04)	(4.25)	(5.42)
Locations/ownership				
USA	–0.22	–0.58*	0.30	0.01
	(0.62)	(1.77)	(0.90)	(0.03)
Japan	0.09	–0.08	0.57	–0.78
	(0.13)	(0.14)	(0.93)	(1.58)
EC	–0.28	–0.51	0.21	–0.20
	(0.76)	(1.51)	(0.62)	(0.73)
UK	–0.10	–0.38	0.50	0.29
	(0.29)	(1.17)	(1.55)	(1.10)
Canada	–0.15	0.52	1.46***	0.60
	(0.26)	(0.94)	(2.63)	(1.35)
Other Europe	–0.21	–0.28	0.85*	–0.08
	(0.43)	(0.64)	(1.93)	(0.23)
Ownership				
USA	–0.50*	–0.48*	–0.29	–0.39
	(1.85)	(1.94)	(1.19)	(1.95)
Japan	–0.56	–0.35	–0.80*	–0.47
	(1.25)	(0.85)	(1.93)	(1.39)
EC	–0.38	0.02	–0.29	–0.59 ***
	(1.52)	(0.08)	(1.27)	(3.16)
UK	–0.41	–0.33	–0.32	–0.20
	(1.58)	(1.40)	(1.32)	(1.03)
Scandinavia	–0.34	–0.47	–0.71	–0.74*
	(0.66)	(0.99)	(1.48)	(1.93)
Canada	–0.48	–0.38	–0.04	–0.11
	(0.92)	(0.78)	(0.07)	(0.27)
Industry				
Pharmaceuticals	0.66***	0.59***	0.56**	0.30*
	(2.72)	(2.71)	(2.56)	(1.72)
Office equipment	0.53	0.21	–0.04	–0.18
	(1.45)	(0.64)	(0.11)	(0.69)
Motor vehicles	–0.34	–0.13	0.20	0.69**
	(0.76)	(0.34)	(0.52)	(2.28)
Professional and	1.09*	1.01*	1.52***	0.17
scientific equipment	(1.80)	(1.81)	(2.70)	(0.38)
Chemicals, etc.	0.43*	0.22	0.52**	0.19
	(1.95)	(1.14)	(2.60)	(1.18)
Engineering	0.40	0.34	0.33	0.24
	(1.47)	(1.40)	(1.34)	(1.22)
F-location	0.21	1.42	1.93*	2.29**
F-ownership	0.75	1.29	0.97	2.21**
F-industry	2.17*	1.92*	2.57**	1.46

Dependent variable	*Local traditions*	*Helpful environment*	*Availability of professionals*	*Diversification*
F-total	1.25	1.66*	1.68*	1.58*
Number of observations	124	131	131	130
R^2	0.18	0.21	0.21	0.20
Mean	1.78	1.73	1.99	1.44

*** significant at 1 per cent level.
** significant at 5 per cent level.
* significant at 10 per cent level.

levels and that shortage problems therefore persist because wages are not raised to encourage additional supply. In a well-functioning market wages would be perceived as more of a constraint than availability because availability problems would be solved by raising the wage. The relatively low wage offered to scientists in certain countries may reflect a culturally-specific view that scientists should be paid less than managers, irrespective of their professional competence and the scarcity of supply. Such cultural influences are considered further in section 6.11.

The emphasis on availability rather than the wage is also consistent with the view that it is the availability of highly specialised personnel that is the problem, and that in the short run firms cannot find such personnel at any price. In this case market imperfection arises from the 'thinness' of the market (that is, from the small number of participants involved).

6.8 THE ORGANISATION OF INTERNATIONAL R & D

One of the major questions raised by the internationalisation of R & D is how overseas laboratories are coordinated with the rest of the group. To examine this issue, respondents were asked to classify their laboratory as a *support laboratory*, promoting the efficient local assimilation of current technology through links with indigenous marketing and production; or as a *locally integrated laboratory*, enjoying some autonomy in product and process development (such a laboratory may hold a world product mandate, endowing it with the responsibility for deriving, producing and marketing a distinctive product for a global, or at least a large regional, market); or as an *internationally integrated laboratory* participating in a general programme of research involving other laboratories; such a laboratory will be linked more closely into the general research programme than it is into the production and marketing activities in the country in which it is located.

The results in Table 6.7 show that it is industry and not location or ownership which is the major influence on the organisation of international R & D. Industries such as pharmaceuticals and office equipment, which involve significant basic research, are disposed to international integration. So too is chemicals which, as noted earlier, is prominent in diversification-oriented research. It is also clear that industries which are disposed to international integration are biased against local integration.

While many laboratories undertake local support of some kind, relatively few respondents classified their laboratories as being primarily of this type. Local support seems to be a fairly ubiquitous activity, in the sense that there are no significant location or ownership differences in the incidence of support laboratories and indeed, even amongst industries, it is only the pharmaceutical industry that is significantly biased against activity of this type. In other words, it is the trade-off between international integration and local integration, rather than between international integration and support, that is crucial for the organisation of R & D.

The only significant location effect relates to the USA. Laboratories in the USA, as well as overseas laboratories owned by US firms, are less likely than others to belong to an internationally interdependent network. This is consistent with other results, which suggest that the internationalisation of R & D is relatively less advanced amongst US firms, and that foreign-owned laboratories in the USA operate in a relatively autonomous manner (Cantwell, 1991; Casson, Pearce and Singh, 1991). It may be that US laboratories like to dominate other laboratories in the group; parent laboratories can do so by formal subordination of overseas laboratories, whilst foreign-owned laboratories in the USA react against foreign ownership by cultivating a high degree of independence.

Another possible explanation of the lack of international integration in US laboratories is that they are geared mainly to product development. It may be that laboratories geared instead to basic research or to diversification lend themselves more to interdependence and that overseas laboratories of this kind are less common in the USA, or within US firms.

TABLE 6.7 *Patterns in the type of overseas laboratory*

Dependent variable	*Internationally interdependent*	*Locally integrated*	*Support*
Intercept	2.00***	2.52***	1.84***
	(4.97)	(4.29)	(5.64)
Locations/ownership			
USA	–0.62*	0.17	0.03
	(1.68)	(0.52)	(0.10)
Japan	0.03	0.39	0.12
	(0.05)	(0.68)	(0.19)
EC	–0.12	–0.03	–0.34
	(0.31)	(0.07)	(0.92)
UK	0.08	–0.17	0.09
	(0.23)	(0.54)	(0.25)
Canada	0.09	–0.27	–0.42
	(0.13)	(0.46)	(0.66)
Other Europe	0.09	–0.45	0.83
	(0.16)	(0.94)	(1.68)
Ownership			
USA	–0.30*	0.24	–0.18
	(1.72)	(0.94)	(0.63)
Japan	0.67	0.32	–0.22
	(1.30)	(0.72)	(0.50)
EC	0.09	–0.06	–0.04
	(0.36)	(0.26)	(0.14)
UK	–0.26	0.23	0.01
	(0.93)	(0.95)	(0.03)
Scandinavia	0.16	0.45	0.30
	(0.30)	(0.97)	(0.61)
Canada	0.15	0.46	–0.24
	(0.27)	(0.99)	(0.48)
Industry			
Pharmaceuticals	1.09***	–1.02 ***	–0.46**
	(4.42)	(4.75)	(2.00)
Office equipment	0.84**	–0.97 ***	–0.48
	(2.41)	(3.26)	(1.48)
Motor vehicles	0.27	–0.18	–0.56
	(0.60)	(0.45)	(1.34)
Professional and scientific equipment	0.96	–0.67	0.25
	(1.56)	(1.27)	(0.32)
Chemicals, etc.	0.65***	–0.65***	0.17
	(2.93)	(3.29)	(0.82)

continued on page 192

TABLE 6.7 *continued*

Dependent variable	*Internationally interdependent*	*Locally integrated*	*Support*
Engineering	0.18 (0.66)	–0.35 (1.46)	0.24 (0.93)
F-location	1.35	0.64	1.02
F-ownership	1.48	1.12	0.23
F-industry	4.20***	4.76**	2.66**
F-total	0.31***	2.29***	1.51
Number of observations	124	119	121
R^2	0.31	0.29	0.21
Mean	2.10	2.05	1.80

*** significant at 1 per cent level.
** significant at 5 per cent level.
* significant at 10 per cent level.

6.9 PATENTING OF INVENTIONS FROM OVERSEAS LABORATORIES

One way of measuring the output of R & D is by the number of patents granted. In cooperation with our colleague John Cantwell and researchers at the Science Policy Research Unit, University of Sussex, it was possible to establish the proportion of a firm's patents granted in the USA that are attributable to research in its overseas laboratories. The limitations of patents as a means for assessing research performance are well known, and these difficulties are compounded in the present instance by the fact that the US Patent Office is 'home ground' to US MNEs, who are therefore likely to register with them relatively trivial inventions that firms would not normally patent outside their home country. While this undermines strict comparability between US and non-US firms, it should not affect comparability between different non-US nationalities, however.

It is reasonable to suppose that firms with extensive overseas production activities are more likely than others to undertake overseas R & D, if only because of their need to adapt products and processes to local markets and local operating conditions. Production experience may also provide a spin-off in identifying sources of cheap scientific labour which can be used in more basic R & D. Data on the proportion of production undertaken overseas is available from a separate data base (Dunning and Pearce, 1985). It was possible to match up the proportion of a firm's US patents originating from overseas laboratories (the overseas patenting ratio) for 1981–3 with the proportion of the firm's world-wide production accounted for by overseas plants (the overseas production ratio) for 1982, for 478 of the firms in the consolidated sample. The same exercise also generated a measure of the overall size of the firm: the logarithm of world-wide sales, 1982.

Table 6.8 shows that when controlling for size of firm, industry and the nationality of the firm, the overseas production ratio does indeed have the expected impact on overseas patenting activity. It also shows that size of firm, as measured by the logarithm of sales, has a negative impact on overseas patenting. This result is surprising as theory suggests that, if anything, the international division of labour in R & D should expand as the size of firm increases, and that as a result overseas patenting would increase with size. It cannot be explained by the fact that US firms are larger than non-US firms and have a bias to patenting their domestic inventions because this effect, though significant, is captured by the US dummy variable. One possible explanation is that the very largest firms operate such a strongly interdependent network of laboratories that it is difficult for them to impute a patent to any specific laboratory, so that patents are attributed by default to the parent laboratory instead.

The coefficients of the industry dummy variables seem to support this interpretation. For example, both the food and drink and the pharmaceutical industries involve quite considerable overseas R & D, but nevertheless the overseas patenting ratio is significantly higher in food and drink than in pharmaceuticals (when other factors are controlled for). This may be because the kind of adaptive work that dominates food and drink research is easily identified as belonging to the overseas subsidiary, whereas the more basic research undertaken by subsidiaries in the pharmaceutical industry is a small part of a long-term project coordinated by the parent laboratory.

The overseas patenting ratio and the overseas production ratio can be considered as potential *firm-specific* influences on global R & D strategies. It is particularly interesting to know whether the parent firm's perception of the general rationale for overseas R & D varies with the degree of internationalisation of the firm. This issue was examined by comparing the importance that parent respondents attached to the following influences on R & D location strategy:

TABLE 6.8 *Regression analysis of overseas patenting ratio using industry and country dummies*

Constant	46.36***
	(5.00)
Overseas production ratio	0.61***
	(11.90)
Logarithm of sales	–2.89***
	(2.60)
Industry dummies	
Food, drink and tobacco	5.89*
	(1.77)
Paper	3.06
	(0.87)
Rubber	3.74
	(0.91)
Chemicals	2.04
	(0.60)
Coal and petroleum	8.01**
	(2.19)
Mechanical and electrical engineering	0.33
	(0.74)
Scientific and professional equipment	–7.15
	(0.73)
Motor vehicles	–3.34
	(0.80)
Office equipment	–3.50
	(0.61)
Pharmaceuticals	–8.78**
	(2.08)
Country dummies	
USA	–30.99***
	(7.91)
UK	–7.94*
	(1.79)
Europe	–17.73***
	(4.20)
Japan	–25.91***
	(5.66)

*** Significant at 1 per cent level.
** Significant at 5 per cent level.
* Significant at 10 per cent level.

NOTE: $N = 478$; $R^2 = 0.48$; $\bar{R}^2 = 0.46$; $F = 26.94$***

(a) a local tradition of research excellence in certain overseas centres;
(b) the availability of low-cost specialist labour in overseas centres;
(c) the question of scale economies, and the possibility of researching using many small laboratories rather than a single large one;
(d) the importance of adapting products to the local market;
(e) the importance of adapting technology to the local market.

These responses were related to the following firm-specific factors:

(a) the overseas patenting ratio;
(b) the overseas production ratio;
(c) the logarithm of total sales;
(d) the parent's R & D expenditure per unit sales.

The last of these factors is used to proxy the firm's overall commitment to research.

Unfortunately, the need to pool data from three separate sources – the patent data base, the production data base and the questionnaire data base – reduced the number of parent firms that could be studied from 163 in the full sample to only 45. This is because most firms had at least one relevant missing observation.

It is perhaps not surprising, therefore, that the results reported in Table 6.9 are rather disappointing. It seems that the overall internationalisation of R & D, as reflected in either patenting or production, does not significantly affect the parent firm's view of the strategic factors involved in decentralising R & D; neither does the size of firm have any significant effect.

The most interesting results concern the influence of the commitment to research, as measured by the R & D/sales ratio. While large firms are not significantly more disposed than others to regard scale economies as either promoting or inhibiting the gains from decentralisation of research, they are more disposed to attach weight to the tradition of excellence in the choice of overseas location, and less inclined to see that location as simply a place in which to carry out adaptive research. This suggests that the firm's perception of global R & D strategy is a reflection more of its commitment to research than to the internationalisation of its production and marketing operations. At the firm level, it seems, R & D strategy in the most committed firms is to some extent separable from production and marketing strategies, although, of course, at the industry level the

TABLE 6.9 *Regression analysis of factors in the location of parent laboratory*

	Local tradition	*Cost*	*Scale labs*	*Adapt product*	*Adapt technology*
Constant	0.49	2.50***	1.42	1.71*	2.87***
	(0.69)	(3.02)	(1.21)	(1.87)	(3.08)
Overseas patenting ratio	0.00	0.01	0.01	0.00	–0.00
	(0.86)	(0.93)	(0.92)	(0.46)	(0.45)
Overseas production ratio	–0.00	0.00	0.00	–0.00	–0.01
	(0.04)	(0.41)	(0.23)	(0.23)	(0.79)
Logarithm of sales	0.09	–0.08	0.06	0.11	–0.04
	(1.13)	(0.86)	(0.43)	(1.06)	(0.37)
R & D expenditure/sales	0.11***	–0.03	–0.03	–0.04	–0.08*
	(3.53)	(0.88)	(0.58)	(1.02)	(1.98)
N	45	45	45	45	45
R^2	0.25	0.11	0.04	0.07	0.95
F	3.47**	1.25	0.47	0.77	1.07

*** Significant at 1 per cent level.
** Significant at 5 per cent level.
** Significant at 10 per cent level.

nature of the product and the structure of global competition will impact on all these strategies simultaneously.

6.10 THE POLICY ENVIRONMENT

This section discusses managerial perceptions of the host-country policy environment, based upon answers to open-ended questions about anticipated changes in the direction of research. Only a minority of respondents bothered to answer these questions, and clearly some of the responses were designed to persuade rather than inform. However, most of those who did respond were very emphatic about their views. Moreover, these views were broadly consistent with those expressed during interviews (see section 6.3), although it cannot, of course, be claimed that these views are necessarily representative of R & D managers as a whole.

Headquarters respondents had relatively little to say about government policy, perhaps because their concerns were global rather than national, or perhaps because they were simply out of touch with the frustrations of managing a foreign-owned subsidiary in an alien environment. Subsidiary respondents, on the other hand, had quite a lot to say. Their views are summarised in Table 6.10.

TABLE 6.10 *Changes in government policy desired by foreign subsidiary respondents*

	Location of laboratory				
	Total	*UK*	*USA*	*Europe*	*Other*
REDUCED REGULATION					
General reduction	6	0	5	1	0
Faster decision-making	3	2	0	1	0
In social matters: relax reporting requirements in					
Product safety and pre-market testing	3	0	2	0	1
Occupational safety	2	0	2	0	0
Animal experiments	2	1	0	0	1
Environment	3	0	1	1	1
In industrial policy					
Fewer anti-trust restrictions on collaborative R & D	1	0	1	0	0
Less pressure for global mandating of subsidiaries	1	0	0	0	1
Less restriction on commercialisation of spin-offs from government funded R & D	1	0	1	0	0
Less restriction on export of key technologies	2	0	2	0	0
In marketing policy					
More flexibility over pricing	1	0	0	1	0
Abolish 'limited list' for prescriptions	2	2	0	0	0
IMPROVEMENT OF EDUCATION AND SCIENCE BASE					
Increased support for university centres of excellence	3	2	0	0	1
More joint fellowships, studentships, etc.	3	2	0	0	1
More science graduates	2	2	0	0	0
Improve social status of engineering	1	1	0	0	0
IMPROVED LABOUR MOBILITY THROUGH EASIER IMMIGRATION OF RESEARCH PROFESSIONALS	2	0	1	1	0

SOURCE: Questionnaire.

The popular view of the USA as a deregulated economy takes a sharp knock. Foreign investors complain about the amount of form-filling involved in US operations, particularly in dealing with social matters. It is the Federal agencies which are most to blame. The

Food and Drug Administration, for example, is considered unnecessarily stringent in its requirements for pre-market testing. The cost of drug trials, for example, can be up to ten times the cost of drug discovery and development. 'Learning by doing' in the application of new drugs in the USA is inhibited by the 'drug lag' (Parker, 1989). Bureaucratic demands absorb resources that could better be employed elsewhere. Occupational safety reporting requirements are also perceived as relatively stringent in the USA.

Industrial policy too is problematic in the USA. Anti-trust measures arc claimed to deter cooperative R & D with other firms. The commercialisation of spin-off from government contracts is unduly inhibited, it is claimed; enforced delays in patenting inventions, and restrictions on the intrafirm export of technology should be eliminated.

Both Switzerland and the USA are perceived as inflexible over the immigration of foreign research workers.

The UK is believed by some to have a too-strict policy on animal experiments but is perceived as fairly liberal over environmental issues. (Whether this policy stance is regarded as satisfactory or problematic will not be considered here.)

Two pharmaceutical subsidiaries in the UK expressed concern about the 'limited list': the reduction in the number of proprietary medicines which doctors are able to prescribe to National Health Service patients, and the consequent switch of government-funded demand to generic products. A related concern over pricing restrictions was expressed by a pharmaceutical subsidiary in Belgium.

Managers of subsidiaries expressed concern over the future of the education system in the UK, and the erosion of the science base. It is worth noting that no complaints of similar nature were made in the USA or elsewhere in Europe. Two firms called for increased support for university centres of excellence, and two for more joint university–industry research posts. There was also a call for increased output of graduate scientists and an improvement in the social status of engineers (from a firm in the office equipment industry).

Strong views were also expressed on funding issues. As might be expected, respondents were generally in favour of more government funding for R & D, though there were differences of opinion as to how this should be done. There was a widespread view – particularly in continental Europe – that governments should increase their funding for fundamental and high-risk research in the corporate sector. This would effectively subsidise long-term projects whose returns were difficult to quantify. The precise rationale for this view was not clear, however. It could reflect a belief that private returns from such projects are difficult to appropriate compared to the social benefits conferred (an externality argument), or that the government's obligation to future generations implied a lower rate of discount than management's obligations to its shareholders.

Some respondents sought more funding for corporate research of all kinds, whilst others suggested that existing schemes to promote cooperative research (within the EC, for example) should be expanded. On the other hand, one UK respondent claimed that government discrimination in favour of cooperative research meant that his laboratory could no longer use government funding because of the threat to secrecy.

Several US-based laboratories favoured an expansion of Federal projects put out to competitive bidding. Another respondent complained, however, that such projects were always awarded to 'Beltway Bandits' (politically-networked firms that specialised in winning contracts but had no coherent research strategy of their own). This sceptical view was shared by several interviewees, who were adamant that governments were very poor judges of the kind of fundamental research that needed to be done. Instead of special projects, they favoured general incentives such as tax credits.

Tax credits on R & D expenditure seem very popular; they are a familiar fiscal instrument which subsidises R & D but leaves the corporation free to decide what research to do. Foreign subsidiaries in Australia seemed very impressed with the commonwealth government's use of tax credits (though they were less impressed by the tight environmental restrictions imposed by some state legislatures). If the case for R & D subsidiaries is accepted by government, then tax credits seem to provide a simple and acceptable mechanism for implementing them.

6.11 CULTURE AND COMPETITIVENESS

The overall competitiveness of Western economies has aroused a good deal of controversy. Much of this has centred on the mismatch between productivity and real wages in the manufacturing sector as a cause of deindustrialisation. A deindustrialised economy can, however, still be a wealthy one if there is a buoyant service sector, and if there are substantial profit remittances from abroad, and R & D can contribute in both of these respects.

The UK service sector appears, in general, to be more competitive than its manufacturing counterpart; statistics on exports of tourism and financial services certainly support this view. One reason may be a relatively low incidence of labour–management conflict, as reflected in strikes, for example. R & D, too, is generally immune from industrial relations problems, even though craft technicians are quite widely employed. Concentration of employment on R & D can therefore be seen as part of a general strategy of strengthening an existing UK comparative advantage in service activity.

The availability of research professionals is a strong point in the UK's favour. A traditional strength of the UK educational system is in the training of specialists, in contrast to the USA, where a more general training is provided at school and undergraduate level. Foreign firms have not been slow to exploit the abundance of specialist researchers. In the photographic industry, for example, four major foreign MNEs successfully carry out research in the UK even though there has never been any major UK competition in this field. A somewhat similar story could be told in other high-technology industries. Under these conditions it is difficult to sustain the argument that foreign firms 'crowd out' UK firms in the scientific labour market. It seems most likely, indeed, that as the major employers, the foreign firms are responsible for maintaining job opportunities in many specialised disciplines.

The real issue is why UK firms perform so badly in the high-technology field. This is true not only of their domestic operations but also of their international operations. Patent statistics show that the main areas of UK corporate strength are in low-technology industries such as food, drink and tobacco, construction equipment and textiles. They are also successful in services: banking, hotels, retailing and so on.

The strongest UK manufacturing industries are, in any case, industries in which patent origination is highly dispersed, so that the UK has done no more than maintain its position amongst the leading countries. In industries where the pattern of patent origination has shown greatest mobility in recent years – such as industrial engines, motor vehicles and nuclear power – the strongest UK firms of 20 years ago have invariably lost out (Cantwell, 1991). In industrial engines and motor vehicles they have lost out to Japan. This is, perhaps, excusable on the grounds that others too have lost out (West Germany, for example, has even lost out to Japan in other key sectors such as office equipment). In nuclear power, however, the UK has lost out to France and Germany as well as Japan.

Even in low-technology industries there is a question mark about the overall efficiency of research. Although UK firms are highly internationalised in their research, this does not seem to imply any great degree of sophistication. It certainly cannot be claimed, on the basis of UK experience, that the globalisation of R & D is *ipso facto* a successful strategy that can be recommended to other firms. The high degree of UK internationalisation is not the result of any special plans that will weaken the UK research base, either. Rather, it seems to be a consequence of the nature of the industries in which UK MNEs operate. Food, drink and tobacco, for example, require considerable adaptive R & D to match technology and products to quality of local inputs and to local consumer tastes, and this is best carried out on the spot in an overseas laboratory.

This heavy involvement in adaptive R & D may also explain why UK firms have been relatively slow to network their international laboratories. UK firms are more disposed than most to maintain the traditional distinction between the headquarters and the subsidiary laboratories. Networking, by contrast, is most often found in high-technology industries where the basic research, once done only by the parent laboratory, has been decentralised. It is this kind of decentralisation that partly accounts for the presence of so many foreign-owned laboratories in the UK. Thus laboratories based in the UK are often networked – reducing the hierarchical dominance of the parent – even though UK laboratories overseas are not.

Further evidence on UK backwardness is that UK-owned firms report higher turnover rates amongst their scientific personnel, which is usually taken as an indication of poor management. One reason for this, suggested by the interviews, is the limited career prospects for scientists in UK firms. Table 6.11 shows that UK firms paid less than their foreign rivals within the UK in 1981 (the last date for which directly comparable data are available).

Part of the explanation may be a cultural one. Some of the laboratory managers we interviewed felt that the boardroom regarded science as a vocation, and expected the scientists who were employed to be biased towards pure research. The attitude was that people who were interested in pay would instead choose management as a career, or at any rate join the firm as a scientist and convert from the laboratory bench to the management ladder later on.

TABLE 6.11 *Average wages and salaries of R & D employees in UK manufacturing industry, 1981*

Industry	*Foreign firms* £	*All firms* £
All products	10 115	8 429
Chemicals	9 956	9 942
Mechanical engineering	9 389	8 195
Electrical engineering (including electronics)	10 539	7 023
Vehicles (including aerospace)	9 218	9 220
Other products	11 228	9 083

SOURCE: Pearce (1987), Table 8, derived from *Business Monitor M014* (1981), Table 16.

There is independent evidence (CEST, 1990) to suggest that UK employers believe that UK scientists are underpaid by European (let alone US) standards and expect to have to raise salaries after 1992, to combat greater mobility; but apparently, while they complain about skill shortages, they are not prepared to raise salaries in the short run.

Cultural attitudes may be of wider significance than scientific pay. The status of engineers is also an important issue. A study of engineering and management in West German firms found not only that engineering graduates enjoy relatively higher status than in the UK (Lawrence, 1980; Hutton and Lawrence, 1981) but they are also more pervasive in senior management positions. Line managers in Germany typically have more specialised engineering expertise than their UK counterparts, and hence have less need to rely on 'back-room specialists' for advice. When experts are employed in specialist roles – notably in industrial design – their influence is much wider than in Britain because the managers they report to share their professional allegiance and value their expertise.

Two major waves of German scientific emigration – before each of the two world wars – transmitted some of these cultural values to the USA. It is not surprising, therefore, that a comparison of interview experiences in UK- and US-owned laboratories suggests that in US firms technology is much more a part of the general business culture. It was in North America that we met the president of a company rather than the R & D manager because the president considered himself the executive in charge of R & D. Senior management in his company was dominated by engineers, who sold the products to other engineers who managed procurement in the client companies. Other evidence suggests that this engineering culture is fairly common amongst US, German and Scandinavian parent firms. We encountered no instance of it in parent firms in the UK.

It may be conjectured that UK firms suffer from a social division between arts and science specialists, in which the former dominate general management and the latter R & D. This suggests that UK firms in marketing-oriented industries and in the service sector may be more successful because there is greater cultural homogeneity within the management team, centred on an arts-based education. Conversely, US, Japanese and German firms may be more successful in high-technology industries because in these firms the technological culture pervades almost the whole of the management.

6.12 CONCLUSIONS

This chapter has examined a wide range of issues relating to the internationalisation of R & D. It is claimed that these are the key issues from the standpoints of both economic theory and the practical problems encountered by managers. Internationally integrated corporate R & D networks are most advanced in high-technology industries where an 'intellectual division of labour' allows research which is relatively remote from the market to be distributed to smaller overseas laboratories where abundant supplies of scientific specialists are available. It is much less advanced in low-technology industries, where overseas research is on a more limited scale and is focused on near-market research geared to local conditions.

In low-technology industries overseas research laboratories are much more subordinated to the headquarters laboratory than is the case in high-technology industries. So far there has been little systematic attempt to pool specific knowledge garnered from adaptive research in different local environments. The recent drive to develop globally acceptable consumer products has so far had relatively little impact, it would seem, on the organisation of international R & D. Consumer product development still seems to be driven by the pull of the major market. In most industries this means that product development is pulled to the USA, although pharmaceuticals is an important exception because of the high degree of Federal regulation of the innovation process in the USA. The pull of the US market may well diminish if the Japanese market becomes more accessible, and if

European integration not only reduces internal barriers to trade but promotes cultural homogeneity in consumer tastes as well. Within Europe, Germany looks increasingly attractive as a geocentric location with a large high-income market, although the UK has traditionally been an important centre in which to adapt foreign products to the European market. The UK's advantage in terms of the use of the English language, good communications infrastructure, and availability of specialists seem to be declining relative to other European centres, however, as the rival centres improve English language teaching in schools and universities and invest in new transport and communications hubs. It remains to be seen whether some of these disadvantages can be offset by a stronger technological orientation in UK business culture, though it seems unlikely that this will occur.

7 Cultural Determinants of Corporate Excellence in an Integrated World Economy: The Impact of National Cultures on Organisational Performance

CHRISTOS S. NICOLAIDIS

7.1 INTRODUCTION

In modern business literature culture is identified as a source of distinct competitive advantage along with proprietary technology (Dunning, 1981) and superior business strategy (Porter, 1985). Culture – unlike proprietary technology and superior business strategy – is difficult for outsiders to understand and imitate, and so a cultural advantage is particularly useful in sustaining the long-run profitability of the firm (Casson, 1990, Chapter 4).

However, little systematic empirical work has been undertaken to explore the way culture creates a superior competitive advantage. Most empirical research has been directed towards testing the so-called 'culture-free' (Haire, Ghiselli and Porter, 1966; Hickson *et al.*, 1974, 1979; Child and Kieser, 1979) or 'convergence' (Cole, 1973; Form, 1979) hypothesis in comparative management rather than towards measuring specific cultural determinants of organisational performance across societal and national boundaries.

Empirical research has been hampered by the absence of a

comprehensive multidisciplinary theoretical framework relating managers' perceptions of strategic issues to their cultural predispositions on the one hand, and the outcomes of their actions on the other. The absence of this framework reflects the Western belief in man's ability objectively to control his environment and the consequent rejection of the idea of culturally-determined perceptions (Adler and Jelinek, 1986). On a more practical level, research into culture is hampered by the proliferation of legal, political and structural differences between countries which makes the isolation of purely cultural factors extremely difficult.

The present chapter contributes to the study of corporate culture in four main ways. On the theoretical side, it integrates concepts from the fields of economics and social psychology by synthesising elements of entrepreneurship theory and social cognition theory. The synthesis of the economic and behavioural perspectives contributes significantly to the discussion of the culture-free as opposed to the culture-specific argument, decisively favouring the latter.

On the empirical side, it combines questionnaire data on attitudes and beliefs (based on Likert-type attitudinal scales, which are well established in sociological research) with corporate accounting data (financial performance ratios) for stratified samples of closely-matched firms from two countries.

It also pioneers the use of Chow tests to test for the influence of nation-specific cultural characteristics on corporate performance. The Chow tests are applied to regressions which control for environmental factors such as industry sector, stage of industry development, size of firm, and other non-cultural firm-specific characteristics that may influence performance. In this way the study overcomes many of the methodological weaknesses of previous research.

Finally, because it considers culture at both the national and organisational levels, this chapter addresses head-on the question of the relative competitive advantages among different national cultures and their impact on national economic performance, an issue attracting great concern in current international business literature (Lodge and Vogel, 1987).

Section 7.2 distinguishes two distinct but related issues at the intersection of organisation theory and corporate culture. The first concerns the validity of the convergence hypothesis alluded to above, and the second the impact of corporate culture on corporate performance. Section 7.3 outlines a synthetic view on culture which integrates concepts from economic and behavioural theories in order to explain the impact of both national and organisational culture on corporate performance. It is argued that an appropriate corporate culture can both improve the quality of the firm's decision-making and economise on its internal transaction costs. This leads to the formulation of the main hypothesis: harmonising corporate culture with both nation- and industry-specific environmental factors motivates excellence in corporate performance. Section 7.4 explains the design of the research while sections 7.5 and 7.6 analyse and interpret the results. Conclusions, policy implications and the scope for further research are discussed in section 7.7.

7.2 CORPORATE CULTURE AND ORGANISATIONAL THEORY

The intersection of organisation theory and corporate culture is particularly evident in two fields: comparative management and theories of corporate excellence.

In comparative management, culture is normally considered to be an independent environmental factor which is specific to each country. The convergence hypothesis asserts that learning will lead intelligent people from different cultures to adopt the same efficient pattern of behaviour. Competitive market forces will eliminate those who resist convergence, so that only the convergent will survive. The speed of the selection process reflects underlying economic fundamentals such as scale economies in production and the pace of technological progress. Thus economic imperatives steadily mould industrial societies into a common pattern.

By contrast, the culture-specific argument claims that even if organisations located within different societies face similar economic problems and adopt similar formal structures, deep-rooted cultural forces passed through generations will still re-assert themselves in the way people actually behave and relate to each other. Hofstede (1980) compared organisational behaviour in 40 countries with respect to four cultural characteristics (uncertainty avoidance, power distance, individualism and masculinity), and found that the different national subsidiaries of the MNE he was studying were very different in cultural terms, despite similar task-environments, the same formal structures and a strong set of corporate values disseminated from headquarters. Similarly, Laurent (1983) found that the collective nationally-bounded perceptions of organisation held by managers in a sample of ten countries resisted convergence effects induced by the increased professionalism of management and the internationalisation of the firm.

Theories of corporate excellence assert that firms which have internal cultures that are supportive of their strategies are more likely to be successful (Schwartz and Davis, 1981). Unlike research in comparative management, which is systematic and empirically driven, research on corporate excellence is dominated by simple theories and casual anecdotal evidence. Corporate culture is regarded as a managerial tool which may be used to optimise performance (Ouchi, 1981; Pascale and Athos, 1981; Deal and Kennedy, 1982; Peters and Waterman, 1982; Wilkins and Ouchi, 1983). However, the claims of some writers that there is a unique and universal optimal culture cannot be substantiated with available evidence. The evidence in this chapter strongly supports the view that the optimal culture varies according to the specifics of the situation. It is the matching of cultural characteristics to non-cultural firm-specific and industry-specific characteristics that is the crucial determinant of performance.

7.3 CORPORATE CULTURE AND PERFORMANCE: A SYNTHETIC VIEW

The tension between these disparate approaches highlights the need for an integrated theoretical framework for the study of corporate culture (Nicolaidis, 1991). The framework should encompass both economic and behavioural perspectives, and consider culture at both the organisational and national levels.

The synthetic view is based on the premise that corporate culture may influence organisational performance by increasing both the *technical* and the *moral* efficiency of the group. Technical and moral efficiency sustain the long-term competitiveness of the firm by maintaining continuous innovation in technology and business strategy. Technical efficiency is associated with improved decision-making abilities (Casson, 1990). Moral efficiency is associated with minimisation of internal transaction costs by effective coordination of resources. Corporate culture can improve technical efficiency by establishing norms which foster members' problem-solving capabilities. Corporate culture also increases moral efficiency by manipulating individuals' preferences so as to cultivate an atmosphere of trust, shared commitment and cooperation directed towards specific goals. This economises on the costs of negotiating, monitoring and enforcing the exchanges between team members (Ouchi, 1980).

Within this synthetic view national culture influences corporate culture by providing the universal values and moral principles which condition organisation members' basic assumptions regarding the nature of the environment, and human nature itself (Schein, 1985). At the firm level, the entrepreneur's assumptions and behaviour provide the values which condition employees' specific goals. The entrepreneur's ability to manipulate goals stems from an apparent competence in making judgemental decisions in highly complex situations where the environment cannot be fully specified (Casson, 1990, Chapter 3). This view implies that skilful entrepreneurs can draw upon their national cultural characteristics to achieve competitive advantages through the synergy of national and corporate cultures. But while they can modify employees' specific goals, they cannot overturn the general values derived from national culture.

7.4 RESEARCH DESIGN

The Hypotheses

This study involves a comparison of UK and Greek companies. Within the previous literature UK companies have been singled out as decentralised enterprises (Graves, 1973; Child and Kieser, 1979), relying on formal roles with intergroup conflict, and high tolerance of dissonance (Laurent, 1983). Greek companies have been identified as having managers with little belief in subordinates' capacity for leadership, and as practising participative management (Haire, Ghiselli and Porter, 1966; Cummings and Schmidt, 1972).

In Hofstede's study the UK was classified as a highly individualistic country (score index 89) with low uncertainty avoidance (score 35) and power distance (score 35) characteristics. Greece was classified as being less individualistic (score 35) and having high uncertainty avoidance (score 112) and high power distance (score 60). These substantial differences were consistent with the different historical, social, religious, economic and political backgrounds of the two countries.

Using his theoretical framework, Hofstede inferred from his empirical results that in the UK organisations would display less centralisation and less structuring of activities, but would employ more generalists, have more flexible risk-taking managers, have more ambitious and primarily calculative employees, perceive people as pro-work in nature, tolerate dissonance and conflict, adopt policies which allow for individual initiative, and make promotions based on market value criteria. In Greece, organisations would demonstrate more centralised structures and higher structuring of activities, employ more specialists, have less ambitious and primarily morally involved employees, perceive people as anti-work in nature, be tolerant of dissonance and conflict, have task-oriented and risk-avoiding managers, adopt policies based on familism, loyalty and a sense of duty, and make promotions based on a seniority basis.

Though recent research has verified some of these differences, no research so far, to the best of our knowledge, has connected these cultural differences with organisational performance. The above propositions provide a suitable framework within which a comparative study of UK and Greek organisations can be undertaken. Two hypotheses are suggested.

1. Corporate cultures in small and medium-size enterprises should reflect the national differences identified by Hofstede. Differences in corporate culture should be reflected in management practices, too.
2. Within each country the firms which adopt managerial practices compatible with their national culture will be the best performers. Controlling for non-cultural industry-specific and firm-specific characteristics, national cultural characteristics will emerge as key determinants of corporate excellence.

Questionnaire Design and Administration

A 23-item questionnaire was administered to a sample of 300 British and 300 Greek companies during the summer of 1989. The companies were matched for size: the sample was stratified for small (up to £5 million turnover for the year 1987), medium (£5–£20 million turnover) and large (in excess of £20 million turnover) companies. The questionnaires were addressed to the chief executive officers (CEOs) of the companies because of their important role as culture creators.

In constructing the questionnaire a great deal of care was taken to avoid words, expressions or sentence construction that could not

TABLE 7.1 *Sectoral distribution of respondents*

Sector	*UK*	*Greece*	*Total*
Manufacturing	60	61	121
Retailing	13	25	38
Services	32	13	45
Total	105	99	204

communicate equivalent meanings in both languages. After translation from English to Greek the questionnaire was translated back to English, and discussed with a bilingual Greek economist working in Britain. The first three questions were purely factual questions about the nature of the firm's business. The next 18 questions concerned their cultural attitudes. They mainly involved Likert-type 1–5 opinion scales. The last two questions were open-ended questions about the mission of the firm and the CEO's assessment of the probable impact of the Single European Market on the firm's position. A copy of the questionnaire is reproduced in the appendix. The response rate was almost identical in both countries – 35 per cent in UK and 33 per cent in Greece – and an almost equal number of replies were received from each sample strata. Table 7.1 summarises the characteristics of the respondents.

Accounting data on each respondent for the period 1984–7 were obtained by desk research in both countries, and the return on total assets (RTA) and growth of sales (GSL) performance indicators calculated. RTA was chosen as an indicator of the overall performance, while GSL was selected as a more dynamic indicator reflecting attitudes towards change and improvement in competitiveness.

Questionnaire Items

Given the considerable overlap in the concepts used by various authors when discussing organisational culture, a review and consolidation was carried out which led to 18 dimensions grouped into five conceptual categories. The first category (addressed in questions 4 and 5) examines CEOs' perceptions of their environment. Question 4 examines how predictable respondents believe their environment to be and question 5 whether they believe the company is better or worse run than its competitors. It is argued that a perception of control over nature and confidence in relation to competitors can help firms to assimilate know-how and to be pro-active. Such confidence can also reinforce high norms and therefore increase performance.

The second conceptual category (questions 6–10), examines aspects of decision-making. Question 6 addresses attitudes towards traditional or scientific decision-making; question 7 examines the reliance on advanced quantitative techniques in assessing situations; question 8 examines the preference for improvised judgements over the use of old well-tried rules in new and complex situations; question 9 asks whether decisions are usually taken by individuals or by a committee; and question 10 investigates attitudes towards delegation.

At the one extreme of this category organisations may have a scientific decision-making system, where reliance on measurement is important in managing sophisticated logistical systems, where judgement and new experimental methods are welcomed and people are encouraged to take responsibility. At the other extreme companies can have a traditional decision-making system, based on the authority of the wise leader, the importance of qualitative factors – such as consideration for people's special interests – and where the implementation of well-tried methods is preferred in complex situations.

The third category (questions 11–14) examines the extent to which moral values are shared within the organisation. Questions in this category examine whether the relationship between members of the same rank in the organisation are based on concepts of group cooperation and group welfare, or individual initiative and personal welfare (question 11), whether recruitment favours personal or formal qualifications (question 12), what benefits employees derive from the organisation, in terms of stable income as opposed to challenging work and participation (question 13), and whether or not promotion is assessed on hard measures of personal performance (question 14).

Theory suggests that individualism encourages independent judgement while collectivism emphasises respect for the leader's opinion. Selective recruitment can help organisations to replicate or mutate themselves. Challenging work versus income stability reflects the CEO's view of whether people are pro-work or anti-work in nature, which will, in turn, influence the main motivation system employed in the firm. Hard assessment of performance indicates attitudes of distrust and low levels of integrity in the organisation. Soft assessment is associated with a trusting view that people will normally avoid opportunistic behaviour.

The fourth category examines attitudes towards flexibility. Question 15 enquires whether the CEO permits employees to break rules at their discretion; question 16 considers whether the basis on which an organisational member can control the activities of another is role prescription, task knowledge or personal influence; question 17 asks about the frequency with which people are moved between tasks.

Theory suggests that compliance with rules and commitment to roles can reduce flexibility. However, they can make monitoring easier. Inflexibility may, indeed, afford economies of scale by promoting a stable division of labour that facilitates concentration on detail. While flexible working practices can increase breadth of experience, they can also decrease the efficiency of mechanistic performance.

Category five concerns cultural attitudes towards the distribution of power within the organisation. Question 18 asks whether the structuring of organisational relationships is premised on paternalism (those in power should take care of those not in power) or partnership. Question 19 is about whether power and information should be shared at all organisational levels or kept at the top. Question 20 asks whether the main feature of people who do well in the company is technical competence or effectiveness in personal relationships and loyalty. Question 21 asks whether the CEO advocates competitive tactics between employees.

Theory suggests that paternalism will result in one particular set of objectives or expectations dominating policy-making, while partnership will seek compromise with other people's objectives too. Participation will better communicate goals and objectives, though at the expense of greater time devoted to information processing. High autonomy will motivate an individual's responsibility, while loyalty will motivate group effectiveness. Finally, a competitive-market-type organisational form will promote achievement by ensuring that the most capable groups are set the highest realistic norms. However, it can also encourage negative attitudes like hostility and aggression, and ultimately decrease intragroup communication.

Response Bias

Despite careful research design, response bias may still be present. Companies which underperform might not be willing to fill in the questionnaire. This does not seem to be important though, since the performance ratios of participant companies indicate that many underperforming companies completed the questionnaire. Another possibility is that companies which favour objective criteria towards decision-making may be more inclined to participate in scientific research. It is possible that this may have affected UK respondents but not Greek ones, as the distribution of UK responses to question 7 was skewed towards objective criteria.

7.5 CORPORATE CULTURE AND MANAGERIAL PRACTICES

Three main differences in cultural characteristics emerged when analysis of variance was performed. The first regards attitudes towards measurement in organisations, the second the internal relationship of members and the third power and leadership structures. Overall the results strongly support the proposition of this chapter regarding differences in managerial practices in the two countries.

Table 7.2 shows that UK companies rely more on objective criteria and hard tangible measures in their approach to management. This is reflected in attitudes towards the use of detailed scientific projections in decision-making (question 7), specific and detailed directions towards instructing subordinates (question 10), and hard appraisal of members' performance and competence (question 14). With respect to internal relationships, UK employees whom CEOs expect to do well are technically competent rather than loyal (question 20). On average UK employees are perceived as pro-work in nature (question 13), and as treating competition among themselves as a natural fair-play phenomenon (question 21). Subordinates who break rules are tolerated if it is clearly for the benefit of the organisation (question 15). It is also preferred that they are versatile across tasks (question 17). Regarding leadership and power distribution within the organisation, a rather paternalistic attitude is evident. The leader is seen more as an outsider of the group who formulates and communicates goals and views through his or her legitimate form of power (question 18). Though not statistically significant, there is a tendency in UK companies for decisions to be taken by individuals rather than committees (question 9), and for individuality in general to be emphasised (question 11). UK employers also place more emphasis on formal qualifications than personal qualities where employees are concerned (question 12).

TABLE 7.2 *Analysis of variance of mean responses for Greek and UK companies*

Question	*Cultural variables*		*Greece*	*UK*	F-*value*
4	control (1)	non-control (5)	2.54	2.68	0.74
5	confidence (1)	non-confidence (3)	1.50	1.45	0.61
6	traditional (1)	scientific (4)	3.06	2.93	0.70
7	subjective experience (1)	objective criteria (5)	3.14	3.50	5.79**
8	simplicity (1)	complexity (5)	3.01	3.16	1.31
9	low problem decomposition (1)	high decomposition (5)	2.77	2.59	1.42
10	low delegation (1)	high delegation (5)	2.49	1.98	10.28***
11	collegiality (1)	individualism (2)	1.17	1.26	2.11
12	screening out (1)	non-screening out (5)	2.04	2.20	1.82
13	lazy people (1)	working people (5)	2.98	3.63	9.92***
14	high trust (1)	low trust (5)	2.95	3.43	9.47**
15	low tolerance (1)	high tolerance (5)	2.40	2.96	14.35***
16	no changing roles (1)	changing roles (3)	2.03	1.91	1.31
17	versatile skills (1)	non-versatile skills (5)	3.44	3.03	9.16**
18	paternalism (1)	partnership (2)	1.82	1.67	5.80*
19	participation (1)	consultation (3)	1.79	1.84	0.48
20	high moral autonomy (1)	low moral autonomy (2)	1.86	1.69	7.98**
21	non-market institution (1)	market form institution (5)	3.09	3.40	4.62***
	Number of respondents		99	105	

* significant at 5 per cent level.
** significant at 1 per cent level.
*** significant at 0.1 per cent level.

On the whole UK companies possess an individualistic attitude. Companies are rather centralised at the strategic level and relatively decentralised and flexible at the operational level. At the strategic level the decision-making process is driven by scientific criteria while implementation is driven by the legitimate power of the leader. At the operational level rules can be changed if they seem inappropriate in the light of the specific situation.

In Greece companies rely more on subjective criteria and experience in decision-making. Companies believe less in hard measures as a basis for their decision-making (question 7), people are assessed more in terms of trust (question 14), and directions and details are not so clear-cut across organisation layers (question 10). Organisational relationships are more of a family type where loyalty is seen as a virtue (question 20), and competitive attitudes are undesirable since they can unleash conflict among members (question 21). People are perceived as having a weak work ethic (question 13) and flexibility is generally lower than in UK; dissenting opinions and breaking of rules are not allowed without previous permission even if they are for the benefit of the company (question 15); and people are more specialised and more attached to their tasks (question 17). Regarding leadership, the leader is seen as being inside the group, formulating goals and strategy by discretion and consensus (question 18) and communicating them through participation (question 19). Though not statistically significant, recruitment in Greek companies emphasises personal qualities rather than formal qualifications (question 12), and the company as a whole operates as a collectivity (question 11).

On the whole Greek companies seem to possess a family-type culture where, after the leader subjectively formulates and communicates the goals, no deviance and no competitive tactics among members are permitted. Some flexibility, however, is evident as companies favour subjective criteria in performance appraisal.

The results support the findings in the literature discussed earlier, in both the UK (Graves, 1973; Child and Kieser, 1979; Hofstede, 1980; Laurent, 1983) and Greece (Cummings and Schmidt, 1972; Hofstede, 1980).

7.6 CORPORATE CULTURE AND CORPORATE PERFORMANCE

Two sets of ordinary and two sets of stepwise regressions were run for each country in order to assess the impact of their cultural characteristics on the RTA and GSL. Dummy variables for the industrial sector (SCT1 = manufacturing, SCT2 = retailing, SCT3 = services), stage of industry development (ILC1 = growth, ILC2 = maturity, ILC3 = decline), and organisational structure (STR1 = functional, STR2 = divisional by product, STR3 = divisional by area, STR4 = matrix) were included in these regressions to control for non-cultural industry-specific and firm-specific characteristics which may influence performance. Size (SZ = log. total assets 1987) was also included as an important contextual characteristic.

Prior to the estimation of these regressions, Chow tests were performed to test for the comparability of the regression lines for the British and Greek samples. This tests for the similarity of the impact of various cultural characteristics on corporate performance in the two countries. For both the RTA and GSL ratios the Chow test indicated that the two regression lines were not comparable, suggesting a significant difference in the way the cultural attitudes influence corporate performance in the two countries (RTA: F (28 112) =

TABLE 7.3 *Regression results for UK companies*

	RTA		*GSL*	
Parameter	*Estimate*	*t*	*Estimate*	*t*
Constant	–0.1987	–1.36	–0.1031	–0.28
SCT1	–0.0256	–0.93	–0.1991	–2.92***
SCT2	–0.0648	–1.65*	–0.2199	–2.25**
STR1	–0.0095	–0.36	–0.0450	–0.69
STR2	0.0123	0.39	0.0170	0.22
STR3	0.0438	0.66	–0.1758	–1.06
SZ	0.0049	0.53	0.0542	2.36**
ILC1	0.0916	1.91*	0.0764	0.64
ILC2	0.0598	1.20	0.0463	0.37
Response 4	–0.0133	–1.20	–0.0032	–0.12
Response 5	–0.0063	–0.32	–0.0027	–0.06
Response 6	–0.0034	–0.26	–0.0317	–0.96
Response 7	0.0061	0.57	–0.0190	–0.72
Response 8	–0.0030	–0.25	–0.0019	–0.06
Response 9	0.0013	0.11	0.0014	0.05
Response 10	0.0110	0.77	–0.0004	–0.01
Response 11	0.0363	1.48	0.0696	1.14
Response 12	0.0120	0.84	–0.0277	–0.78
Response 13	–0.0081	–1.05	–0.0207	–1.07
Response 14	0.0316	3.09***	0.0426	1.68*
Response 15	–0.0005	–0.05	0.0201	0.68
Response 16	–0.0163	–1.10	–0.0302	–0.82
Response 17	–0.0030	–0.28	–0.0031	–0.12
Response 18	0.0087	0.31	0.1242	1.74*
Response 19	0.0294	1.66*	0.0179	0.41
Response 20	0.0360	1.59	–0.1016	–1.80*
Response 21	–0.0076	–0.63	–0.0348	–1.15
Sample size		89		89
R^2		0.41		0.43
F statistic		1.65**		1.81**

*** significant at 1 per cent level.
** significant at 5 per cent level.
* significant at 10 per cent level.

NOTES: SCT1 and SCT2 are dummy variables for manufacturing and retailing sectors respectively. ILC1 and ILC2 are dummy variables for growing and maturing stages of industry development. STR1, STR2 and STR3 are dummy variables for functional, divisional by product and divisional by area organisational structures.

1.63, $p < 0.05$; GSL: F (28 100) = 1.48, $p < 0.10$). Tables 7.3 and 7.4 report the ordinary regression results for UK and Greek companies respectively. Tables 7.5 and 7.6 report the stepwise regression results for each country.

TABLE 7.4 *Regression results for Greek companies*

	RTA		*GSL*	
Parameter	*Estimate*	*t*	*Estimate*	*t*
Constant	0.5732	2.03**	–0.3958	–1.08
SCT1	0.0038	0.08	–0.0899	–1.23
SCT2	0.0055	0.11	–0.1641	–2.23**
STR1	0.1932	1.32	0.2362	1.29
STR2	0.0072	0.03	–0.8892	–3.32***
STR4	0.1458	1.00	0.2377	1.31
SZ	–0.0293	–2.25**	–0.0126	–0.75
ILC1	–0.1079	–1.03	0.0561	1.27
ILC2	–0.1011	–1.01	–	·
Response 4	0.0074	0.51	0.0134	0.66
Response 5	–0.0792	–2.74***	0.0040	0.10
Response 6	–0.0156	–1.02	0.0141	0.65
Response 7	–0.0052	–0.33	0.0258	1.25
Response 8	–0.0232	–1.49	–0.0007	–0.04
Response 9	–0.0003	–0.03	–0.0096	–0.56
Response 10	–0.0009	–0.08	–0.0108	–0.60
Response 11	0.0487	1.16	0.0120	0.19
Response 12	–0.0167	–0.78	0.0029	0.11
Response 13	0.0070	0.60	0.0256	1.63
Response 14	–0.0047	–0.31	0.0124	0.63
Response 15	–0.0275	–1.67*	0.0277	1.29
Response 16	0.0101	0.41	0.0401	1.19
Response 17	0.0024	0.13	0.0011	0.04
Response 18	–0.0121	–0.26	–0.0945	–1.56
Response 19	–0.0269	–1.15	0.0572	1.88*
Response 20	0.0226	0.54	0.0127	0.22
Response 21	–0.0064	–0.43	0.0169	0.87
Sample size		79		67
R^2		0.50		0.62
F statistic		2.00*		2.69*

*** significant at 1 per cent level.
** significant at 5 per cent level.
** significant at 10 per cent level.

NOTES: SCT1 and SCT2 are dummy variables for manufacturing and retailing sectors respectively. ILC1 and ILC2 are dummy variables for growing and maturing stages of industry development respectively. STR1, STR2, and STR4 are dummy variables for functional, divisional by product and matrix organisational structures.

TABLE 7.5 *Stepwise regression results for UK companies*

	RTA		*GSL*	
Parameter	*Estimate*	*t*	*Estimate*	*t*
Constant	−0.0899		0.0123	
ILC1	0.0499	2.66***		
Response 4	−0.0148	−1.72*		
Response 11	0.0395	1.88*		
Response 12	0.0221	1.91*		
Response 14	0.0291	3.32*	0.0481	2.18**
SCT1			−0.2177	−4.10***
SCT2			−0.2499	−3.33***
SCT3			−0.2668	−1.99**
SZ			0.0446	2.46***
Response 20			−0.1080	−2.15**
Sample size		89		89
R^2		0.29		0.34
F statistic		5.56***		5.86***

*** significant at 1 per cent level.
** significant at 5 per cent level.
** significant at 10 per cent level.

NOTES: SCT1 and SCT2 are dummy variables for manufacturing and retailing sectors respectively. ILC1 is a dummy variable for the growth stage of industry development. STR3 is a dummy variable for divisional by area organisational structure.

Return on Total Assets

The cultural characteristics of distrust (question 14) and power concentration (question 19) emerged as significant predictors of corporate performance in UK companies. As the theoretical part predicted, 'hard' objective criteria of performance appraisal had a positive effect on a company's performance (question 14). Also a concentration of power positively influences performance (question 19). The dummy variables indicated a lower performance for the retailing sector (SCT2) and a higher one for growing industries (ILC1).

The stepwise regression results indicate that individualistic attitudes (question 11), perception of control over the environment (question 4), recruitment based on formal rather than personal qualifications (question 12), and hard objective criteria for the assessment individuals' performance (question 14) were good predictors of

TABLE 7.6 *Stepwise regression results for Greek companies*

	RTA		*GSL*	
Parameter	*Estimate*	t	*Estimate*	t
Constant	0.7331		−0.1554	
STR1	0.0676	2.64***		
SZ	−0.0321	− 3.83***		
Response 5	−0.0966	− 4.20***		
Response 6	−0.0221	− 1.84*		
Response 8	−0.0230	− 1.77*		
Response 15	−0.0200	− 1.62	0.0333	1.96*
Response 19	−0.0354	− 2.00**	0.0572	2.33**
SCT1			−0.1029	− 1.88*
SCT2			−0.1503	− 2.56**
ILC1			0.0734	2.05**
STR2			−1.0234	− 7.06***
Response 13			0.0328	2.88***
Sample size		79		67
R^2		0.45		0.54
F statistic		8.21***		9.72***

*** significant at 1 per cent level.
** significant at 5 per cent level.
* significant at 10 per cent level.

NOTES: SCT1 and SCT2 are dummy variables for manufacturing and retailing industry sectors respectively. ILC1 is a dummy variable for the growth stage of industry development STR1 and STR2 are dummy variables for functional and divisional organisational structures respectively.

RTA. The dummy variables indicated a higher performance for growing industries (ILC1).

The results for Greek companies suggested an important role for size (SZ), confidence (question 5) and intolerance (question 15) in motivating performance. The Greek companies that achieved the best results were smaller, had a higher level of confidence relative to their competitors and possessed a lower degree of tolerance. Confidence and high norms are often necessary innovation prerequisites. Low levels of tolerance are important in reducing dissent and deviance within family-type Greek companies.

Stepwise regression results suggest that functionally-organised (STR1), more centralised companies in Greece outperformed their competitors, as did smaller companies (SZ). Regarding cultural characteristics, high levels of confidence (question 5), traditionalism in decision-making (question 6), and reliance on well-tried rules in dealing with new and complex situations (question 8) also increased performance. Low tolerance levels (question 15) and diffusion of power (question 19) were also good predictors of company performance, although the former are just insignificant in the statistical sense. The importance of tradition and continuity may reflect employees' concern for uncertainty avoidance in Greek firms.

Overall the results support the hypothesis that each country's most successful companies will adapt their organisational culture to the cultural idiosyncrasies of their national culture. Individualistic attitudes and objective criteria motivate performance in Britain. Familism and intolerance of dissent give the best results in Greece.

Growth of Sales

This result must be modified substantially in respect of the growth of the firm, however. In the case of the UK, objective criteria towards performance appraisal (question 14) were again important. However, technical competence (question 20) emerged as a good predictor of companies' performance even though personal loyalty appeared as more important in achieving profitability. Also important was a partnership attitude in structuring organisational relationships (question 18). This does not fit well with the general attitude of UK firms (Table 7.2). A possible explanation is that a partnership attitude towards technically competent team members reduces administrative pressures on the leader in a high-growth situation. A leader who trusts his partners can attenuate the problems of growth through increased delegation. The dummy variables indicated that large companies (SZ) performed well and that organisational structures based on functions and products did not (SCT1, SCT2).

The stepwise regression results provided corroboration. The results confirm that size (SZ), objective criteria in performance appraisal (question 14) and technical competence (question 20) are significant motivators of performance. The manufacturing and retailing sectors performed worse than the service sector (SCT1, SCT2), as did geographically divisionalised organisational structures (STR3).

The results for GSL were very different from those for RTA in the case of Greek companies. Manufacturing and retailing sectors underperformed (SCT1, SCT2) along with firms divisionalised by product (STR2). A concentration of power rather than participation (question 19), while incompatible with national culture, nevertheless contributed significantly to the increase of sales. This may be because leaders of high-growth Greek firms need to 'break the mould' of traditional attitudes by 'leading from the front'. They cannot afford to compromise their goals by consulting too extensively with people who have a negative attitude to work. This interpretation is corroborated by the stepwise results, which show that not only concentration of power but also pro-work attitudes are significant facilitators of growth in Greek firms. The fastest-growing Greek companies perceived people as pro-working (question 13), had a higher degree of tolerance (question 15) and again favoured the concentration of power (question 19). The fastest-growing Greek companies therefore tended to resemble the more profitable UK companies. This suggests that while profitability is enhanced by harmonising corporate culture and national culture, growth requires more uniform corporate cultural characteristics. These characteristics allow the CEO to take a high profile in setting corporate goals while encouraging him or her to delegate responsibility to internally competitive managers who have clearly-defined responsibilities of their own.

It is interesting to note that the correlation between profitability and growth is much higher among UK firms than it is among Greek firms. The Spearman correlation coefficient between GSL and RTA was 0.50 ($p < 0.0001$) for UK firms but only 0.20 ($p < 0.07$) for Greek firms. This suggests that adaptation to national culture facilitates both profitability and growth of sales in the UK, but facilitates only profitability in Greece. The UK approach of delegating responsibility to competitive subordinates who are subjected to hard performance appraisal affords profitability in the UK because it satisfies the ambitions of the most able employees and facilitates growth by mitigating bureaucratic diseconomies of scale. It does not generate profitability in Greece because it does not satisfy the desire of Greek employees for a familial structure, but it is a necessary evil for those Greek firms which desire to keep up with, or catch up on, faster growing international rivals. This in turn suggests that because the costs of 'going for growth' are greater in Greece than in the UK, Greek firms generally have a lower growth potential. Indeed, with the sample, the average growth rate for the Greek firms was less than half that of the UK firms. Furthermore, if large size is regarded as a legacy of fast growth in the past, then the negative association between profitability and size in Greece confirms the very real nature of the profit penalty of going for growth. While fast-growing Greek firms may resemble fast-growing UK firms, there may never be sufficient fast-growing Greek firms to dominate Greek industry and influence Greek business culture.

7.7 CONCLUSIONS AND IMPLICATIONS FOR FURTHER RESEARCH

The chapter shows that both national and corporate cultures affect organisational performance. Evidence from a sample of 105 British and 99 Greek enterprises supports the hypothesis that in each country the most profitable companies adapt their organisational culture to the idiosyncracies of their national culture. Individualistic attitudes linked to objective measurements promote profitability in the UK, while familism and intolerance of dissent enhance profitability in Greece. The profitable strategies in Greece, however, are not so consistent with growth of sales as are the profitable strategies in the UK. Unless Greek culture changes, Greek firms will remain small. If convergence occurs, it is unlikely to come from the growing dominance of large Greek-owned firms. It will come, rather, from the impact of foreign firms investing in Greece and bringing their more impersonal and quantitative management techniques with them.

These differences between the UK and Greek firms cannot be explained away by the different structures of the national economies, since the cultural effects reported control for differences in the companies' lines of business, and even in their organisational structures. All the evidence points to the importance of a few key factors which are deeply ingrained in the national culture, and are likely to change only with prolonged exposure to foreign influence. Such influence may well intensify, however, following the completion of the single market in 1992.

More generally, this chapter has outlined a methodology for investigating the dynamics of competitive advantage of nations, by explicitly relating culture to performance at both the organisational and national levels. Since national wealth is not only inherited but also created (Porter 1990; Casson, 1991), the proposed methodology can go beyond conventional economic factors in explaining why some firms from some nations are systematically better than others in creating advantages based on quality and innovation. Key aspects of source-country culture may be synergised with industry-specific factors through the activities of a country's entrepreneurial elite to generate national level competitive advantages. Further research is clearly needed to clarify the impact of national cultures on strategy, structure and performance at both the corporate and national levels.

Appendix: Questionnaire on Cultural Assumptions Underlying Corporate Behaviour

Please place one tick only in the position which reflects your view on how your organisation conducts its operations.

1. *Please indicate the primary activity of your organisation:* a. Manufacturing; b. Retailing; c. Other. Please describe
2. *Which of the following descriptions best characterises the way your company is structured?* a. Organised by functional areas (e.g. marketing, finance); b. Organised by product; c. Organised by geographic divisions; d. Organised by both functional areas and product or geographical divisions; e. Other.
3. *Which of the following statements best describes the stage of the development of the major industry you operate within?* a. Growth stage; b. Maturity stage: c. Aging stage.
4. *On the whole, how predictable do you find the environment you operate within?* a. Predictable; b. Fairly predictable; c. Neutral; d. Fairly unpredictable; e. Unpredictable.
5. *Compared to your competitors, is your organisation:* a. Better run; b. Run just as well; c. Not so well run.
6. *Which of the following statements best describes the process of decision-making in your organisation?* a. This is the right way, it has always been this way; b. We should ask consultants or experts to advise us what to do; c. Let's try and see; d. Our research will show us what to do.
7. *When a problem is investigated by your organisation, how important are hard measures of assessment like detailed forecasts or other scientific projections?* a. No such indicators are available; b. They are not very important; c. They are fairly important; d. They are very important; e. They are extremely important.
8. '*In novel and complex situations old well-tried methods perform better than new unproven methods based on judgement*'*:* a. I strongly agree; b. I agree; c. Neutral; d. I disagree; e. I strongly disagree.
9. '*Decisions made by individuals are of higher quality than decisions made by appointed committees*'*;* a. I strongly agree; b. I agree; c. Neutral; d. I disagree; e. I strongly disagree.
10. '*A manager instructing a subordinate should always give explicit and detailed directions*'*;* a. I strongly agree; b. I agree; c. Neutral; d. I disagree; e. I strongly disagree.
11. *In your organisation, are relationships between members of the same rank based on:* a. Group cooperation, group consensus, and group welfare; b. Individuality, competition, individual rights and individual welfare; c. Other, please describe.

12. *When your organisation recruits new members how are personal qualities rated in relation to formal qualifications?* a. Overriding importance; b. More important; c. Of the same importance; d. Less important; e. No importance.
13. *The most important benefit your employees derive from your company is:* a. Income stability; b. Job security; c. Promotion; d. Interesting and challenging work; e. Involvement and participation; f. Other, please describe.
14. *When a member of your organisation is promoted, how important are hard measures of his performance, such as sales generated, output per day, etc?* a. No such indicators are available; b. They are not very important; c. They are fairly important; d. They are very important; e. They are extremely important.
15. *In your company rules and procedures should not be broken even if the employee thinks it is for company's best interest;* a. I strongly agree; b. I agree; c. Neutral; d. I disagree; e. I strongly disagree.
16. *In your company it is legitimate for a person to control other's activities:* a. If he has power or his role prescribes so; b. If he has the knowledge relevant to the task at hand; c. It is influence not control that is important.
17. *In your company members are transferred across tasks:* a. Very frequently; b. Frequently; c. Usually; d. Seldom; e. Not at all.
18. *Which of the following ways is the most important for structuring your organisational relationships:* a. Those in power should take care of those who are not in power; b. Organisational members are partners who share full responsibility for the performance of the organisation whatever their role; c. Other, please describe.
19. *Power in your organisation:* a. Must be shared at all levels because information and skills at all levels are relevant to company performance; b. Must be placed where information and skill reside, but responsibility should remain in managerial roles; c. Should remain in the hands of the leaders, but some relevant information should be available to all organisational levels; d. Other, please describe.
20. *Most people who do well in your company are:* a. Technically competent; they like taking risks and operating on their own; b. Effective in personal relationships with a strong sense of loyalty to the organisation; c. Other, please describe.
21. *'Competition among employees usually does more harm than good'.* a. I strongly agree; b. I agree; c. Neutral; d. I disagree; e. I strongly disagree.
22. *Please comment briefly on the mission of your company.*
23. *With respect of 1992 how do you foresee your company's position in the market place? Please describe briefly.*

Thank you for answering this questionnaire. Please return using the enclosed envelope.

8 The Prospects for European Investment in LDCs

ALLAN WEBSTER

8.1 INTRODUCTION

This chapter examines likely future developments in the outward direct investment of EC firms in LDCs. In particular, it considers the implications of various policy changes by governments which seem likely to influence the outward direct investment of the EC in LDCs.

Section 8.2 shows that EC investment is of less significance to LDCs than that of the USA and Japan. Further examination suggests that the very existence of the EC leads firms in its member states to channel a high proportion of their investment to other EC member states. More generally, outward investment for each of the three main sources (EC, USA and Japan) tends to be geographically focused upon neighbouring regions: there is a 'back yard' effect. Both of these characteristics have implications in a changing policy environment, particularly with respect to 1992 and East European liberalisation.

Section 8.3 discusses the general impact of host-country policy on incentives for FDI in LDCs, while section 8.4 focuses on the specific implications of microeconomic reforms. Section 8.5 considers the investment incentives implicit in macroeconomic reform programmes in LDCs. Section 8.6 argues that the presence of large public sector debt in many LDCs may actually lead to an improved climate for FDI. Section 8.7 uses the example of Mexico to suggest that recent changes in host-government policy towards FDI are leading to a more favourable climate for investment in LDCs.

It is a central argument of this chapter that indirect incentives (those policies which affect the general economic climate rather than FDI specifically) have been significantly changed by both microeconomic and macroeconomic reforms by LDC governments. The incentives to undertake direct investment in LDCs have, therefore, been dramatically improved in a manner which would be likely to generate more investment were all other things to be equal.

Other things will not remain equal, however. Developments in Europe (East and West) are quite likely to overshadow improvements made in LDC policies. Section 8.8 addresses these issues, while section 8.9 draws some tentative conclusions concerning the prospects for European investment in LDCs based upon this analysis.

8.2 PAST DIRECT INVESTMENT BY EC COUNTRIES IN LDCs

Figure 8.1 compares the stocks of direct investment in developed economies and LDCs over the period 1975–87 for the USA, Japan and those EC countries for which there are available data. It can be seen that outward investment by, say, the Federal Republic of Germany in developed economies is comparable in volume to that of Japan. Moreover, its growth has tended to keep pace with that of US FDI stocks. However, EC countries have increasingly fallen behind Japanese and US levels of investment in LDCs. Indeed, given that stocks of investment by the EC countries involved have tended to grow slowly in nominal terms, the real value of their stocks has in some cases declined. This is in contrast to a fairly steady growth in the nominal value of US stocks and an accelerating growth in the nominal value of Japanese stocks.

Whilst not conclusive, the data suggest an increasing marginalisation of EC investment in LDCs to an extent that does not occur for direct investment in developed economies. This implies that EC investment is disproportionately and increasingly focused upon developed economies. Table 8.1, which reports average annual percentage changes in the nominal (dollar) value of stocks, illustrates this point further. Moreover, this table incorporates data for the UK (excluded from Figure 8.1 as UK stock data is not reported annually). This confirms that outward investment by EC countries in LDCs has tended to decline relative to investment in developed economies. This is in contrast to US outward stocks in LDCs which have increased in importance relative to those in developed econ-

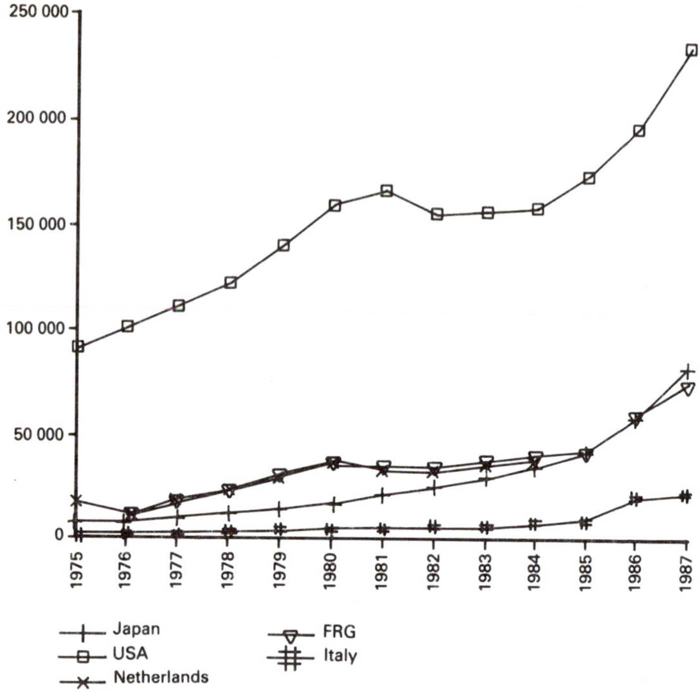

SOURCE: UNCTC data base.

FIGURE 8.1 (a) Outward direct investment stocks in developed economies (US$ million)

TABLE 8.1 *Average annual increases in outward FDI stocks (current US$) 1977–87*

Source country	*Host region* *LDCs (a)*	*Developed (b)*	*Ratio (a/b)*
Japan	17.51	22.28	0.79
USA	10.47	8.43	1.24
Netherlands (1977–84)	7.81	10.01	0.78
FRG (1978–87)	10.97	16.77	0.65
Italy	19.98	23.97	0.83
UK (1978–84)	23.45	26.36	0.89

SOURCE: UNCTC data base.

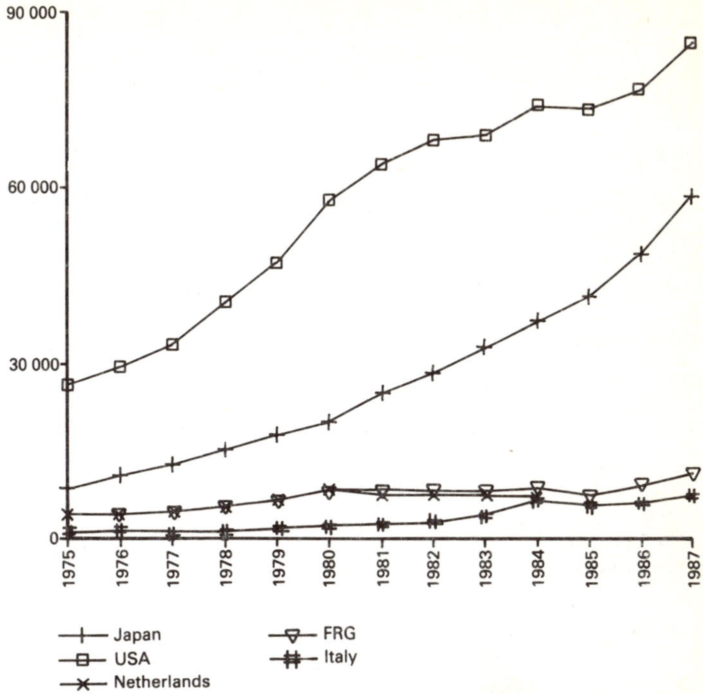

SOURCE: UNCTC data base.

(b) Outward direct investment in LDCs (US$ million)

omies. Although Japanese outward stocks in LDCs show a similar tendency to decline relative to those in developed economies, it must be remembered that Japanese investment, unlike that of EC countries, exhibited a much greater initial focus upon LDC hosts.

Table 8.2, which compares the geographical composition of outward stocks for the FRG, the Netherlands, UK, USA and Japan, illustrates this process in more detail. All three of the EC economies exhibit a similar trend: a marked increase in the relative importance of North America as a host for investment. In each case this is partially at the expense of European hosts, but it also represents a clear switch in emphasis away from LDCs. In comparison, Japan exhibits a similar growth in the *relative* importance of North America as a recipient of investment, but this is almost entirely at the expense of investment in LDCs and Asia. The principal contrast between Japan and EC countries is again a much greater initial emphasis on LDCs.

TABLE 8.2 *Geographical composition of outward stocks (percentages based on current values in national currencies)*

	1977	*1984*	*1987*
Netherlands			
EC	45.80	38.12	na
Other European	5.57	4.21	na
North America	18.19	30.84	na
Other Developed	10.94	10.16	na
Asia	3.67	4.80	na
Latin America	12.06	9.10	na
Mediterranean LDCs	3.77	2.76	na
FRG			
EC	41.60	33.79	40.67
Other European	14.26	8.72	10.35
North America	19.56	34.89	30.86
Other Developed	4.10	4.54	4.78
Asia	3.23	3.16	2.38
Latin America	13.76	11.79	8.97
Mediterranean LDCs	1.45	1.47	0.90
Other LDCs	2.03	1.63	1.09
*UK**			
EC	25.77	21.07	na
Other European	5.20	3.56	na
North America	25.20	41.59	na
Other Developed	23.25	15.39	na
Asia	8.37	7.61	na
Latin America	5.01	7.63	na
Mediterranean LDCs	2.64	0.05	na
Other LDCs	4.55	3.10	na
USA			
EC	34.34	37.97	39.32
Other European	9.36	9.16	8.59
North America	24.49	19.37	18.29
Other Developed	8.74	5.51	8.84
Asia	3.84	6.24	6.11
Latin America	18.66	20.61	17.96
Other LDCs	0.56	1.15	0.89
Japan			
Europe†	13.85	12.70	15.11
North America	24.32	30.06	37.87
Other Developed	5.66	5.21	4.77
Asia	28.49	25.24	19.13
Latin America	16.92	18.23	18.08
Other LDCs	10.77	8.57	5.05

* 1978 replaces 1977.
† including EC.

NOTE: na = not available.
SOURCE: UNCTC data base.

The USA, by contrast, does not exhibit a decline in the share of its outward stocks in LDCs. Indeed its outward stocks in 1987 represent a marginally increased emphasis on LDCs over 1977. The pattern, then, has been for the composition of US and Japanese stocks to converge in their geographical distributions. This convergence is evident at the regional level as well as in the North–South distribution, since US investment in Latin America has declined in relative importance and that in Asia has increased. The picture for Japan is the reverse.

If the geographical distribution of US and Japanese investment has tended to converge, investment from the three EC economies has tended to diverge from both. The trend, therefore, is for the USA and Japan to converge by the former increasing its (relatively modest) emphasis on LDCs whilst Japan reduces its strong emphasis. The EC economies, in contrast, exhibit a weakening of an already light emphasis on LDCs.

The geographical breakdowns of the LDC totals are also of interest. Japanese stocks have traditionally focused on Asia although this has now considerably diminished. US stocks have tended to focus on Latin America. This suggests a tendency for investment in LDCs to be initially focused on a back-yard region before becoming more global in nature. The feature that distinguishes Dutch and German stocks of investment in LDCs from those of the USA and Japan is the absence of this back yard element. The best approximation to the EC's LDC back yard is the Mediterranean basin. However, investment by the Netherlands and West Germany shows little evidence of a particular focus in the Mediterranean. This is probably because the overall market size of the Mediterranean basin is small in relation to that of Asia or Latin America and because costs (and, in particular, labour costs) are high in the Mediterranean in relation to other LDCs. In short, the EC's back yard has been the least suitable location for outward direct investment in LDCs.

Thus, the limited evidence available for the period 1977–87 suggests two trends relevance:

(a) EC countries have tended to exploit investment opportunities within EC boundaries or in North America before investing elsewhere;
(b) most source countries exploit investment opportunities in neighbouring, back-yard LDCs before investing in more distant economies.

Both of these trends share a common strand: a focus on the more familiar environment as a host for investment. This pattern has already been observed in an empirical context by the UNCTC (1988) in the investment of small- to medium-sized MNEs. The reasons derive from some well known theoretical propositions. First, the internalisation approach of Buckley and Casson (1976, 1985) identifies a crucial role for transactions costs. Second, within this paradigm Caves (1982) identifies the trade-off between internalisation economies and the high information costs and increased risk to the investor as a potential disincentive to investment.

Johanson and Vahlne (1977) focus on the role of information in the dynamics of the internationalisation process. They argue that the markets which are most likely to be exploited first in a gradual process of internationalisation are those with the shortest psychic distance as such markets offer a better transaction cost/risk trade-off. From the viewpoint of outward investment in LDCs (which, typically, exhibit significant cultural, linguistic and market differences), geographical distance is likely to approximate closely to psychic distance. As the most profitable projects in familiar locations become exhausted the more profitable projects in the high (perceived) risk locations become attractive in relation to the remaining less profitable projects in familiar locations. We should, therefore, expect a tendency for investment to spread outwards from familiar localities over time.

This process is, however, only one dimension of a multidimensional phenomenon. Thus the argument of the investment–development cycle (Dunning, 1982, 1986), that levels of inward investment are related to levels of economic development, and Kojima's (1978) claim that early Japanese investment was attracted to LDCs by the relative lack of technological sophistication of Japanese firms at that time, can be seen as more general arguments in favour of initial investment in more familiar economies. Similarly, the argument of Svedberg (1981) that former colonial powers enjoy favourable conditions for FDI in former colonies due to common cultural, linguistic or institutional factors, and the traditional emphasis of British FDI on former dominions and colonies reported by Stopford (1974), can be seen as variations of essentially the same argument: the investment projects that are most likely to be undertaken first are those where knowledge of local conditions is most readily available.

A decomposition of changes in aggregate stocks of outward FDI by type of investment – resource-seeking, import-substituting, export

TABLE 8.3 *Percentage Shares of LDCs in Outward Stocks of FDI, by Industry*

	Agriculture	*Mining*	*Chemicals*	*Transport equipment*	*Electrical engineering*	*Textiles*	*Food, drink and tobacco*
Japan							
1975	73.4	61.2	78.7	83.5	68.8	92.4	58.5
1984	55.0	72.3	76.8	44.6	34.0	79.0	41.7
1987	51.1	69.6	65.9	35.9	27.2	72.4	41.4
USA							
1970	na	11.0	24.7	12.5	11.6	na	21.1
1980	na	4.2	23.5	16.6	15.0	na	23.7
1987	na	na	19.1	16.1	15.1	na	19.6
Netherlands							
1973	47.8	42.4	na	na	na	na	18.8
1979	10.8	33.2	na	na	na	na	17.5
1984	na	40.8	na	na	na	na	30.3
West Germany							
1976	na	62.4	14.6	61.4	24.6	na	na
1981	na	44.6	16.0	42.8	23.6	na	na
1986	na	44.2	13.3	29.0	18.1	na	na
UK							
1971	na	na	14.8	2.9	10.5	8.5	34.5
1981	na	na	26.6	4.4	8.5	4.7	28.0
1984	na	na	32.4	3.8	5.5	na	32.7

NOTE: na = not available.
SOURCE: UNCTC data base.

platform and rationalised – would cast further light on recent trends. However, such categories are difficult to measure directly. Table 8.3 attempts to measure such types of investment by reference to a number of 'indicator' industries. Thus to capture movements in resource-seeking investment it reports changes in the LDC share in outward investment in agriculture and mining. Textiles are used as an indicator for export platform investment and food, drink and tobacco for import-substituting investment. For rationalised investment, transport equipment and electrical engineering were selected as indicator industries. Finally, chemicals were included as a hybrid of the resource-seeking and rationalised categories. Clearly certain chemical activities (petro-chemicals and fertilisers, for example) are likely to be resource-based whereas others (for example, pharmaceuticals) are much more likely to be amenable to vertically disintegrated production, and hence rationalised investment.

The evidence of agriculture and mining reveals a tendency for LDCs to have become less important in resource-seeking investment from all sources. In most cases this relative decline exceeds the average for all investment. For the import-substitution indicator (food, drink and tobacco) there is some slight decline in the significance of LDCs in the outward investment of the USA and Japan. For the Netherlands this industry exhibits an increase in the significance of LDCs, whereas the position for the UK shows little change between 1971 and 1984. For the indicator industries for rationalised investment the position is very mixed. For Japan there appears to have been a major switch in emphasis away from LDCs, whereas LDCs have become slightly more important in US outward investment in these industries. Information on the export platform indicator industry (textiles) is sufficiently meagre to make any firm conclusions difficult. However, the limited evidence would seem to suggest that the role of LDCs as hosts has not increased for this type of investment.

Thus the principal trend common to all source countries is a tendency for LDCs to have become less important in resource-seeking investment. The role of LDCs in rationalised investment appears to have diminished for Germany, the UK and Japan but to have been enhanced for the USA. However, these trends in rationalised investment are not markedly divergent from trends in aggregate investment stocks in LDCs.

8.3 ASSESSING THE IMPORTANCE OF HOST-COUNTRY POLICIES

Clearly the policies of host governments have the potential to affect direct investment in their economies. Whether, in practice, this has a significant impact on investment is an empirical question that this section seeks to address.

It is also germane to ask which sort of policies are likely to affect FDI in LDCs. Obviously, policies which are specifically addressed to FDI (for example, local content restrictions) are likely to exert some influence. For convenience these are referred to as 'direct' (dis)incentives. However, as Marsden and Belot (1987) argue, FDI can be affected by economic policies which are not specifically directed at it.

TABLE 8.4 *Important factors affecting the locational decision of the outward investment of Japanese multinationals, 1987*

Factor	*Percentage of total responses*	
	Large firms	*Small firms*
Markets	41.2	28.7
Labour	18.9	18.0
Local taxes	12.3	17.2
Supply of materials	8.4	11.5
Political situation	4.5	12.3
Other	14.7	12.3

SOURCE: Long Term Credit Bank of Japan.

So, for example, it could be argued that much import-substituting investment is attracted by market considerations rather than by direct policy incentives. But it would be remarkable if macroeconomic policies (such as government budget deficits) and microeconomic policies (such as consumption taxes) did not affect the available market. Similarly, macro and micro policy is likely to affect local operating costs and hence all other forms of investment. For convenience, these are referred to as 'indirect' incentives.

Japanese FDI provides an interesting illustration of the combined influence of direct and indirect incentives. Table 8.4 reports the responses of Japanese firms to a questionnaire about which factors affect their foreign location decision. Local taxation has an important but not dominant role in the location decision. Moreover, to the extent that government macroeconomic policy can significantly affect market size, this, too, has a potentially significant influence.

Table 8.5 lists a selection of policy or policy-related factors which Japanese multinationals have reported as difficulties in operating current FDI projects. This also gives a guide to those disincentives likely to influence future investment; in short, it reports disincentives measured at the post-investment rather than pre-investment stage.

Host-government policy on FDI itself (direct incentives) is, as expected, reported as a major factor leading to operating difficulties. There is a significantly greater propensity for this type of difficulty to arise in LDCs. Inflation can also provide a significant degree of difficulty but this appears not to be a specifically LDC problem except in the case of Latin America. Similarly, Japanese multinationals do

TABLE 8.5 *Problems in the operation of investment projects reported by Japanese multinationals (1986)*

Category	*Percentage of total responses by region*			
	Asia	*Latin America*	*Africa*	*World*
Host-government FDI policy	29.2	27.4	37.6	23.1
Inflation	10.4	28.8	12.0	11.2
Import policy	4.6	13.6	14.3	4.8
Infrastructure	1.5	2.1	3.3	1.4

SOURCE: Ministry of International Trade and Industry.

not seem to have experienced much difficulty with host-government policy with respect to imports, although such difficulties are significant for projects in Africa and Latin America.

Turning to direct policy incentives, Guisinger and associates (1985) provide a comprehensive review of policy incentives and disincentives which is accompanied by some detailed industry case studies. Guisinger identifies two main types of direct incentive: explicit and implicit. Explicit incentives or disincentives are formal policies which are openly applied to all relevant firms, whereas implicit (dis)incentives are those which the host government may use in a discretionary fashion to provide incentives or disincentives for particular projects.

In general, Guisinger finds a substantial difference between the policies of LDCs and developed countries towards inward investment. A wide range of quite stringent direct policy disincentives is common in LDCs, whereas the emphasis in developed market economies is much more towards providing incentives for inward FDI. Moreover, Guisinger provides some further survey evidence that (dis)incentive policies exert a significant influence on the location decision (see Table 8.6).

This suggests a significant role for direct policy incentives in the location decision for all types of investment project. Across types of investment project, those intended to supply world export markets seem to be the least sensitive to direct incentives, whilst those intended to supply only the domestic market appear to be the most sensitive. Across types of incentive, implicit incentives are, in general, the least likely to affect the location decision, while commodity incentives are the most likely to affect investments to supply domestic

TABLE 8.6 *Dominant factors in the location decision*

Influences	*Type of investment project (number of cases)* Domestic market	Local export	World export	All
Incentive-unrelated	8	9	7	24
Implicit incentives	3	6	0	9
Explicit incentives:				
Commodity	23	0	1	24
Factor	2	11	4	17
Total	36	26	12	74

SOURCE: Guisinger and associates (1985).

markets. Investment to supply export markets, in contrast, is more sensitive to explicit factor incentives.

Finally, Contractor's econometric study (1989) finds a significant relationship between the liberalisation of direct policy disincentives and the tendency of US firms to undertake new direct investment. To summarise, then, evidence from a wide range of sources suggests that host-government policy – both direct and indirect – has a significant effect on investment.

8.4 THE IMPLICATIONS OF MICROECONOMIC STRUCTURAL ADJUSTMENT PROGRAMMES IN LDCs

Microeconomic structural adjustment programmes have been promoted by both the World Bank and the International Monetary Fund since the mid-1980s. The focus of these programmes is the freeing of markets in LDCs as a means of stimulating economic development. Typical features of these programmes include:

(a) liberalisation of international trade;
(b) privatisation;
(c) deregulation of domestic economic activity;
(d) restructuring the domestic tax system to render it less discriminatory by product or factor of production.

The ultimate goal of these measures as expounded by, for example, Bruno (1988), is an improvement in both allocative and productive efficiency. FDI is clearly likely to both influence and be influenced by extensive change of this type.

The liberalisation of international trade is likely to have a number of consequences for investment in the liberalising economy. First, the removal of protection from current economic activity reduces the returns to protected activities and hence acts as a disincentive for further import-substituting investment. This effect need not be strong because it is industrial production which tends to receive the highest protection, and most LDCs have a relatively small industrial sector. Moreover, many LDCs give most protection to activities which process local raw materials (spinning of yarn, for example). Despite high nominal tariff rates on the next stage of the production process (say, cloth weaving), this stage is frequently disprotected because the increase in costs resulting from tariffs on inputs exceeds the increase in revenue from the output tariff (that is, negative effective protection). Thus it is often the case that several of the (relatively few industrial) activities that are apparently heavily protected are, in effective terms, disprotected. These are likely to benefit from liberalisation.

Protection can only serve to increase revenues on the domestic market, usually by raising prices; it cannot raise export prices. Protection, therefore, reduces the incentive for protected industries to export as it raises the price of domestic relative to export supply. In other words, it is likely to encourage import-substituting investment at the expense of all other forms of indirect investment. To summarise, then, the removal or reduction of protection does not unambiguously worsen incentives for import-substituting investment in the liberalised activity. This is because in many instances it will have faced effective disprotection. It removes disincentives for all other types of investment and, in particular, export platform investment.

Given that protection tends to concentrate on *existing* industry which is often limited to a relatively narrow range of products, the effects of protecting these activities upon other activities – that is, the general equilibrium effects of protection – are of considerable importance. Raising the price of a fairly narrow range of existing industrial products by protection of the domestic market changes incentives. In particular, the rise in the price of protected importables by definition lowers several other relative prices. It not only lowers the relative price of exports within the same industry (as already discussed) but also of other exportable products. Protection, therefore, lowers incentives to invest in predominantly export industries. Moreover, as the most protected industries are invariably ones that actually exist at present, it lowers the relative price of those industries that do not currently exist, and so discourages their establishment. This is a particularly acute problem in respect of manufacturing industry as it is in the nature of LDCs that they have a small and undiversified industrial sector.

The effects of trade liberalisation are 'long run' in the sense that they require resources to be moved from previously protected activities to new or previously disprotected activities. In the short run there is a possibility that this adjustment process could lead to a contraction in output and demand as labour is displaced from one activity before being taken on in another. However, there a number of reasons why these 'short-run' effects are unlikely to be particularly adverse. First, the World Bank and the International Monetary Fund often provide financing for reform programmes to offset precisely these factors. Second, because the sector most vulnerable to these effects – industry – is typically small, its temporary contraction will not necessarily have much aggregate impact. Lastly, there is some limited evidence that adjustment programmes start to achieve long-run results quickly (this is discussed in more detail in section 8.5). Thus the short run appears to be sufficiently short for adverse effects to be limited.

Deregulation of industrial and commercial activity in LDCs is also likely to reduce disincentives to FDI. Relaxation of price and profit controls therefore tends not only to improve incentives for domestically-owned production but for foreign direct investment too. Privatisation is unlikely to generate any net increases in physical capital but does offer increased opportunities for foreign firms to 'buy in' to the privatised sector.

Restructuring domestic taxation policies to render them more uniform across products or across factors of production is also likely to improve incentives. Clearly, LDC governments must impose some taxes to finance government expenditure and debt repayments. However, in the past this has been done in a way that has tended to provide disincentives to produce locally. For example, domestic turnover taxes are a common way to raise revenue. However, such taxes have the reverse effect of tariffs: they discriminate against local production. Given that many industries in LDCs involve a small value-added component (that is, they are simple processing industries) the effective rate of taxation upon the local value-added component is often very high indeed.

Similarly, taxes on labour tend to offset one of the important attractions of production in a LDC location, that of low labour costs. Adopting a different structure of domestic taxation – raising revenue through a uniform consumption tax (one that applies at the same rate to all goods and services whether imported or locally produced) and cutting taxes which discriminate against domestic production or against labour – is likely to also significantly improve incentives for investment.

The object of microeconomic reforms is to reduce disincentives to undertake new or expand existing production (that is, to improve the allocation of resources). They do not, therefore, have a direct impact upon productivity. However, they would be likely to improve physical productivity in two ways, by increasing competitive pressure and by encouraging the adoption of improved technology. The first of these, competitive pressure, applies particularly to trade liberalisation. Removing protection increases competitive pressure on the domestic market and is therefore likely to improve productivity in previously protected industries. Reform is also likely to lead to improved technology. The principal mechanism for this would be technology transfer through FDI. However, the real point of microeconomic reform is to stimulate greater industrial and export diversification. Removing protection does not affect the competitive pressure in export markets, and neither does the stimulation of new industries guarantee a productivity improvement.

8.5 THE IMPLICATIONS OF MACROECONOMIC REFORM (STABILISATION) PROGRAMMES IN LDCs

A common focus of these programmes is (a) the devaluation (depreciation) of heavily overvalued exchange rates and (b) an attack on inflation by means of a restrictive monetary policy. Like the microeconomic reform programmes, these date from the mid-1980s, and are a result of IMF influence.

Dornbusch (1988) summarises the costs of overvalued exchange rates as follows:

(a) a loss in external competitiveness (reduced exports and higher imports);

(b) a consequent loss of domestic employment and output;
(c) balance of payments crises;
(d) adverse effects on domestic financial markets.

Similar costs may be imputed to inflation because, with a fixed but overvalued currency, inflation raises the real exchange rate (domestic prices relative to world prices in, say, dollar terms) and so competitiveness declines.

As discussed in section 8.3, there is some evidence that investing firms find high local rates of inflation to be a powerful disincentive to FDI. This, presumably, is for several reasons. First, as the currencies of many LDCs are pegged to one or more of the 'major' currencies, local inflation which is higher than world inflation means a decline in the price competitiveness of local value added and local resources. Second, inflation introduces uncertainty and, therefore, exchange risk. Increasing the risk of any investment in a particular location is likely to reduce the attractiveness of any project in that location.

Reducing the difference between local inflation and world rates can, therefore, provide a more favourable economic climate for FDI. However, the restrictive monetary policy used to tackle inflation reduces aggregate demand and thus reduces the available market for FDI. It may therefore also provide disincentives.

These incentives and disincentives vary between the short run and the long run, and according to type of investment. For instance, investment in a particular location which is intended to supply export markets is sensitive to local inflation (which affects the competitiveness of local value-added) but, as it seeks to supply markets other than the local domestic one, it is not sensitive to changes in aggregate demand in the host economy.

Restrictive monetary policies take time to reduce inflation. More importantly, there is a lag before the effects of reduced inflation can be expected to improve the overall level of economic activity through reduced inflationary expectations generating new investment (whether domestic or foreign in origin). The conflict in incentives between the demand and supply sides is consequently most acute in the short run. Thus the incentive effects on investment that is intended partially or wholly to supply the host-country market are more likely to be favourable in the long run than the short run.

This begs the question that also arose in the discussion of microeconomic reform: 'How short is the short run?' Evidence on both types of reform programme is thin because the first reform programmes were

TABLE 8.7 *Performance indicators of African reform programmes (average annual percentage changes)*

	All countries		*Countries not affected by strong shocks*	
Indicator	*With strong reform*	*Weak or no reform*	*With strong reform*	*Weak or no reform*
Real GDP growth:				
1980–4	1.4	1.1	1.2	0.7
1985–7	2.8	2.6	3.8	1.5
Export volume growth:				
1980–4	−1.3	−3.1	−0.7	−5.7
1985–7	4.2	0.2	4.9	−3.3
Real domestic investment:				
1980–4	−8.1	−3.7	−3.5	−7.0
1985–7	−0.9	−7.0	1.9	−4.8
Real per capita consumption:				
1980–4	−2.3	−1.1	−2.4	−1.5
1985–7	−0.4	−0.5	0.7	−0.9

SOURCE: World Bank (1989).

only initiated in the mid-1980s. Some countries have adopted reform programmes more recently and others have yet to do so (indeed, some may never do so). Even where reform programmes were adopted early it takes time for data to emerge and, in any case, the programmes are intended to secure long-run improvements.

However, the World Bank (1989) has produced some information on the results of reform programmes. This is reproduced in Table 8.7. These data refer to Africa but the problems – debt, high levels of microeconomic intervention, inflation and overvalued exchange rates – are common to many LDCs, particularly those in Latin America.

Countries were classified according to the changes in their policies during the period 1985–7; in short, whether they adopted the types of structural adjustment programme discussed earlier. The following countries, therefore, were treated as having 'strong' reform programmes: Burundi, Central African Republic, Congo, Ivory Coast, Gambia, Ghana, Guinea, Guinea-Bissau, Kenya, Madagascar, Malawi,

Mauritania, Mauritius, Niger, Nigeria, Senegal, Tanzania, Togo and Zaire. Strong shocks were classified as abnormally large variations in agricultural growth and exceptional variations in export prices. The countries classified by the World Bank as having been subjected to strong external shocks were: Burkina Faso, Burundi, Congo, Ethiopia, Malawi, Niger, Nigeria, Sudan and Zimbabwe.

The most relevant column is that relating to countries not affected by strong shocks; to identify the effects of reform it helps to eliminate as far as possible 'noise' from the data. From these data it can be seen that countries with strong reform programmes exhibit significantly increased growth rates in real GDP. These rates considerably exceed those for unreformed economies and, moreover, the change in the growth rate between the pre-reform and post-reform periods greatly exceeds that of the unreformed countries.

A similar picture emerges for export volume. For reformed countries post-reform growth in export volumes represents a much more considerable improvement than for the unreformed ones. For real domestic investment in reformed economies, the post-reform period exhibits increasing real investment in contrast to the pre-reform period. This again compares very favourably with the performance of the unreformed economies. Lastly, reformed economies exhibited a greater contraction in real per capitum consumption in the pre-reform period than did the unreformed economies. In the post-reform period reformed economies exhibit growth in real per capita consumption whereas the unreformed ones exhibit continued (but reduced) contraction.

Whilst these data are not sufficient to provide a conclusive picture of the effects of reform programmes they do suggest that reform is capable of producing the results that it claims to. Moreover, it suggests that these results are achieved with surprising rapidity. The evidence, therefore, suggests short-run adverse effects are limited both in magnitude and duration (that is, the short run is shorter than might be expected).

This view is far from uncontroversial. A number of authors – for example, Hamilton (1989) – have challenged the rationale for adjustment programmes involving economic liberalisation. Given that opinions vary at the conceptual level, the issue is essentially an empirical one. On the empirical side, the World Bank study (1989) receives support from Balassa (1990). Balassa does not directly measure the impact of liberalisation programmes but, using a sample of Sub-Saharan African economies over three periods – 1965–82, 1965–73 and 1974–82 – he conducts an empirical study of the effects of policy upon export performance. Countries are classified in one of three categories according to their policy emphasis: market-oriented, interventionist and hybrid. Balassa finds that there is a general tendency for market-oriented economies to gain export market share whilst interventionist ones lose it. This, therefore, provides some indirect evidence that liberalisation in Africa may indeed achieve the results that the World Bank claims.

8.6 LDC DEBT

The substantial size of public sector debt in many LDCs has a number of implications for inward direct investment. A large debt burden reduces market demand in host economies but at the same time is likely to induce a more favourable policy stance towards inward investment. It has also encouraged, through debt–equity swaps, a new and more favourable method of financing direct investment in LDCs.

Servicing and repaying the debts to foreign banks requires an outflow of public sector funds from the LDC. In practice, this has led LDC governments to increase overall fiscal receipts or to reduce government expenditure or, in most cases, both. Thus, financing the debt has led to significant fiscal contraction of the economies concerned.

This clearly affects the domestic market size adversely and hence is likely to have a disincentive effect upon inward investment. This is not uniform across types of investment project. Obviously it constitutes a disincentive for import-substituting investment as this, by definition, is intended to supply the domestic market. Export platform investment is, in principle, independent of domestic levels of demand as the intended markets are elsewhere.

However, the impact on export platform investment depends on which export markets the investment is intended to supply. Export platform investment to supply developed economy markets is unlikely to suffer any loss of available markets. In contrast, investment intended to supply neighbouring LDC export markets will almost certainly face contracting markets because trading partners also face the need for domestic contraction to finance external debt. Resource-seeking investment and rationalised investment both aim to supply global markets and are therefore unlikely to be strongly affected by the contraction of aggregate demand in LDCs.

On the supply side, however, the effects of debt are less ambiguous. As debts are usually denominated in foreign currencies, the need to finance the debt leads to a shortage of foreign exchange. Foreign investment is, therefore, particularly attractive as it brings much-needed foreign exchange.

Moreover, the contractionary impact of debt financing implies increased difficulty in financing new investment from domestic sources. This may be manifested in a direct shortage of investment funds in the host economy or increased domestic interest rates, or both. This, in turn, implies a lower rate of new investment from domestic sources. Host governments wishing to promote industrial growth are therefore increasingly likely to seek private investment projects from foreign sources in attempts to increase or maintain investment in their economies.

The effect on supply-side incentives for inward FDI is not limited to the pressures that debt brings to bear upon host governments. As Kume and Ito (1989) note, external debt has led to a new mechanism of direct investment: the debt–equity swap. They list 17 LDCs which have either adopted or are considering adopting such a policy: Argentina, Brazil, Chile, Colombia, Costa Rica, Dominican Republic, Ecuador, Egypt, Honduras, Jamaica, Mexico, Morocco, Nigeria, Peru, the Philippines, Uruguay and Venezuela.

Debt–equity swaps involve the new investor purchasing some portion of the outstanding liability of the host government from its creditors (usually a commercial bank in a developed economy). This is purchased at a discount as the creditor is able to reduce its risk exposure. The central bank of the LDC then exchanges the debt for its face value in local currency for the purposes of local investment. Many host governments place restrictions upon the type of inward investment or attach performance requirements on qualifying investments.

From the viewpoint of the outward investor, debt–equity swaps are a clear incentive in that the cost of the investment is reduced by the discount offered by the original creditor. However, the way in which the host government funds the purchase of the debt from the inward investor may lead to some secondary effects which are less favourable. The two principal ways in which the host central bank could finance debt–equity swaps are by (a) printing more money and (b) issuing bonds. The former could lead to further inflationary pressure and the latter to higher interest rates (and, hence, a higher cost of any local financing of the project). It seems unlikely than any negative secondary effect of this type would be sufficient to offset the positive incentive effect of the debt–equity swap itself, however. Moreover, in some cases (such as Mexico), equity in previously nationalised industries has been involved. This avoids the possibility of adverse secondary effects as there is no net financing requirement on the part of the host central bank.

8.7 IMPROVING DIRECT POLICY INCENTIVES: THE EXAMPLE OF MEXICO

The Mexican economy has a number of characteristics which make it intrinsically attractive of foreign investors (see, for example, Blomstrom and Persson, 1983). It has a relatively large domestic market in its own right and its geographical location makes a very suitable platform for exporting to the USA. On the supply side it is abundant in a number of natural resources and labour is relatively cheap even by Latin American standards. Moreover, its relatively high degree of political stability helps to reduce potential risks for investors.

However, the emphasis of Mexican government policy towards inward FDI from the late 1960s to the late 1980s was one of tight regulation and stringent performance requirements. These direct disincentives reflected a more general policy emphasis of intervention-regulation and nationalisation in domestic markets and an interventionist import-substitution approach to international trade.

From 1985 to 1986 the Mexican government began to adopt a more market-oriented strategy. This started with a series of macroeconomic reforms, privatisations and reductions in tax rates. In 1988 this was followed by liberalisation of international trade, and then by a relaxation of the regulations concerning inward investment in May 1989. Foreign investors became permitted to own up to 100 per cent of firms in certain 'restricted' sectors. Permission is automatic if the project exceeds US$100 million, is funded from abroad, is located outside the three largest cities, is anticipated to create new jobs and satisfies environment requirements. If not, permission is discretionary. For activities where foreign direct investment remains restricted or prohibited, foreign investment can be undertaken through temporary (20 year maximum) local investment trusts. Permission to expand existing investments which are export-oriented or result from merger is no longer required. Restrictions on acquisitions by foreign firms in unrestricted sectors have been relaxed.

The application of these revised regulations varies according to the industrial sector. Six categories of industry are defined:

(a) those reserved for the state (principally mineral extraction, banking, electricity, railways and telegraphs);
(b) those reserved for Mexicans (transportation, forestry, financial services and broadcasting);
(c) those in which FDI is limited to 34 per cent (mineral processing);
(d) those where FDI is limited to 40 per cent (petrochemicals, automative parts);
(e) those where FDI is limited to 49 per cent (fishing, extraction of ores, explosives, firearms, telecommunications, rental agencies);
(f) those where up to 100 per cent is permitted subject to authorisation (agriculture, publishing, construction, various services).

All other activities are free from regulation.

Thus Mexican liberalisation represents a move away from quite stringent disincentives, but is clearly far from complete. Nonetheless, a significant improvement in both direct and indirect policy incentives for inward investment is the clear result.

Mexico is only one of many LDCs where such policy changes are in evidence. Indonesia, for example, has much in common with Mexico: natural resources, cheap labour, a large domestic market, geographical proximity to large export markets and substantial debt. Moreover, from the 1960s to the mid-1980s it shared Mexico's policy emphasis on domestic intervention, protectionism and stringent disincentives for inward FDI. As in the Mexican case, Indonesia started to liberalise its domestic economy and its external trade in the mid-1980s. This was followed in late 1987 and late 1988 by two rounds of liberalisation of its policies towards inward FDI.

Several African countries (for example, Cameroon, Togo and Benin) have introduced investment codes which offer tax breaks for inward investors. Venezuela has recently introduced a similar reform programme to that of Mexico. In conclusion, the Mexican example can be seen as broadly representative of an emerging trend in LDCs toward a more favourable policy environment. As yet, liberalisation is only partial, which suggests that further changes are probable.

8.8 1992 AND EAST EUROPEAN LIBERALISATION

Liberalisation in Eastern European economies offers new opportunities for investment by EC firms in low labour cost locations. Similarly, 1992 is likely to improve the attractiveness of supplying other national markets within EC boundaries. The purpose of this section is to discuss the implications of these changes for EC investment in LDCs.

Although 1992 should make the supply of other national markets within the EC more attractive to EC firms it does not follow that it will increase FDI. Production in a foreign location is to a large extent a substitute for exporting. Harmonisation of EC markets reduces the cost of exporting and would be likely to promote exports in place of foreign production. However, certain types of FDI are complements to rather than substitutes for exporting: subsidiaries to provide sales outlets or after-sales services would be examples of this. In these cases the tendency of harmonisation to promote exports would also promote FDI. To the extent that FDI and exporting are independent activities (that is, they neither complement nor substitute), the harmonisation of the 1992 programme would remove remaining barriers to intra-EC investment and would, therefore, tend to increase it.

Eastern European liberalisation differs from 1992 in its implications for FDI. First, the magnitude of the reduction in barriers to trade and investment is likely to greatly exceed that involved with 1992. Second, as East European economies are being increasingly opened to trade as well as FDI it is most likely that both will be stimulated simultaneously rather than one at the expense of another. Thus both 1992 and East European liberalisation are likely to make FDI in Europe more attractive to EC investors. As the magnitude of the change is more considerable in the case of Eastern Europe it is likely that this will generate more new FDI than the 1992 programme. Moreover, the greater difference in costs (especially for labour) between West and East Europe also suggests that East European liberalisation will prove the greater stimulus.

The question now arises as to how far any increases in FDI generated by these changes will be at the expense of FDI in LDCs (that is, how far will it be 'crowded out'?). The crowding out of investment in one location by investment in another location is possible through one of two routes. To borrow a term from consumer theory – Lancaster (1979) – there is a possibility of both 'inside' and 'outside' substitution effects. An 'inside' substitution effect is where a particular project could be located in one of several competing locations. A typical scenario would be a single project which could be placed in one of several locations. The decision to choose one, by definition, excludes the others.

The strength of this effect depends on the nature of the investment. An import-substituting investment is intended to supply only the host-country market and so there is no substitution by definition. Similarly, resource-based investment is only likely to face a choice of locations between those that share similar natural resources. East European and EC economies typically do not share the same natural resources as LDCs, so this effect is not likely to be significant.

Investment which is intended either to supply export markets or to be a rationalised investment will typically select one of many possible locations according to its particular characteristics. So, for example, the choice of an 'export platform' may be decided on a number of criteria including low labour costs, the local availability of supplies, and so on. It is these types of FDI which are most likely to generate inside substitution effects between Europe and LDCs.

However, given that an inside substitution effect is most likely between economies that share common characteristics (for example, low labour costs), we can differentiate between the likely impacts of 1992 and East European liberalisation. Eastern Europe possesses more characteristics in common with LDCs, particularly low labour costs, than do most EC economies. Inside substitution is, therefore, considerably more likely between investment in Eastern Europe and that in LDCs. Perhaps the greatest area of possible inside substitution likely to result from 1992 (due to geographical proximity, common climate and broadly similar labour costs) is that between Mediterranean LDCs and Mediterranean regions of the EC.

To summarise, Eastern European liberalisation is likely to lead to strong inside substitution effects at the expense of export platform and rationalised investments in LDCs. In contrast, 1992 is unlikely to lead to strong effects to this type except between EC Mediterranean economies and Mediterranean LDCs.

An outside substitution effect occurs where, say, two different projects exist which are not inside substitutes (because they are not trying to exploit the same market or the same resources) but, due to certain constraints, only the more profitable of the two may be chosen. More generally, when a financing constraint is binding on firms that have a variety of possible projects, the selection of one particular project implies another cannot be chosen. This applies to all types of investment (market-seeking, export platform and so on).

The constraints upon the growth of a firm are well known from the work of Marris (1964). Financing and managerial constraints are of particular relevance here. It is not difficult to justify financing constraints: retained profits are clearly likely to be finite and neither new share issues (with a consequent increase in the risk of takeover) nor additional borrowing (given the increased risk of bankruptcy in a highly-geared firm) can avoid them altogether. Moreover, finance is not the only constraint upon the expansion of the firm: FDI is also constrained by the ability of management to absorb the running of new subsidiaries.

However, an outside substitution effect is principally a short-run effect, as the constraints to the expansion of firms are less binding in the long run than the short. We should, therefore, expect East European liberalisation to produce powerful short-run (outside substitution) and long-run (inside substitution) effects, diverting FDI away from LDCs. However, 1992 is unlikely to produce major investment diversion effects in the long run other than in respect of Mediterranean LDCs. In the short run there may be some diversion, but this is unlikely to be anywhere near the magnitude of East European effects.

8.9 CONCLUSIONS

In terms of supply-side incentives the economic climate for FDI in LDCs has undergone considerable improvement in recent years. Indirect supply-side incentives have been considerably improved by microeconomic and macroeconomic reform programmes. There is an observable trend, exemplified by Mexico, for direct policy incentives to be improved as well. The existence of debt provides an inducement for host governments to improve direct incentives further, so that liberalisation of LDCs' policies seems likely to continue.

Evidence suggests that host-government policy can have a significant influence upon the location decision of outward investors. As some LDCs liberalise faster or further than others the locational effects may simply redistribute investment from one LDC to another. However, the pace of liberalisation and the number of LDCs involved suggest that a net increase in investment in LDCs *relative to that which would otherwise have occurred* is the most probable outcome. In short, the changes in the economic environment make

LDC locations relatively more attractive than existing developed economy locations (and, hence, may induce some substitution), but also make some potential projects in LDCs more profitable than before (and thus are likely to generate entirely new investment).

The evidence of the past behaviour of EC outward investment, although limited, suggests that member states' firms tend to exploit investment opportunities in other EC member states before exploiting those available elsewhere. To the extent that 1992 increases the attraction of investment in other EC member states this would be likely to involve some diversion of investment away from LDCs. However, the extent to which 1992 will induce FDI rather than exporting as a means of supplying European markets is unclear and, in any case, any diversionary effect away from LDCs is unlikely to be strong.

There is a back-yard effect in outward investment (a tendency to exploit investment opportunities first in neighbouring and more familiar regions before exploiting those in more distant regions). One reason for the lower propensity of EC countries to invest in LDCs is the absence of a back yard comprising LDCs with sufficiently large markets and cost advantages to offer extensive investment opportunities.

The liberalisation of Eastern European economies is likely to provide EC firms with exactly such a back yard in which to invest. Thus liberalisation provides entirely new and substantial opportunities for investment in relatively large markets offering cheap labour. The geographical proximity of these markets, their cultural similarity and, in some cases, political reunification all add to the attractiveness of these locations. It is difficult to see liberalisation not resulting in significant investment from EC countries.

If so, the potential of these new markets for outward investment to divert projects away from LDCs is strong. First, cheap labour means that projects in Eastern Europe are more likely to be direct substitutes for those in an LDC location. Second, even where there is not direct substitution, constraints upon the rate at which firms can expand are likely to cause a 'crowding out' effect on outward investment in LDCs. All of this suggests that the net effect will be a further decline in the EC's propensity to undertake outward direct investment in LDCs.

Bibliography

Adler, N.J. and M. Jelinek (1986) Is organisational culture 'culture bound'?, *Human Resource Management*, 25, 73–90.

Anderson, E. and H. Gatignon (1986) Modes of foreign entry: A transaction cost analysis and propositions, *Journal of International Business Studies*, 27(3), 1–26.

Anderson, R.W. and C.J. Harris (1986) A model of innovation with application to new financial products, *Oxford Economic Papers*, 38, Nov. supplement, 205–17.

Arthur, W.B., Y.M. Ermoliev and Y.M. Kanioviski (1987) Path-dependent processes and the emergence of macro-structure, *European Journal of Operational Research*, 30, 294–303.

Balassa, B. (1990) Incentive policies and export performance in Sub-Saharan Africa, *World Development*, 18, 383–91.

Ball, C.A. and A.E. Tschoegl (1982) The decision to establish a foreign bank branch or subsidiary: an application of binary classification procedures, *Journal of Financial and Quantitative Analysis*, 17, 411–24.

Bartlett, C.A. and S. Ghoshal (1990) Managing innovation in the transnational corporation, in C.A. Bartlett, Y. Doz and G. Hedlund (eds), *Managing the Global Firm*, London: Routledge & Kegan Paul, 215–55.

Bhagwati, J. (1986) Trade in services and developing countries, *Columbia University Discussion Paper*, no. 307, New York.

Blomstrom, M. and H. Persson (1983) Foreign investment and spillover efficiency in an underdeveloped economy: evidence from the Mexican manufacturing industry, *World Development*, 11, 493–502.

Boddewyn, J.J., M.B. Halbrich and A.C. Perry (1986) Service multinationals: conceptualisation, measurement and theory, *Journal of International Business Studies*, 17(3), 41–57.

Bowker (1987) *Directory of American Research and Technology 1988*, 22nd edn, New York: R.R. Bowker.

Brooke, M.Z. (1984) *Centralization and Autonomy: A Study in Organization Behaviour*, London: Holt, Rinehart & Winston.

Bruno, M. (1988) Opening up: liberalization with stabilization, in Dornbusch, R. and F.L.C.H. Helmers (eds), *The Open Economy: Tools for Policymakers in Developing Countries*, Oxford: Oxford University Press, 223–48.

Buckley, P.J. and M.C. Casson (1976) *The Future of the Multinational Enterprise*, London: Macmillan.

Buckley, P.J. and M.C. Casson (1981) The optimal timing of a foreign direct investment, *Economic Journal*, 91, 75–87.

Buckley, P.J. and M.C. Casson (1985) *The Economic Theory of the Multinational Enterprise: Selected Papers*, London: Macmillan.

Burstall, M.L., J.H. Dunning and A. Lake (1981) *Multinational Enterprises, Governments and Technology: Pharmaceutical Industry*, Paris: OECD.

Campayne, P. (1990) An analysis of some determinants of multinational bank performance, *University of Reading Discussion Papers in International Investment and Business Studies*, No. 146.

Campbell, N. (1988) *China's Business Strategies*, Oxford: Pergamon Press.

Campbell, N. (1989) *A Strategic Guide to Equity Joint Ventures in China*, Oxford: Pergamon Press.

Cantwell, J. (1987) Historical trends in international patterns of technological innovation, *University of Reading Discussion Papers in Economics*, Series A, no. 191.

Cantwell, J.A. (1991) The international agglomeration of technological activity, in M.C. Casson (ed.), *Global Research Strategy and International Competitiveness*, Oxford: Blackwell, 133–82.

Casson, M.C. (1982) The Theory of Foreign Direct Investment, in J. Black and J.H. Dunning (eds), *International Capital Movements*, London: Macmillan, reprinted in Buckley and Casson (1985), 113–43.

Casson, M.C. (1987) *The Firm and the Market: Studies on Multinational Enterprise and the Scope of the Firm*, Oxford: Blackwell.

Casson, M.C. (1989) The economic theory of multinational banking: an internalisation approach, *University of Reading Discussion Papers in International Investment and Business Studies*, no. 133.

Casson, M.C. (1990) *Enterprise and Competitiveness: A Systems View of International Business*, Oxford: Clarendon Press.

Casson, M.C. (1991) *Economics of Business Culture: Game Theory, Transaction Costs and Economic Performance*: Oxford: Clarendon Press.

Casson, M.C., R.D. Pearce and S. Singh (1991) A review of recent trends, in M.C. Casson (ed.), *Global Research Strategy and International Competitiveness*, Oxford: Blackwell, 250–71.

Caves, R.E. (1982) *Multinational Enterprise and Economic Analysis*, Cambridge: Cambridge University Press.

CEST (1990) *Attitudes to the Exploitation of Science and Technology: Final Report*, Manchester: Centre for Exploitation of Science and Technology.

Chandler, A.D., Jr. (1977) *The Visible Hand: The Managerial Revolution in American Business*, Cambridge, Mass.: Belknap Press of Harvard University Press.

Chandler, A.D. and F. Redlich (1961) Recent developments in American business administration and their conceptualisation, *Business History Review*, 35.

Chen, N-R (1986) *Foreign Investment in China: Current Trends*, Washington, DC: US Department of Commerce.

Chesnais, F. (1988) Technical cooperation agreements between firms, *STI Review* no. 4, Paris: OECD, 51–119.

Chesnais, F. (1990) The network firm, Paris: OECD, *mimeo*.

Child, J. and A. Kieser (1979) Organisational and managerial roles in British and German companies: an examination of the culture-free thesis, in

C.J. Lammers and D.J. Hickson (eds), *Organisations Alike and Unlike*, London: Routledge & Kegan Paul, 251–71.
Cho, K.R. (1985) *Multinational Banks: Their Identities and Determinants*, Ann Arbor, Michigan: University of Michigan Press.
Choi, S.R., A.E. Tschoegl and C.M. Yu (1986) Banks and the world's major financial centres, 1970–1980, *Weltwirtschaftliches Archiv*, 122(1), 48–64.
Christaller, W. (1933) *Central Places in Southern Germany*, Englewood Cliffs, New Jersey: Prentice-Hall.
CITIC (1984, 1985, 1986) *China Investment Guide*, London: Longman.
Coffey, W.J. and M. Polese (1987) Trade and location of producer services: a Canadian perspective, *Environment and Planning A*, 19, 597–611.
Cohen, J.M. (1956) *The Life of Ludwig Mond*, London: Methuen.
Cole, R.E. (1973) Functional alternatives and economic development: an empirical example of permanent employment in Japan, *American Sociological Review*, 38, 424–38.
Contractor, F.J. (1989) The liberalisation of foreign ownership regulations in the 1980s, *State University of New Jersey School of Management Working Paper* no. 89–01.
Contractor, J. and P. Lorange (eds) (1988) *Cooperative Strategies in International Business*, Lexington, Mass.: Lexington Books.
Cummings, L.L. and S.M. Schmidt (1972) Managerial attitudes of Greeks: the roles of culture and industrialisation, *Administrative Science Quarterly*, 17, 265–72.
Dave, U. (1984) US multinational involvement in the international hotel sector: an analysis, *The Service Industries Journal*, 4, 48–63.
Davidson, W.H. (1980) The location of FDI activity: country characteristics and experience effects, *Journal of International Business Studies*, 11(3), 9–22.
Davidson, W.H. (1982) *Global Strategic Management*, New York: John Wiley.
Davidson, W.H. and D.G. McFetridge (1985) Key characteristics in the choice of international technology transfer mode, *Journal of International Business Studies*, 16(2), 5–21.
Davis, E.P. (1990) International financial centres: an industrial analysis, *Bank of England Discussion Paper* 51, September.
Deal, T.E. and A.A. Kennedy (1982) *Corporate Cultures*, Reading, Mass.: Addison-Wesley.
Dicken, P. (1986) *Global Shift: Industrial Change in a Turbulent World*, London: Harper & Row.
Dornbusch, R. (1988) Overvaluation and trade balance, in Dornbusch, R. and F.L.C.H. Helmers (eds), *The Open Economy: Tools for Policymakers in Developing Countries*, Oxford: Oxford University Press, 80–107.
Doz, Y.L. (1986) *Strategic Management in Multinational Companies*, London: Pergamon.
Dunning, J.H. (1969) The City of London: a case study in urban economics, *Town Planning Review*, 40, 207–33.
Dunning, J.H. (1977) Trade, location of economic activity and the multinational enterprise: a search for an eclectic approach, in B. Ohlin, P.O.

Hesselborn and P.M. Wijkman (eds), *The International Allocation of Economic Activity*, London: Macmillan, 395–418.
Dunning, J.H. (1980) Towards an eclectic theory of international production: some empirical tests, *Journal of International Business Studies*, 11(1), 9–31.
Dunning, J.H. (1981) *International Production and the Multinational Enterprise*, London: Allen & Unwin.
Dunning, J.H. (1982) Explaining the international direct investment position of countries: towards a dynamic or developmental approach, in J. Black and J.H. Dunning (eds), *International Capital Movements*, London: Macmillan.
Dunning, J.H. (1986) The investment development cycle and Third World multinationals, in K.M. Khan (ed.), *Multinationals of the South: New Actors in the International Economy*, London: Frances Pinter.
Dunning, J.H. (1988a) *Explaining International Production*, London: Unwin Hyman.
Dunning, J.H. (1988b) The eclectic paradigm of international production: a restatement and some possible extensions, *Journal of International Business Studies*, 19(1), 1–31.
Dunning, J.H. (1989) Multinational enterprises and the growth of services: some conceptual and theoretical issues, *The Service Industries Journal*, 9(1), 5–39.
Dunning, J.H. and M. McQueen (1981) The eclectic theory of international production: a case study of the international hotel industry, *Managerial and Decision Economics*, 21, 197–210.
Dunning, J.H. and G. Norman (1987) The location choice of offices of international companies, *Environment and Planning A*, 19, 613–31.
Dunning, J.H. and R.D. Pearce (1985) *The World's Largest Industrial Enterprises, 1962–1983*, Aldershot: Gower.
Edgerton, D.E.H. (1988) Industrial research in the British photographic industry, 1879–1939, in J. Liebenau (ed.), *The Challenge of New Technology: Innovation in British Business since 1850*, Aldershot: Gower, 106–34.
Fagre, N. and L.T. Wells, Jr (1982) Bargaining power of multinational enterprises and host governments, *Journal of International Business Studies*, 13(3), 9–32.
Fieldhouse, D.K. (1978) *Unilever Overseas: The Anatomy of a Multinational 1895–1965*, London: Croom Helm.
Form, W. (1979) Comparative industrial sociology and the convergence hypotheses, *Annual Review of Sociology*, 5, 1–25.
Franko, L.G. (1987) New forms of investment in developing countries: a five industry comparison, *Columbia Journal of World Business*, Summer, 39–56.
Franko, L.G. (1989) Use of minority and 50–50 joint ventures by US multinationals in the 1970s: the interaction of host country policies and corporate strategies, *Journal of International Business Studies*, 20(1), 19–40.
Garnier , G. (1984) The autonomy of foreign subsidiaries: environmental

and national influences, *Journal of General Management*, 4(1), 57–82.
Gates, S.R. and W.G. Egelhoff (1986) Centralisation in headquarters–subsidiary relationships, *Journal of International Business Studies*, 17(2), 71–91.
Gatignon, H. and E. Anderson (1988) The multinational corporation's degree of control over subsidiaries: an empirical test of a transaction cost explanation, *Journal of Law, Economics and Organisation*, 4, 305–36.
Germidis, D. and C.A. Michalet (1984) *International Banks and Financial Markets in Developing Countries*, Paris: OECD.
Goldberg, L.G. and A. Saunders (1980) The causes of US bank expansion overseas: the case of Great Britain, *Journal of Money Credit and Banking*, 12, 630–43.
Goldberg, L.G. and A. Saunders (1981) The growth of organisational forms of foreign banks in the US, *Journal of Money Credit and Banking*, 13, 304–74.
Gomes-Casseres, B. (1989) Ownership structure of foreign subsidiaries: theory and evidence, *Journal of Economic Behaviour and Organisation*, 11, 1–26.
Graves, D. (1973) The impact of culture upon managerial attitudes, beliefs and behaviour in England and France, in G. Graves (ed.), *Management Research: A Cross Cultural Perspective*, San Francisco: Jossey Bass, 282–304.
Guisinger, S.E. and associates (1985) *Investment Incentives and Performance Requirements*, New York: Praeger.
Haire, M., E.E. Ghiselli, and L.W. Porter (1966) *Managerial Thinking: An International Study*, New York: John Wiley.
Hakanson, L. (1990) International decentralisation of R & D – the organizational challenges, in C.A. Bartlett, Y. Doz and G. Hedlund (eds), *Managing the Global Firm*, London: Routledge & Kegan Paul 256–78.
Hamilton, C. (1989) The irrelevance of economic liberalisation in the Third World, *World Development*, 10, 1523–30.
Hansen, S-O. (1981) *Studies in Internationalisation of the Pharmaceutical Industry – A Taxonomic Approach*, Abo: Abo Akademi.
Hennart, J.F. (1990) The transaction costs theory of equity joint ventures: an empirical study of Japanese subsidiaries in the US, *mimeo*.
Hewson, J. (1986) The internationalisation of banking, in Tan and Kapur (1986).
Hickson, D.J., C.R. Hinings, C.J. McMillan and J.P. Schwitter (1974) The culture-free context of organisation structure: a tri-national comparison, *Sociology*, 8, 59–80.
Hickson, D.J., C.H. McMillan, K. Asumi and D. Howard (1979) Grounds for comparative organisation theory: quick sand or hardcore, in C.J. Lammers and D.J. Hickson (eds), *Organisations Alike and Unlike*, London: Routledge & Kegan Paul, 25–41.
Hirsch, S. (1987) International Transactions in Services and in Service Intensive Goods; paper presented at the Academy of International Business, annual meeting.
Hladik, K.J. (1988) R & D and international joint ventures, in Contractor and Lorange (1988), 187–204.

Hofstede, G. (1980) *Culture's Consequences*, Beverly Hills, California: Sage Publications.

Hounshell, D.A. and J.K. Smith, Jr (1988) *Science and Corporate Strategy: Du Pont R & D, 1902–1980*, Cambridge: Cambridge University Press.

Hsu, J.C. (1989) *China's Foreign Trade Reforms: Impact on Growth and Stability*, Cambridge: Cambridge University Press.

Hutton, S. and P. Lawrence (1981) *German Engineers: The Anatomy of a Profession*, Oxford: Clarendon Press.

Hymer, S.H. (1971) The multinational corporation and the law of uneven development, in J. Bhagwati (ed.), *Economics and World Order*, New York: World Law Fund.

Isard, W. (1960) *Methods of Regional Analysis*, Cambridge, Mass.: MIT Press.

James, B.G. (1977) *The Future of the Multinational Pharmaceutical Industry to 1990*, London: Associated Business Programmes.

James, F.A.J.L. (ed.) (1989) *The Development of the Laboratory: Essays on the Place of Experiment in Industrial Civilization*, London: Macmillan.

Johanson, J. and J.E. Vahlne (1977) The internationalisation process of the firm – a model of knowledge development and increasing foreign market commitments, *Journal of International Business Studies*, 8, 23–32.

Kaku, S. (1980) The development and structure of the German coal-tar dyestuffs firms, in A. Okochi and H. Uchida (eds), *Development and Diffusion of Technology: Electrical and Chemical Industries*, Tokyo: University of Tokyo Press, 77–94.

Kelly, M. and G. Philippatos (1982) Comparative analysis of the foreign investment evaluation practices by US manufacturing MNCs, *Journal of International Business Studies*, 13(3), 19–42.

Khambata, D.M. (1986) *The Practice of Multinational Banking; Macro-Policy Issues and Key International Concepts*, London: Quorum Books.

Khoury, S.J. (1980) *Dynamics of International Banking*, New York: Praeger.

Kindleberger, C.P. (1983) International banks as leaders or followers of international business, *Journal of Banking and Finance*, 7, 583–95.

Kindleberger, C.P. (1974) *The Formation of Financial Centres: A Study in Comparative Economic History*, Princeton, NJ: Princeton Studies in International Finance, No. 36.

Kogut, B. (1983) FDI as a sequential process, in C.P. Kindleberger and D.B. Audretsch (eds), *The Multinational Corporation in the 1980s*, Cambridge, Mass.: MIT Press.

Kogut, B. (1988) A study of the life cycle of joint ventures, in Contractor and Lorange (1988), 169–85.

Kojima, K. (1978) *Direct Foreign Investment: A Japanese Model of Multinational Business Operations*, London: Croom Helm.

Kume, G. and K. Ito (1989) International Direct Investment and Debt Problems in Developing Countries in OECD, *International Direct Investment and the New Economic Environment*, Paris: OECD, 71–94.

Lall, S. (1982) *Developing Countries as Exporters of Technology*, London: Macmillan.

Lancaster, K. (1979) *Variety, Equity and Efficiency*, Oxford: Basil Blackwell.

Laurent, A. (1983) The cultural diversity of Western conceptions of management, *International Studies of Management and Organisation*, 13(1–2), 75–96.

Lawrence, P. (1980) *Managers and Management in West Germany*, London: Croom Helm.

Lazonick, W. (1986) Strategy, structure and management development in the United States and Britain, in K. Kobayashi and H. Morikawa (eds), *Development of Managerial Enterprise*, Tokyo: University of Tokyo Press, 101–46.

Lodge, G.C. and E.F. Vogel (eds) (1987) *Ideology and National Competitiveness: An Analysis of Nine Countries*, Boston, Mass.: Harvard Business School Press.

Longman (1987) *Industrial Research in the United Kingdom: A Guide to Organizations and Programmes*, 12th edn, Harlow, Essex: Longman.

Longman (1988a) *European Research Centres: A Directory of Scientific, Technological, Agricultural and Medical Laboratories*, 7th edn, Harlow, Essex: Longman.

Longman (1988b) *Pacific Research Centres: A Directory of Organizations in Science, Technology, Agriculture and Medicine*, 2nd edn, Harlow, Essex: Longman.

Losch, A. (1954) *The Economics of Location*, New Haven, Conn.: Yale University Press.

Machlup, F. (1977) *A History of Thought on Economic Integration*, London: Macmillan.

Marris, R. (1964) *The Economic Theory of Managerial Capitalism*, London: Macmillan.

Marsden, K. and T. Belot (1987) Private Enterprise in Africa, *World Bank Discussion Paper*, no. 17.

MOFERT (1987) *Almanac of China's Foreign Economic Relations and Trade*, Beijing: China Prospect Publishing House.

Nair, A. (1987) New drug policy: will it meet national objectives?, *Economic Times*, 2 April.

Nicolaidis, C.S. (1991) Cultural Determinants of Corporate Excellence: The Impact of National Cultures on Corporate Performance, PhD Thesis, University of Reading, UK.

Nigh, D., K.R. Cho and S. Krishnan (1986) The role of location-related factors in US banking involvement abroad; an empirical examination, *Journal of International Business Studies*, 17(3), 59–72.

OECD (1990) *Main Economic Indicators*, Paris: OECD.

Ouchi, W.G. (1980) Markets, Bureaucracies and Clans, *Administrative Science Quarterly*, 25, 129–141.

Ouchi, W.G. (1981) *Theory Z: How American Business can Meet the Japanese Challenge*, Reading, Mass.: Addison-Wesley.

Parker, J.E.S. (1984) *The International Diffusion of Pharmaceuticals*, London: Macmillan.

Parker, J.E.S. (1989) Who Has a Drug Lag?, *Managerial and Decision Economics*, 10, 299–309.

Pascale R.T. and A.G. Athos (1981) *The Art of Japanese Management*, New York: Simon & Schuster.

Pearce, R.D. (1987) Host countries and the R & D of multinationals, *University of Reading Discussion Papers in International Investment and Business Studies*, no. 101.

Pearce, R.D. (1989a) *Internationalisation of Research and Development by Multinational Enterprises*, London: Macmillan.

Pearce, R.D. (1989b) The internationalisation of sales by leading enterprises: some firm, industry and country determinants, *University of Reading Discussion Papers in International Investment and Business Studies*, no. 135.

Pecchioli, R.M. (1983) *The Internationalisation of Banking*, Paris: OECD.

Peters, T.J. and R.H. Waterman (1982) *In Search of Excellence*, London: Harper & Row.

Porter, M.E. (1985) *Competitive Advantage*, New York: Free Press.

Porter, M.E. (1986) Competition in global industries: a conceptual framework, in M.E. Porter (ed.), *Competition in Global Industries*, Cambridge, Mass.: Harvard University Press.

Porter, M.E. (1990) *The Competitive Advantage of Nations*, London: Macmillan.

Reader, W.J. (1975) *Imperial Chemical Industries: A History, Vol. II*, Oxford: Oxford University Press.

Reed, H.C. (1981) *The Pre-eminence of International Financial Centres*, New York: Praeger.

Reed, H.C. (1983) Appraising corporate investment policy: a financial centre theory of foreign direct investment, in C.P. Kindleberger and D.B. Audretsch (eds), *The Multinational Corporation in the 1980s*, Cambridge, Mass.: MIT Press.

Reich, L.S. (1985) *The Making of American Industrial Research: Science and Business at GE and Bell*, Cambridge: Cambridge University Press.

Root, F.R. (1987) *Entry Strategies for International Markets*, Lexington, Mass.: Lexington Books.

Rugman, A.M. (1987) The firm-specific advantages of Canadian multinationals, *Journal of International Economic Studies*, 2, 1–14.

Rybcynski, T.M. (1988) The internationalisation of finance and business, *Business Economics*, 23(3), 14–20.

Sauvant, K.P. and Z. Zbigniew (1985) Foreign direct investment and transnational corporations in services, *CTC Reporter*, 20, Autumn.

Schein, E. (1985) *Organisational Culture and Leadership*, San Francisco: Jossey Bass.

Schnee, J.E. and E. Caglarcan (1978) The Changing Pharmaceutical Research and Development Environment, in C.M. Lindsay (ed.), *The Pharmaceutical Industry*, New York: Wiley, 91–104.

Schwartzman, D. (1976) *Innovations in the Pharmaceutical Industry*, Baltimore: Johns Hopkins University Press.

Schwartz, H. and S.M. Davis, (1981) Matching corporate culture and business strategy, *Organisational Dynamics*, 23 Summer, 30–48.

Scott, J.D. (1962) *Vickers: A History*, London: Weidenfeld & Nicolson.

Segal-Horn, S. (1988) Global service delivery – managing the critical interdependencies, in R. Johnson (ed.), *The Management of Service Operations*, Coventry: University of Warwick, 99–127.

Singh, S. (1985) *Multinational Corporations and the Indian Drug Industry*, New Delhi: Criterion Publications.

Smith, D.M. (1966) A theoretical framework for geographical studies of industrial location, *Economic Geography*, 42, 95–113.

Smith, D.M. (1981) *Industrial Location: An Economic Geographical Analysis*, Chichester: John Wiley.

Stafford, D.C. and R.H.A. Purkis (1989) *Macmillan Directory of Multinationals*, London: Macmillan.

Stopford, J.M. (1974) The origins of British-based multinational manufacturing enterprises, *Business History Review*, 48, 303–35.

Stopford, J.M. (1987) European practices and policies, in R.D. Robinson (ed.), *Direct Foreign Investment: Costs and Benefits*, Westport Conn.: Praeger.

Stopford, J.M. and K. Haberich (1978) Ownership and control of foreign operations, in M. Ghertman and J. Leontiades (eds), *European Research in International Business*, New York: North Holland, 141–67.

Stopford, J.M. and L.T. Wells (1972) *Management of the Multinational Enterprise: Organisation of the Firm and Ownership of the Subsidiaries*, New York: Basic Books.

Svedberg, P. (1981) Colonial enforcement of foreign direct investment, *The Manchester School*, 49, 21–38.

Tan, A.H.H. and B. Kapur (1986) *Pacific Growth and Financial Interdependence*, London: Allen & Unwin.

Telesio, P. (1979) *Technology Licensing and Multinational Enterprises*, New York: Praeger.

Temin, P. (1979) Technology, regulation and market structure in the modern pharmaceutical industry, *Bell Journal of Economics*, 10, 429–46.

Terpstra, V. and C.-M. Yu (1988) Determinants of foreign direct investment of multinational advertising agencies, *Journal of International Business Studies*, 19(1), 33–46.

Terrell, H. (1979) US banks in Japan and Japanese banks in the US: an empirical comparison, *Federal Reserve Bank of San Francisco Economic Review*, Summer, 18–30.

Thoburn, J.T., H.M. Leung, E. Chau and S.H. Tang (1990) *Foreign Investment in China under the Open Door Policy*, Aldershot: Avebury.

Trebilcock, C. (1977) *The Vickers Brothers: Armaments and Enterprise 1854–1914*, London: Europa.

Tschoegl, A.E. (1987) International retail banking as a strategy: an assessment, *Journal of International Business Studies*, 19(2), 67–88.

UNCTAD (1989) *Handbook of International Trade and Development Statistics 1988*, New York: UNCTC.

UNCTC (1979) *Transnational Corporations and the Pharmaceutical Industry*, New York: UNCTC.

UNCTC (1985) *Transnational Corporations in the Pharmaceutical Industry of Developing Countries*, New York: UNCTC.

UNCTC (1988) *Foreign Direct Investment and Transnational Corporations in Services*, New York: UNCTC.

UNCTC (1991) *Recent Developments related to Transnational Corporations and International Economic Relations: The Triad in Foreign Direct Investment*, New York: United Nations Economic and Social Council.

von Weiher, S. (1980) The rise and development of electrical engineering and industry in Germany in the nineteenth century: a case study – Siemens & Halske, in A. Okochi and H. Uchida (eds), *Development and Diffusion of Technology: Electrical and Chemical Industries*, Tokyo: University of Tokyo Press, 23–44.

Weber, A. (1929) *Theory of the Location of Industries*, Chicago: University of Chicago Press.

Weinstein, A.K. (1974) The international expansion of US multinational advertising agencies, *MSU Business Topics*, Summer, 29–35.

Weinstein, A.K. (1977) Foreign investments by service firms: the case of multinational advertising agencies, *Journal of International Business Studies*, 8(1), 83–91.

Wilkins, A.L. and W.G. Ouchi (1983) Efficient cultures: exploring the relationship between culture and organisational performance, *Administrative Science Quarterly*, 28, 468–81.

Wilkins, M. (1989) *The History of Foreign Investment in the United States to 1914*, Cambridge, Mass.: Harvard University Press.

Wilson, C. (1954) *The History of Unilever: A Study in Economic Growth and Social Change*, 2 vols, London: Cassell.

Wilson, C. (1968) *Unilever 1945–1965: Challenge and Response in the Post-war Industrial Revolution*, London: Cassell.

World Bank (1989) *Africa's Adjustment and Growth in the 1980*s, New York: World Bank.

Wrigley, J. (1986) Technical education and industry in the nineteenth century, in B. Elbaum and W. Lazonick (eds), *The Decline of the British Economy*, Oxford: Clarendon Press, 162–88.

Yannopoulos, G.N. (1983) The growth of transnational banking, in M.C. Casson (ed.), *The Growth of International Business*, London: Allen & Unwin, 236–57.

Index